Developing Generic Support for Doctoral Students

This multidisciplinary, multi-voiced book looks at the practice and pedagogy of generic, across-campus support for doctoral students. With a global imperative for increased doctoral completions, universities around the world are providing more generic support. This book represents collegial cross-fertilization focussed on generic pedagogy, provided by contributors who are practitioners working and researching at the pan-disciplinary level that complements supervision.

In the UK, funding for two weeks of annual training in transferable skills for each doctoral scholarship recipient has caused an explosion of such teaching, which is now flourishing elsewhere too; endorsed by the Carnegie Initiative on the Doctorate in the USA and developed extensively in Australia. Generic doctoral support is expanding, yet it is a relatively new kind of teaching, practised extensively only in the last decade and with its own ethical, practical and pedagogical complexities. These raise a number of questions:

- How is generic support funded and situated within institutions?
- Should some sessions be compulsory for doctoral students?
- Where do the boundaries lie between what can be taught generically or left to supervisors as discipline-specific?
- To what extent is generic work pastoral?
- What are its main benefits? Its challenges? Its objectives?

Over the last two decades supervision has been investigated and theorized as a teaching practice, a discussion this book extends to generic doctoral support.

This edited book has contributions from a wide range of authors and includes short inset narratives from academic authorities, accumulatively enabling discussion of practice and the establishment of a benchmark for this growing topic.

Susan Carter coordinated a generic doctoral programme from 2004–2012 and now works with supervisors as an academic developer within the recently established Centre for Learning and Research in Higher Education at the University of Auckland, New Zealand.

Deborah Laurs is a senior learning advisor at Victoria University of Wellington, New Zealand, where she runs research skills seminars and thesis writing workshops, as well as providing one-to-one support to students from all disciplines and at all stages of their doctoral journey.

Developing Generic Support for Doctoral Students

Practice and pedagogy

Edited by
Susan Carter and Deborah Laurs

LONDON AND NEW YORK

First published 2014
by Routledge
2 Park Square, Milton Park, Abingdon, Oxon OX14 4RN

and by Routledge
711 Third Avenue, New York, NY 10017

Routledge is an imprint of the Taylor & Francis Group, an informa business

© 2014 Susan Carter and Deborah Laurs

The right of the editors to be identified as the authors of the editorial material, and of the authors for their individual chapters, has been asserted in accordance with sections 77 and 78 of the Copyright, Designs and Patents Act 1988.

All rights reserved. No part of this book may be reprinted or reproduced or utilized in any form or by any electronic, mechanical, or other means, now known or hereafter invented, including photocopying and recording, or in any information storage or retrieval system, without permission in writing from the publishers.

Trademark notice: Product or corporate names may be trademarks or registered trademarks, and are used only for identification and explanation without intent to infringe.

British Library Cataloguing in Publication Data
A catalogue record for this book is available from the British Library

Library of Congress Cataloging in Publication Data
A catalog record for this book has been requested

ISBN: 978-0-415-66232-1 (hbk)
ISBN: 978-0-415-66233-8 (pbk)
ISBN: 978-1-315-77911-9 (ebk)

Typeset in ITC Galliard Std
by Saxon Graphics Ltd, Derby

Contents

Contributors	vii
Acknowledgements	xv
Introduction: mapping this book	1

PART I
Generic support's inception — 5

1 Context — 7
2 Putting together a doctoral skills programme — 19

PART II
Developing generic support's potential — 33

3 Responding to cross-campus student requirements — 35
4 Acknowledging values, identity and equity — 51
5 Generic support for English as an Additional Language (EAL) students — 69
6 Writing: intrinsic to research — 85
7 Writing: process, product and identity development — 103

PART III
Ensuring generic support's sustainability — 119

8 Part-time and digital support — 121

9 Preparation for careers	133
10 Evaluation of generic doctoral support	147
Conclusion	165
References	169
Index	189

Contributors

Claire Aitchison works in the Office of the Pro Vice Chancellor Research at the University of Western Sydney, Australia, where she supports writing development for higher degree researchers and academics, and contributes to supervisor training and policy. She has published widely on pedagogies for doctoral writing. Her edited books include with Cally Guerin *Writing Groups for Doctoral Education and Beyond: Innovations in Theory and Practice* (2014) and with Barbara Kamler and Alison Lee *Publishing Pedagogies for the Doctorate and Beyond* (2010). Her work in research education has been recognized with a university Vice Chancellor's Award (2010) and an Australian Teaching and Learning Council Award (2008).

Ian Brailsford is an independent training advisor who has worked with doctoral students for over ten years in teaching and career development and published in the area of doctoral education. He coordinates a year-long programme for doctoral candidates aspiring for an academic career and facilitates workshops on academic writing, presentation skills and academic integrity within the Doctoral Skills Programme at the University of Auckland, New Zealand.

Tony Bromley is responsible for the Graduate Training and Support Centre (GTSC) within Staff and Departmental Development at the University of Leeds, UK, which offers a wide range of training and development opportunities for researchers. Tony was lead author of the UK sector impact framework for researcher development, led the implementation of the framework nationally and has authored subsequent sector update reports on the impact of researcher development. Tony was part of the founding group of the *International Journal for Researcher Development*, the first specialist journal for the area (he is currently an Associate Editor) and was also one of three editors for the first published book for researcher development.

Susan Carter coordinated a generic doctoral programme at the University of Auckland, New Zealand from 2004–2012, and now works with supervisors within the recently established Centre for Learning and Research in Higher Education at the University of Auckland. She remains fascinated by the doctorate as a transformative learning experience that manoeuvres through complex semiotics in its social negotiation. Amongst extensive publication resulting from these interests, she is lead author of *How to Structure your Research Thesis* (2012).

Amy Cartwright has worked in researcher development since 2005, first at Strathclyde University in Glasgow, UK, and then at the University of Edinburgh, UK, providing strategic leadership and expertise in the training and development of research students and staff. She is currently deputy director of the Graduate School at Glasgow Caledonian University, UK, taking an active role in the ongoing enhancement of training and development of researchers, and the sharing of practice at a national and international level.

Lisa Chant, Ngati Whatua iwi, has supported and trained many Māori community-based researchers, and community researchers wishing to work with Māori communities, for Māori and community and academic research initiatives since the mid-1990s. She has worked with, trained, and supported indigenous academic researchers and academic researchers working with indigenous communities globally since 2002, advising on graduate and postgraduate indigenous knowledge-based academic endeavours. She is passionate about linking indigenous communities with academia, and academia with indigenous communities.

Meeta Chatterjee-Padmanabhan is a lecturer in Learning Development at the University of Wollongong, NSW, Australia. She has degrees in English literatures, Applied Linguistics and the Teaching of English as a Second Language. She provides academic language and literacy support across faculties. Her doctoral thesis examines the identity and textual engagement experiences of three international students writing a doctoral thesis in EAL. Her research interests include doctoral writing and pedagogy; identity and intertextuality in academic writing; development of English language proficiency in EAL students; multicultural writing in Australia; and humour in women's writing and poetry.

Karen Commons is a senior learning advisor at Victoria University of Wellington, New Zealand. She has much experience in both language teaching and learning support. Her research interests include internationalization of tertiary education and the enhancement of student experience, especially for international and other migrant students.

Catherine Cook is a lecturer in the College of Health at Massey University, Auckland, New Zealand. She developed an interest in postgraduate students' academic trajectories during 12 years as a counsellor in a university setting, in which time she undertook her own doctoral study.

Sara Cotterall is associate professor at the American University of Sharjah in the United Arab Emirates where she teaches postgraduate Teachers of English to

Speakers of Other Languages (TESOL) and research writing courses. She has been teaching and conducting research with tertiary students for whom English is an additional language since 1985 and has published extensively in the field of language education, including several papers from her longitudinal study of the learning experiences of six international PhD students.

Linda Evans is professor of leadership and professional learning at the UK's University of Leeds. She has researched and published widely in the broad field of professional working life, focusing in particular on workplace morale, job satisfaction and motivation, professorial academic leadership in higher education, professionalism, professional development and researcher development. Her books include *Reflective Practice in Educational Research* (2002) and *Teaching and Learning in Higher Education* (1998). She is the editor of the *International Journal for Researcher Development*.

Terry Evans is a professor in the School of Education at Deakin University in Geelong, Australia. He is recognized internationally for his publications, research and scholarship in doctoral education and policy, and in open and distance education. He is a member of ten editorial boards of international journals and is the editor or co-editor of 14 books including *Doctorates Downunder: Key to Successful Doctoral Study in Australia and New Zealand Second Edition* (with C. Denholm, 2012); *Supervising Doctorates Downunder: Keys to Successful Supervision in Australia and New Zealand* (with C. Denholm, 2007) and *International Handbook of Distance Education* (with M. Haughey and D. Murphy, 2008).

Cath Fraser is an educational consultant, working with a number of different organizations in New Zealand's tertiary sector. Current projects include contracted research, teaching and learning resource development, and programme documentation and review. Research interests include mentoring, especially of staff academic writing, supporting diversity and biculturalism, and international students.

Xiaodan Gao is a senior learning advisor at Student Learning Support Service, Victoria University of Wellington, New Zealand. She has taught English, study skills and academic writing to international students in a number of New Zealand and Chinese tertiary institutions. Her research interests and publications mostly relate to second language acquisition, international education, transition for international students and cross-cultural communication.

Cally Guerin is a lecturer in the School of Education at the University of Adelaide, Australia. She coordinates and teaches into a comprehensive suite of research skills training opportunities and academic development programmes for research students and their supervisors. Her research interests are in doctoral education, the multicultural academy, thesis-writing groups, and academic integrity.

Vicky Gunn is director of the Learning and Teaching Centre at the University of Glasgow, UK. She has a long-standing interest in the psycho-social aspects of the PhD experience, particularly in how generic sessions might enable postgraduates to reflect on the impact these have on the writing process.

Heather Hamerton is a Pākeha New Zealander with an extensive background in teaching and supervising postgraduate students. She is manager of a small research centre at a regional polytechnic, and is actively involved in all aspects of research practice and policy. She lives in the sunny Bay of Plenty by the sea.

Bronwyn James' research is in the area of research student writing. Her PhD thesis *Silences, voices, negotiations: Becoming a postgraduate research writer* focused on the decisions higher degree research students make at different points in the drafting process. In 2012, her thesis was recognized nationally, receiving a special commendation in the Australian Association for Research in Education Award for Doctoral Research in Education. She has taught thesis writing in a number of universities and is currently head of the Learning Centre at the University of Sydney, Australia.

Sally Knowles is a research development advisor in the Office of Research and Innovation at Edith Cowan University, Perth, Australia, where she supports staff with their writing for research and publication. Sally seeks to create a vibrant research writing culture that is socially robust and collegial. Since 2003, following Barbara Grant's retreat model, she has facilitated over 50 academic writing retreats for several Australian universities and research institutes. Sally has a strong interest in how artistic research from the creative and performing arts can infuse the research and writing practices of so-called 'traditional' researchers.

Deborah Laurs is a senior learning advisor at Victoria University of Wellington, New Zealand, where she runs research skills seminars and thesis writing workshops, as well as providing one-to-one support to students at all stages of their doctoral journey. She has also taught academic, business and creative writing. She has published journal articles on peer support programmes, student leadership and graduate attributes, and the uncertain demarcation between generic advisors and doctoral supervisors in relation to the thesis-writing process. In 2010, she was recognized as 'most influential staff member' by her university's postgraduate students' association, and in 2011, received a 'staff excellence' award.

Anne Lee works as an independent academic developer with universities around the world. She was previously senior academic development advisor at the University of Surrey, UK. Her book *Successful Research Supervision* was published by Routledge in 2012.

Shosh Leshem was a visiting lecturer at Anglia Ruskin University, UK, for eight years. She worked with doctoral candidates, supervisors and examiners and conducted research on the nature of doctorateness. She is author (with Vernon Trafford) of the book *Stepping Stones to Achieving Your Doctorate* (4th edition, 2012). She is head of the Teacher Education Faculty at Oranim, Academic College of Education, Israel, lectures at Haifa University, and is currently a visiting lecturer in South Africa conducting workshops on the doctorate and its dimensions.

Natalie Lundsteen coordinates career services and programmes for PhD researchers at Massachusetts Institute of Technology, in Cambridge, Massachusetts, USA. Previously, she was a careers advisor at Oxford University and a career counsellor at Stanford University. She is a research associate in two Oxford University Department of Education research centres: The ESRC Research Centre on Skills, Knowledge and Organisational Performance (SKOPE) with a focus on workplace learning, skills, and the economics of education; and the Centre for Sociocultural and Activity Theory Research (OSAT) focusing on student development and expertise in practices.

Catherine Manathunga is an associate professor in the School of Education Policy Implementation at Victoria University of Wellington, Aotearoa/New Zealand. She is a historian, who draws together expertise in historical, sociological and cultural studies research to bring an innovative perspective to educational research. She is currently researching projects on doctoral supervision pedagogy, doctoral graduate outcomes and attributes, interdisciplinarity and the history of university teaching and learning in Australia and Aotearoa/New Zealand.

Inger Mewburn has been a research fellow specializing in research education for the last six years. She is interested in exploring research degree experience through analysis of conversations and material semiotics. Currently director of Research Training at the Australian National University, Canberra, ACT, Australia, she is most well known as the managing editor at the Thesis Whisperer blog and can be found on Twitter as @thesiswhisperer.

Brian Paltridge is professor of TESOL at the University of Sydney, New South Wales, Australia. With Sue Starfield, he is co-author of *Thesis and Dissertation Writing in a Second Language* (2007) and with his TESOL colleagues at the University of Sydney, *Teaching Academic Writing* (2009). With Aek Phakiti, he edited the *Companion to Research Methods in Applied Linguistics* (2010), with Ken Hyland, the *Companion to Discourse Analysis* (2011) and with Diane Belcher and Ann Johns, *New Directions in English for Specific Purposes Research* (2011). His most recent publications are the second edition of his book *Discourse Analysis* (2012) and the *Handbook of English for Specific Purposes*, edited with Sue Starfield (2013).

Alison Phipps is professor of languages and intercultural studies, and co-convener of Glasgow Refugee, Asylum and Migration Network (GRAMNET) at the University of Glasgow, UK, where she teaches modern languages, religious education, anthropology and intercultural education. From 2001 until 2010 she was director of the Graduate School, first for Arts and Humanities and then for Education as well, latterly, as convening the University Heads of Graduate School Committee. In 2011 she was voted Best College Teacher by students and given a Teaching Excellence Award by the university for her innovative work in doctoral pedagogy and researcher development. In 2012 she received an OBE for services to education, intercultural and interreligious relations in the Queen's Birthday Honours.

Jean Rath is a senior lecturer in the Centre for Tertiary Teaching and Learning at the University of Waikato, New Zealand. Originally trained in zoology and anthropology, Jean has led a range of academic and professional development initiatives in both the United Kingdom and New Zealand. Jean has a long-standing interest in and commitment to enhancing the experiences of people new to research and supervision. Recent projects include a review of supervisor development practices within New Zealand, implementation of the University of Oxford's Code of Practice for the Employment and Career Development of Research Staff, working with research supervisors, and facilitating career and personal development events for research active staff and students.

Mary Roberts completed her doctorate in sociolinguistics at Victoria University of Wellington, New Zealand, and has taught at the University of Otago, the University of Canberra and with English Language Partners. Her most recent position was as senior learning advisor at Victoria University of Wellington where, amongst other activities, she ran short courses on critical thinking for postgraduates. Her current research interests include the learning advice session as a cultural event and the teaching of critical thinking.

Gillian Robinson is reader emerita at Anglia Ruskin University, UK, where she was director of research degrees and coordinator of an international PhD programme for 12 years. Her research interests are in doctoral learning and issues of supervision, particularly in cross-cultural contexts.

Miki Seifert completed her PhD on her development of a decolonizing performative research methodology at School of Māori Studies (Te Kawa a Māui) at Victoria University of Wellington in 2011. She is co-founder and artistic director of With Lime, an international, interdisciplinary arts company that explores the interface between cultures, conducts research to develop performative methodologies and practices, and offers training in the use of creative practices for personal and societal transformation.

Sue Starfield is associate professor in the School of Education and director of The Learning Centre at the University of New South Wales, Australia. She is co-author with Brian Paltridge of *Thesis and Dissertation Writing in a Second Language: A Handbook for Supervisors* (2007) and co-editor of the *Handbook of*

English for Specific Purposes (2013). She is co-editor of the journal *English for Specific Purposes*. She is the recipient of a 2008 *Australian Learning and Teaching Council* citation for an Outstanding Contribution to Student Learning for the development of a research-led innovative curriculum to support postgraduate research students' writing; she has taught courses on thesis writing for a number of years. She is a regular contributor to her university's Supervisor Development programme on the topic of thesis writing and runs writing for publication workshops as part of her university's Researcher Development programme. She is co-authoring a book titled *Getting Published in Academic Journals: Negotiating the Peer Review Process* for University of Michigan Press.

Vernon Trafford is professor emeritus at Anglia Ruskin University, UK. He has held international visiting professorships, undertaken consultancies with the British Council, OECD, UNICEF, the World Bank and universities in the UK and other countries. Since 2001 his research, publications and conference presentations have concerned the nature of doctorateness. His 2008 book, with Shosh Leshem, *Stepping Stones to Achieving Your Doctorate* has been reprinted three times.

Chris Trevitt is a consultant in educational design with the Australian National University College of Law, Canberra, ACT, Australia, where he offers individual advice and assistance on a wide range of educational and academic practices, including assessment and curriculum design, practice-based learning, clinical teaching, and work-based learning. Chris recently returned to the ANU after five years at the University of Oxford, where he was director of the Developing Academic Practice Programme. He fosters reflective professional practice. Assessment *for* learning, assessment as a way of understanding the curriculum, and the use of portfolios as a case in point, have become an important focus in recent years.

Jean Webb is professor of international children's literature and director of the International Forum for Research in Children's Literature at the University of Worcester, UK. Jean was associate head of the Graduate School for a number of years and wrote and taught the generic research student training programmes for over a decade. She is still very much engaged with the research student experience as research student coordinator for the Institute of Humanities and Creative Arts. She is well-published and internationally recognized in children's literature.

Gina Wisker is head of the Centre for Learning and Teaching at the University of Brighton, UK, where she is professor of higher education and contemporary literature. Gina has worked with supervisors and postgraduates since the 1990s and runs workshops and teaches on supervision programmes in the UK, Sweden, South Africa, Ireland, Norway, Australia and New Zealand. Gina's books include *The Postgraduate Research Handbook* (2001, 2008) and *The Good Supervisor* (2005, 2012). She is currently writing a book on writing for academic publication and teaching writing for academic publication.

Acknowledgements

First, we thank each other. Our shared journey has been exhilarating and daunting, but always interesting. We are grateful to our contributors for their voices and expertise; many of them have grown to be friends in the process of writing this book. Editor and author exchanges during the shaping of this book figure amongst the aspects of academia that make our lives cheerful. The people involved have made producing this book a pleasure.

We acknowledge the Centre for Learning and Research (CLeaR) at the University of Auckland, and Student Learning Support Services (SLSS) at Victoria University of Wellington for their support with time, funding and encouragement. Colleagues within both centres have been energizingly enthusiastic. We thank Mara Mulrooney for her rigorous editing, her sharp eyes, her care and the cleanness of her integrity. Others have also aided and abetted: Andrew Lavery applied his formatting expertise to the final draft; while writing group members pointed out blind spots in our prose with friendly rigour.

Finally, we thank Routledge, and in particular, Vicky Parting, for her support throughout the publication process, and Laurie Duboucheix-Saunders, whose diligent scrutiny brought to light a few more stow-away proofreading glitches. Blame us if you spot any more.

Susan Carter and Deborah Laurs

Introduction: mapping this book

This book speaks with many voices. Within an overview framework, each chapter has several insets: teaching vignettes, examples of courses, accounts from experience and opinions about the pedagogy of generic doctoral support from a range of different educators. Often, although not always, these are learning advisors in central units. Contributors work in disparate places, mostly in the UK, Australia and New Zealand. Together, their combined discussion shows the complexities of practice involved in working with students by complementing supervisory support, and building relationships with staff within and across institutional hierarchies. Practitioners describe their work in the borderlands between disciplines. Like all borderlands, this one is charged with risks and potentials.

The extensive framework joining the pastiche of contributors' accounts is written by the co-editors Susan Carter and Deborah Laurs; its first-person 'we' refers to us. This introduction and the conclusion are ours. Nonetheless, where as individuals we contribute a short inset, we name ourselves. This book is not a manual on how to teach generic sessions or develop a programme. We do not seek to take the high ground in this emerging field of teaching. There are many others who might have contributed who are not here; just as a doctoral thesis must live within its reasonable perimeters, so must this book. However, here we bring together a group of engaged reflective practitioners sharing their experience in a bricolage of perspectives on generic doctoral support. Pedagogy for generic doctoral teaching is ready to come of age.

There are three parts to the book following the progression of generic support through past (Part I), present (Part II) and future (Part III). Part II is much the largest of the three because it concerns itself with experience from current practice.

Part I: Generic support's inception

Part I (chapters 1 and 2) relates to generic doctoral support's context and inception. It considers the international discussion of what the doctorate is and should be, and the institutional frameworks in which people began to build workshops and courses. Examples of starting from scratch show how generic support emerged under close scrutiny from institutional governance (a significant difference from supervision's historic privacy). Like new supervisors in the past before supervision was discussed, generic advisors have usually been guided mostly by their own experience and their commitment to research students, with very little literature to go by. In Chapter 1, we defend our deliberate use of the word 'generic,' which is often pejorative in educational discourse. We argue that so much about the doctorate is generic – the same criteria, hurdles, and processes across all disciplines – that a clear overview perspective is important for student support. The prescribed nature of the examination criteria makes it useful to regard the doctorate as a textual genre; meeting generic expectations is easier when someone makes it clear how precisely to do this in writing. We aim to show that the borderlands between disciplines give a promising new niche in education. Yet, the limitations and boundaries of generic work are also delineated as we, educators working in this field, define our place in the doctoral process.

Chapter 2 looks at some of the considerations in setting up generic programmes. We describe programme-level workshops, institution-wide programmes, postgraduate 'research skills' degrees and individual learning advisor consultations with students to show how these complement supervision. The thinking behind the emergence of generic support, we suggest, is more relevant than ever with increased doctoral study internationally.

Part II: Developing generic support's potential

From there, Part II (Chapters 3, 4, 5, 6 and 7) shows the development of generic support into multiple dimensions. Since generic support's inception, it has become apparent that an across-campus perspective has potential beyond its foundational goal of teaching transferable skills and competency for faster completion. It can enable doctoral students to build an authentic academic identity based on a deeper understanding of their epistemology within a wider framework. Sureness of their position generates more competent authorial control of thesis writing. Generic support also sustains students through the psychological challenges of undertaking a large project (almost always for the first time), including when their specific identity problematizes this process, as it may do around gender or culture. Chapter 3 showcases a few examples of sessions built in response to the increased understanding of doctoral threshold-crossing that a pan-discipline perspective allows. Looking at the generic processes lets you see much more clearly where the sticking points are. We include sessions on theory and one on accuracy of definition as examples of how a generic approach can teach research methods in terms of precision in the ability to 'demonstrate critical evaluation.' We argue that when doctoral students have the opportunity to contextualize their own work in a broader context through talking to students from different disciplines, they become aware of the meta-levels of their research's methods, theory, and writing.

Chapter 4 turns to the varying possibilities for generic support to address equity and identity. Our examples highlight support for the social constructs of gender, the provision of postgraduate networks in New Zealand for Māori and indigenous students and the overall importance of acknowledging student success. Chapter 5 is devoted to doctoral candidates whose first language is not English. These students are often international, so have the challenge of acclimatizing to an alien culture and finding confidence there. Although often generic support is envisioned as 'correcting non-standard grammar,' we take a broader identity and cultural angle to the support of these students.

Writing the thesis remains a central challenge of doctoral research; teaching writing is core business for many generic doctoral programmes. For this reason, two chapters are devoted to writing. In Chapter 6, several learning advisors and one student reflect on how writing inheres in the entire doctoral process. Chapter 7 includes some examples of writing workshops that explicate and clarify generic thesis requirements. These two chapters map out the complementarity of generic writing support and supervision.

Part III: Ensuring generic support's sustainability

Part III (Chapters 8, 9 and 10) deals with aspects relating to the immediate future. Chapter 8 addresses the challenges of sustaining the increasing cohorts of part-timers, and accommodating the changing media of teaching. We acknowledge both the cost to teachers of the digital environment and its exhilarating emancipation potential, one we see as changing the politics of doctoral pedagogy. The increasing number of doctoral graduates means a shift in the rubrics of their future employment, and thus Chapter 9 looks at support for future careers. Changing contexts mean that graduates need to be flexible: how can the generic skills of adaptability for a future career be taught?

Finally, this book seeks to address the question of how we might account for ourselves as teachers. It is difficult to show causality: given the lengthy time frame and multiple factors involved in a doctorate, we cannot easily show that our contribution was the cause of improved completion rates and retention, or high employment uptake, or improved publication rates. Chapter 10 broaches the vexing topic of the assessment of generic support, closing the book with some suggestions for how we might satisfy bean counters that our work makes a significant contribution, and with a model for measuring good practice based on descriptors from practitioners. The measurement model reflects back the book's multiple voiced accounts and in doing so articulates a practitioner pedagogy for generic doctoral support.

PART I

Generic support's inception

Chapter 1

Context

> If particular skills are useful across a range of fields, then there may be efficiencies in regarding them as generic and teaching them as such.
>
> (Rob Gilbert *et al.* 2004: 386)

Generic doctoral support has lurched into being in response to the desire for increased expertise in a knowledge economy. Conspicuously, in the UK there has been a nationwide drive to provide doctoral students with transferable skills, prompted by the Sir Gareth Roberts' Review (2002), which recommended two weeks' training annually for doctoral candidates. Initial generous government seed funding put generic support in real focus, one this book aims to widen. In New Zealand, Australia, the USA and Canada, individual universities put together their own programmes too, with slightly different frameworks, but the same awareness that students 'want focused "insider" discussion about "the rules of the game"…and the purposes and practices of higher education' (Walker and Thomson 2010: 3). However, such programmes occupy

> an ambiguous space, floating between the margins and the centre, between the student, the faculty and the institution, between a liberal notion of equity and the values of the market place, between fixing the problem and changing the culture.
>
> (Percy 2011: 1–2)

Within this borderlands space, a relatively new niche, learning advisors seek to develop expertise in the field of generic doctoral pedagogy.

We define pedagogy broadly as engagement with teaching and learning. Like Aitchison, Kamler and Lee (2010), we recognize pedagogy as linked to theory, played out against a backdrop 'already replete with goals, values, assumptions, principles and rules, implicit and explicit, and sets of expectations about relationships and outcomes' (p. 6). The social complexities of researcher teaching and learning are multiple, and include a process of becoming within an environment marked by 'supercomplexity' (Barnett 2000). Doctoral students must float, adapting so that they 'fruitfully learn despite not "knowing" (where "not knowing" is framed as an obstacle to be overcome) but [also] deliberately cultivate and sustain a state of not knowing as a learning strategy' (Cherry 2005: 316). During their emergence, doctoral learners will be supervised from within the discipline but are likely to also be taught in generic induction sessions and research skills workshops. Research attention has probed supervisory teaching, intriguingly and promisingly in terms of better practice.

However, in contrast to the many navigational books for doctoral students and supervisors, there is little on generic support, despite the number of academics engaged in its delivery. The UK context of the Roberts' Report funding and its effect on practice and politics has produced one volume of shared accounts about what was then called doctoral 'skills training' (Hinchcliffe, Bromley and Hutchinson 2007); our book extends this conversation about the development, pedagogy and practice of generic doctoral support.

Background

A declaration signed in Bologna in 1999 led to the creation of the European Higher Education Area (EHEA), an international sharing of educational practice whose influence extends beyond geographical boundaries. The term 'Bologna Process' includes the Bologna Declaration (1999) as well as subsequent ratifications at Prague (2001), Berlin (2003), Bergen (2005) and London (2007). With the Berlin Communiqué (2003), the Bologna discussion shifted its sights to doctoral pedagogy.

Most countries outside of Europe also recognize the need to keep up with emerging trends: 'The Bologna Process and subsequent policy development have a wide-ranging effect in bringing doctoral education into a global conversation beyond the boundaries of Europe' (Boud and Lee 2009: 8). As a Canadian Education report (Subcommittee 2008: 349–350) points out,

> Observers from all continents are monitoring with much interest the major changes being implemented in Europe. Countries in Africa, South America, Asia, and North America are analyzing the reform process and trying to determine what influence the Bologna Process will have on their educational systems.

The world is paying attention, with governments in many countries formulating responses according to their own needs.

Similarly, academics are becoming increasingly aware of opportunities to improve the doctoral student experience (Carter 2010; Carter *et al.* 2010; Geraldo, Trevitt and Carter 2011; Lee 2012). Perhaps one of the benefits of such an exercise is that it prompts a critique of practice, within a context that, as Barnett and Hallam (1999) remind us, entails super-complexity, involving forms of 'social practice' (Lee and Boud 2009a: 5), and frequently bound by social restraints due to many different perspectives, different stakeholders, and different institutional objectives. Barrie (Barrie, Jain and Carew 2003; Barrie 2004, and 2006 and 2007) terms generic support a 'complement' model, which typically involves teaching computer skills, information literacy, critical thinking, writing skills, time management and other strategies for aspects of doctoral production that affect most candidates; we aim to show that it enables deep level learning and threshold crossing as well.

Teaching graduate attributes?

The growing awareness of 'graduate attributes' – qualities that students acquire regardless of discipline, which they didn't have before studying – also throws emphasis on what is generic. Yet, 'university teachers charged with responsibility for developing students' generic graduate attributes do not share a common understanding of…the teaching and learning processes that might facilitate the development of these outcomes' (Barrie 2004: 262). Barrie urges that academics should be figuring how to teach these attributes within faculties in a student-focused way. But this book argues that generic courses can enable students to better contextualize their own research when made aware of discipline boundaries, institutional practice, and societal needs by a pan-disciplinary perspective. In this way, generic support can complement discipline-specific engagement, providing a complete scaffold for novice researchers.

As learning advisors, we are 'passionately committed to anything that can assist research graduates to find meaningful and continuing employment' (Manathunga 2007b: 30–31) so that the doctoral endeavour pays off socially. Yet, an additional central theme of this book is that the doctoral thesis is a genre: its moves (evaluating literature, establishing a gap, contextualizing new knowledge, defending choices) are made by all theses, regardless of discipline. It makes good economic sense to have experts in the generic dimensions of the doctorate teaching from this perspective, so that every individual supervisor need not do it all alone. This begs for talk in which 'research is discussed generically, or across discipline boundaries' (Rowland 2006: 10).

Two key terms: genre (noun), generic (adjective)

A defence of the use of the term 'generic' is probably necessary: generic tends to be a pejorative term in education, suspected to be a 'bolt-on' that is never relevant enough to be worth the time (Wingate 2006). Does the adjective generic really come from the noun genre (as smoothly and simply, say, as 'chronological' comes from 'chronology')? Ambiguously, generic can mean either 'of a type' or 'non-specific.' Both genre and generic come from *genus*, meaning in Latin 'a race, stock, family, birth, descent, origin' (Lewis 1995). 'Generic,' the word comes via the French *générique*, is defined as 'characteristic of or belonging to a genus or class' (Trumble *et al.* 2002: 1083).

The vehicle of the 'genre' metaphor is the family, which invokes a sharing of characteristics: sameness. The *Concise Oxford Companion to the English Language*, however, defines 'generic' as '[b]elonging to or designating a genus (as opposed to *a species*) [our emphasis]' (McArthur 1998). This definition, with genus being broader than species, accentuates breadth rather than shared similarities, an apparent contradiction.

In marketing, for example, 'generic' means non-specific rather than belonging to a branded category. As such, it has a slightly negative 'no frills, possibly unreliable' connotation. Generic doctoral support is suspected by some of undermining the traditional supervisory relationship by slightly altering the existing, or traditional, PhD model (Reeves 2007). Yet generic doctoral support complements rather than replaces tailor-made supervision, providing further assurance that a doctoral student will not go blindly through the process. It's been noted that many supervisors 'do not see writing support as their responsibility, but as the responsibility of those in writing centres, since...writing is a generic skill rather than rooted within academic exchanges within each field' (McAlpine and Amundsen 2011: 10). A centralized generic programme covers any shortfall in the disciplines by providing a different kind of expertise focused on the processes of completing a doctorate.

Borthwick and Wissler (2003: 15–16) note the slippage of the term 'generic support' regarding doctoral education: 'A descriptor such as generic, core, transferable, employability, or personal may be attached to abilities, attributes, qualities, or competencies, each of which carries overtones relating to skill and performance'. Gail Craswell (2007: 377) sees 'an obvious demarcation between "research training" (university domain) and "generic capabilities" (industry domain),' but we consider the two ideas are more interconnected.

We believe that doctoral skills and capacities for writing, thinking, theorizing, planning and managing time, project and self are necessary for completion and future research, and that support for their acquisition should come from the supervisor, the department and also from generic learning advisors. The generic perspective is not the only one, but it adds a helpful dimension that many supervisors lack because they work tightly within a discipline framework (a view supported by Paré 2011). With data gathered from 156 doctoral students, McAlpine and Amundsen (2011: 179) found to their surprise that 'supervisors seemed less central to students' experience than is often cited in the literature,' and that this seemed due to students having an increasing range of resources. A wider network is healthy.

Transferable skills or doctoral skills?

Doctoral candidates are expected to learn, and then demonstrate, a whole range of personal, interpersonal, organizational and research skills, exemplified, for example, by the UK Research Council's six-point list:

- research environment
- research management
- personal effectiveness
- communication skills
- networking and team working
- career management.

Green and Bowden (2010: 136) map a three levelled model of research training, calling for the middle level, universities, to provide

> a central program offering seminars and workshops on a range of topics from research higher degree policy and procedures, progress, thesis writing, publication, ethics and intellectual property, research literacies, quantitative approaches, qualitative approaches, career opportunities, stress management, examination and supervision matters.

Much of what doctoral students learn that develops them into fully fledged researchers is useful both within the doctoral process and beyond it. Borthwick and Wissler (2003: 17) point out that 'Many universities tend to interpret generic skills for postgraduate students as being to do with the research process…[yet] many (if not all) of these skills are in fact "transferable" to the workplace' – with a bit of strategizing and luck. The word 'generic', then, can be applied both to the genre of the thesis and to the transferable, employability competencies that the thesis-writing process develops.

The learning of skills has psychological and social dimensions. Undergraduate students have multiple papers and teachers, whereas many doctoral students are locked for three or four years into a single learning relationship primarily with one supervisor, or, increasingly, two. The factor of isolation further validates the place of generic advice, offering comprehensive avenues of support for the lengthy research journey and its associated identity transformation and psychological challenges.

Cross-fertilization complements disciplinary savvy. A suggestion to humanities students, for example, that they overtly discuss methods and methodology can help shift them from opaque rhetoric (often their strength as essayists) to seeing what might be made helpfully explicit. At the same time, science and engineering students sometimes lack the narrative techniques to tell the story of their research project. In a research thesis, the connections between literature, research questions or hypotheses, data and findings are essential: they must be pegged together securely. The curiously defensive nature of the thesis justifies both science's straightforward categorizations *and* humanities' discursive narrative. That all examiners receive the same directives for identifying a successful doctorate signals that the thesis is a genre. Treating it as such accords with a methodology of textual analysis: 'contemporary genre analysis views texts…comprehensively, focussing not only on their forms and textual conventions, but, more importantly, on their purpose and on how components of the text contribute to that purpose' (Clark 2007: xxi). Research by Johnston (1997) shows how doctoral examiners' questions inevitably probe at a deeper level than the discipline specific. Cross-campus discussions amongst students allow the *moves* the thesis makes to meet generic requirements to become clearer, more readily able to be expressed. This form of learning equips students with better understanding of the meta-dimensions of their work.

Gina Wisker (2008: 140–156) highlights how students can use salient learning styles (Honey and Mumford 1986; Kolb 1984; Marton and Säljö 1976; Ramsden 1979) as lenses to learn about themselves as research *learners*. Barbara Lovitts (2007) has gathered descriptors of what makes an outstanding, very good, acceptable and unacceptable thesis, which are useful for generic workshops' objectives in part because they are so similar across disciplines. Sharon Parry (2007: 237) acknowledges that the doctorate is a complex game whose rules are sometimes covert:

> the idea that doctoral study is in a sense a game, or a meaningful social setting with rules, seemed bizarre at first...[but] many of the doctoral students interviewed appeared to identify very strongly with it....in fact, doctoral study does resemble the combination of written and unwritten rules in any complex game.

Many of these rules and expectations belong to the genre of the thesis rather than to the conventions of the discipline.

Institutional frameworks and fault-lines

The practice of generic doctoral support has political and managerial complexities. Practical issues such as funding and location within the institutional infrastructure vary. We argue that it is more advantageous for generic learning advisors to have academic positions rather than being general staff, because they are teaching at the highest student level. Moreover, doctoral pedagogy is a rich laboratory for educational research.

Institutions need to decide whether generic support will be compulsory or optional. Anecdotal evidence (for example student evaluations of the University of Auckland's compulsory doctoral induction) suggests advantages in making core sessions compulsory, despite seeming counter-intuitive at this higher level of teaching. Supervisors may feel vaguely threatened by generic support, discouraging their students from taking it up, which can compromise participation if generic sessions are optional (Reeves 2007). Supervisor buy-in is thus crucial. Those providing generic support often encounter students who are having difficulty with supervisors, a situation that requires considerable diplomacy and care. Ensuring that each workshop or session, be it compulsory or optional, has practical application and relevance to all participants is also necessary, and sometimes challenging.

In the last decade, supervision's 'secret garden' (Park 2007) has received attention as critical to success in doctoral completions. Wisker's (2012) second edition of *The Good Supervisor* is almost twice as long as her first because, in the intervening six years, so much more had been added to the discussion. One agenda of our book is to suggest that generic doctoral support is an area of academic teaching of similar importance as supervision: similarly fruitful; challenging; sometimes fraught and sometimes a source of deep satisfaction. It is time we opened a discourse on its practice, tensions and problems.

This seems especially pressing because generic support is more vulnerable to institutional disruption than supervision – programmes are often canned, devolved, or amalgamated in seemingly random configurations. It is not unheard of for the student cohort, colleagues, the HoD, the Dean etc. all to be aware of inadequate supervisory practice – yet that supervisor to be allowed to continue carelessly, remaining fully entitled as an expert in the field. On the other hand, generic work that is recognized as excellent may be arbitrarily shut down because change at senior management level means a shift in interest or funding provisions. Several of our contributors have had this experience. There are also 'back stories' not discussed here because they represent the dirty linen of institutional politics. Nevertheless, the underpinning reality of our work means instability is a constant. Any pedagogy for generic support must acknowledge that we work on the side of an active volcano. Somehow, we need to stake out the perimeters of our area of expertise, our *modus operandi*, our criteria for curricula, and at the same time find ways to anchor ourselves sustainably within our institutions.

This book benefits from lessons learned from the UK experience. For us in New Zealand, the UK work has provided a lodestar. Thus, we close our contextual chapter with Anne Lee's account of UK focus on the purpose of the doctorate, whether it is fulfilling that purpose, and how it might.

Generic support for doctoral researchers: the UK experience

For some time, there has been a debate in the UK about whether the doctorate is fit for purpose and what that purpose should be (Denicolo and Park 2013; Park 2007; QAA 2011, UK GRAD Programme 2002). In the 1990s there was increasing government concern about the supply of researchers with STEM skills (science, technology, engineering and maths) and in 2001 the UK government commissioned a report that made a number of recommendations, including direct funding for career development and transferable skills training for doctoral students and research staff (Roberts 2002). Many in the UK would argue that there was one man (Sir Gareth Roberts) who set in motion a policy initiative that provided £120 million over ten years of new government funding to support the skills development of research students and postdoctoral research staff (Hodge 2010).

Although Roberts' name has become closely associated with generic skills training and employability issues in the UK, the investment in this area also coincided with the aforementioned concern about technical competitiveness and the relatively benign economic conditions which meant that money was available for investment in higher education. At the same time phenomenographic research was being carried out in Australia to try to identify how academics conceptualized generic graduate attributes (Barrie 2004, 2006; Cumming and Kiley 2009).

There were other key changes happening around this period: especially the growth and evolution of graduate schools (and later the creation by the Research Councils of Doctoral Training Schools or Centres for Doctoral Training). This grouping of cohorts of doctoral researchers made their common needs more visible. There was also increasing harmony about the nature and process of the doctorate across Europe through the Bologna Process and the Salzburg Principles and substantial growth in the numbers of international students coming to study in the UK. By 2009, the majority of UK Higher Education Institutions had at least one graduate school and the gender balance had continued to shift to more adequately represent women (45 percent) (Denicolo, Fuller and Berry 2010). The diversification of doctoral programmes, including a proliferation of professional doctorates was also emerging, and alongside them institutions developed their range of graduate schools to provide them (Denicolo, Fuller and Berry 2010; Woodward *et al.* 2004).

At this time, the UK's higher education audit body, the Quality Assurance Agency (QAA) saw three possible purposes for the doctorate: firstly to lead into an academic career, secondly to be able to bring research skills to bear in professional contexts in jobs across all sectors and thirdly as a personal challenge or interest (QAA 2011). The QAA code of practice for research degrees noted that 'The PhD has also changed over time so that, irrespective of their degree, research students now experience and expect structured research training as part of their programme' (QAA 2012: 3).

Nationally available generic 'GRAD schools' offering careers development had been run by the Careers Research and Advice Centre (CRAC), a charitable career development organization (http://www.crac.org.uk/) since 1968, funded by the Research Councils. This funding was extended in 2003 to create the UK GRAD Programme, which continued running these short courses and worked directly with UK institutions. This was rebranded as Vitae (http://www.vitae.ac.uk/) in 2008 and its remit and funding extended to include research staff.

The creation of the UK GRAD Programme had coincided with government funding, known as 'Roberts money,' being guaranteed for five years, the equivalent of £800 per annum per Research Council funded research student being given (not bid for) to universities provided they ring-fenced it for the professional development of postgraduate researchers and research staff and made a suitably robust annual report on progress.

Thus Vitae emerged as a partnership organization funded largely by the UK Research Councils and managed by the CRAC. It has several key principles: first it aims to build human capital by influencing policy. It has had significant input into various policy documents including the QAA new Quality Code for Research

Degrees (2012) and Concordat to Support the Career Development of Researchers (2008), and was involved in and consulted on the Salzburg Principles (European Knowledge Society 2005) and European Charter and Code. Second it works directly with institutions to build their capacity and capability to provide professional development opportunities for researchers through a network of eight regional Hubs located in partner universities across the UK. Third it creates professional development resources and programmes. Fourth it aims to create an evidence base by evaluating the effectiveness of skills development provision and research into the landscape of researchers' careers, through its 'What do researchers do?' publications. The 'Impact and Evaluation Group' (the IEG, formerly known as the Rugby Group) has created a ladder of evaluation terminology, which it calls 'Impact Framework' (Vitae 2008). This looks at 'Foundations,' 'Reaction,' 'Learning,' 'Behaviour,' and 'Outcomes,' based on the Kirkpatrick model, although any evaluation of training (linking to outcomes) is fraught with complexity, not least because of the difficulty of identifying all the variables (Holton 1996).

Vitae aims to get researcher development embedded within the policies and practice of funders and universities, and often works in collaborations with organizations with similar interests of related agendas through memoranda of understanding that articulate common objectives, for example with the UK Council of Graduate Education and the Associate of Careers Advisory Services.

It also aims to get researcher development embedded within the thinking and practice of funders and universities, and in order to do this, its most recent tool has been the creation of the Vitae Researcher Development Framework (RDF), a framework that articulates the knowledge and attributes of successful researchers at various stages of their career (Reeves *et al.* 2012). The RDF was developed in conjunction with institutions, through consultation with employers, professional bodies and other key stakeholders.

An independent report demonstrated considerable acclaim for the work of Vitae, with many of its institutional stakeholders praising its pioneering role (McWhinnie 2010). The research for this report was commissioned by Vitae as part of a mid-contract review of its progress and impact and was based on interviews with international and UK stakeholders who had all had recent contact with Vitae. The report particularly notes the importance of Vitae's work with all researchers, not just doctoral researchers. Many of the interviewees were in senior positions and the report identified two groups from whom more influence and engagement would be valuable: human resources professionals (particularly important for supporting research staff careers) and university academics who are the Principal Investigators (PIs) and doctoral supervisors. A natural place for engaging academics in the skills development of doctoral researchers is through the process of supervisor development. Many research supervisors that I meet in my workshops are keen to develop their supervisory skills and feel themselves inadequately prepared for (and sometimes not very interested in) preparing their research students for careers outside academia. Vitae and the UK Council for

Graduate Education (UKCGE), the two leading organizations concerned with postgraduate research in the UK have signed a memorandum of understanding to support and collaborate with each other in efforts in supervision development. The editors of this book write of 'working on the side of an active volcano'; those who support doctoral students in generic sessions also need a pedagogy.

The long term future for these two organizations will be interesting: UKCGE is a membership organization and Vitae is currently planning to become independent of its existing central funding streams (at the time of writing guaranteed for the next three years). The conundrum about how to manage supervisors' development of both specific and generic skills is reflected in many universities where the responsibility sits variously with academic development centres, directors of research, human resources departments, libraries and graduate schools. Generic doctoral support must mesh into institutional frameworks.

The Australian and UK approaches to understanding generic skills and attributes are linked in their interest in understanding 'contextualized performance' (Kiley and Cumming 2010), the enactment of skills in particularly challenging and unfamiliar settings. Vitae's Research Development Framework is a research-based attempt to codify these skills and different RDF lenses are being developed to interpret these skills in different contexts. The lenses currently include leadership, enterprise, intrapreneurship, teaching, information literacy, supervision and employability: this area of work has substantial potential to contextualize researchers' skills for researchers, academics and employers.

The strengths of Vitae's work are all linked to its ability to raise the profile of researcher professional development by working with UK institutions and key organizations, and increasingly at an international level, to change policy culture and provide practical resources for institutional staff supporting researchers and individual researchers to use. Vitae's international collaborations include:

1. Exploring the knowledge, behaviour and attributes of researchers in different national contexts, including in Europe, the US and Australia.
2. Working with the European Commission to embed the HR Excellence in Research Award for institutions.
3. Designing trans-national training modules to support transitions from academia to local enterprises.
4. Supporting capacity building programmes to train trainers and provide career development courses.

However, there is more to be done on developing and embedding career paths for research staff and in engaging academics in their professional development.

Vitae avoids using the terms 'generic skills,' 'training' and 'education' when describing its own work, preferring to use 'expertise' and 'competencies,' and to take a holistic approach to the professional development of researchers. However, increasing the focus on rigorous academic inquiry (for example: multi-disciplinary research into how high level skills are identified and developed) might help in engaging academics in the future. The most recent QAA Quality Code calls for training in developing both research and generic skills, and it recommends structured and integrated approaches (QAA 2012: 23). More research in this (contested) area of learning and development might help to provide a hitherto missing link between policy, research and practice. The Vitae annual conferences are successful in bringing together different organizations and international perspectives; increasingly they could also be used to debate the type of academic inquiry I have recommended above. The conferences have already begun to demonstrate that they can enable dialogue between academics and skills trainers.

Vitae has been very successful in gaining and retaining funding for its work as political regimes and economic circumstances have changed over the last ten years. To maintain this position in the future will be a continuing challenge, but it has built a solid base of resources and expertise to draw upon.

There are some criticisms of Vitae's work and one of them is that it is too instrumental; it buys into the language of performativity, measuring outcomes and impact agendas. Since it is supported by RCUK which itself is subject to politico-economic pressures, this is not surprising. Ironically, in the long run, however, a focus on instrumentality might limit the influence of its work. As we saw with the McWhinnie report, Vitae itself recognizes that it has not yet fully engaged front-line academics with its agenda, and this somewhat limiting approach could explain why.

Although the original aim of the Roberts agenda (increasing the quality and number of those engaged in researching STEM subjects) is still a key government objective and it is not clear how much progress has been made towards it, Vitae's work has a much broader objective to support the professional and career development of all researchers, irrespective of discipline. Anecdotal evidence suggests that international research students have been the group that has engaged most enthusiastically with generic skills support programmes, while cases in reports from the IEG and in the Vitae website Database of Practice signals that students' engagement with skills training supports rather than delays timely completion. Vitae still has difficult work to do to engage mainstream academics and make research careers in higher education less fractured, more attractive and coherent. Nevertheless, its many useful resources and even more useful contacts established in the first ten years mean that Vitae's international influence in raising the agenda of the career development of doctoral researchers is growing.

Anne Lee

Layered within Anne's account are the complexities of doctoral support: the contentions of national and institutional politics, discipline demands and the individuality of doctoral students. That universities not bound by the UK's national drivers also provide generic support indicates the universal importance of this work. The next chapter follows the development of generic support as it establishes its perimeters in response to a better understanding of the doctoral process.

Chapter 2

Putting together a doctoral skills programme

> ...the simultaneous fears and reassurances experienced by doctoral researchers are constructed within wider cultural and institutional processes, not simply in advisory relationships.
> (Barbara Kamler and Pat Thomson 2008: 512)

Invariably, generic doctoral support has arisen after successive cohorts of students have struggled in isolation to decipher the academy's rules. Expecting students to find their own way through the administrative and intellectual maze of higher degree research was never a good idea, and is less so in today's environment where economic forces demand timely completion. In the words of Alex Barthel, 'it is the moral and ethical duty of care of an institution to look after its students' and 'every student needs [academic learning] development' (2007, n.p. cited in Percy 2011: 37). Many universities begin with discussion on boards and committees identifying the need, then considering where such support will most logically be situated within their structure, and who will best undertake work that is driven by practical, ethical and, perhaps more pressingly, fiscal needs for retention and timely completion. In other cases, programmes have arisen out of single departments, or counseling and 'student support' agencies. Often one or two committed visionaries initially put some events together. Such programmes can begin within departments, as Cally Guerin's experience demonstrates, and spread out from there. Many who engage in such construction did their own research in disciplines other than education (common backgrounds for tertiary learning advisors, for example, tend to be English literature studies, linguistics, and history), and from that starting point, intuitively develop a form of support. They then need to make sure workshops work equally well for all disciplines. As learning developers, generic doctoral supporters must hunt for central ground shared by all, justifying their complementary role vis-à-vis the supervisory relationship, to provide the best curriculum and pedagogy for those on the cusp of becoming independent researchers.

Ideally, over time, generic support evolves into a cohesive undertaking, as shown by Ian Brailsford's and Susan Carter's accounts. Often uncertainties and financial pressures encroach, as they do even when an institution commits to a fully-fledged course, such as the postgraduate certificate in research skills described by Jean Webb. Irrespective of the workshops and seminars, the bulk of generic support in many institutions comprises one-to-one consultations with learning advisors such as Deborah Laurs who, through their daily encounters with students from across all disciplines, become extremely well versed in the genre of thesis writing. Here we introduce experiences that chart the establishment and development of doctoral skills programmes, both formal and informal. Moreover, doctoral skills preparation programmes have the potential to foster an inclusive research culture within the institution as a whole. Cally Guerin begins by describing a workshop design based on her own experience (a common source of impetus), before going on to reflect on the development potential of the support she provides.

'I wish someone had told me...'

In the days of relatively 'hands-off' supervision (Sinclair 2004) in the late 1980s, I was an unsophisticated doctoral candidate thrilled at the prospect of spending time researching a topic that fascinated me – yet utterly baffled as to how to go about it. How was this project different from writing a very long essay? And how could I ask such a question without revealing my naivety, when everybody else seemed to know exactly what they were doing? Inefficient hunches and guesswork, along with some more hands-on supervision towards the end and a lively and supportive cohort of PhD students, eventually resulted in an acceptable thesis.

It turns out my experience was not unusual, and a range of doctoral pedagogies and strategies have since been called for and introduced across disciplines to create more structured programmes in order to facilitate timely completions. Attempts to map out the desirable pedagogies of supervision have resulted in general frameworks being outlined (see, for example, Bruce and Stoodley 2009; Maxwell and Smyth 2010; Vitae 2010; Willison and O'Regan 2008) from which supervisors are encouraged to develop semi-structured programmes for their doctoral candidates. As an academic developer working with research students, my role is, of course, quite different, but shares a similar desire to provide some structure to ensure that students receive the information and skills I wish I'd had much earlier as a doctoral candidate. The result is a programme that offers both specific skills training and promotes the collegial aspect of university research life; in my aim to facilitate the building of collaborative communities, I sometimes wonder if I've become a kind of 'Mrs Dalloway' of the University in 'bringing together interesting people' (Woolf 1947) to talk about their work and intellectual pursuits.

Faculty-based vs centralized workshops

The current programme attempts to demystify the process of undertaking a research degree and is organized around three main areas: research writing;

research tools; and management of the research process. While the various workshops under each of these topics were originally intended as individual, stand-alone units rather than a 'course' as such, many candidates enrol in all (or most of) the units as if it were a series. This in itself suggested that such registrants might have been looking for some kind of structured programme to organize their learning and academic development above and beyond what can be offered by their supervisors (Cumming 2010; Grover 2007). Capitalizing on this, three workshops (On being supervised, Reviewing literature, and Effective writing strategies) are now packaged together as a series for commencing research students and offered within faculties, allowing for more targeted content. Looking ahead, the plan is to introduce a second series of workshops for students in their second year of candidature, focusing on argument and voice in doctoral writing, introductions and conclusions in the thesis, and examiners and their expectations.

My focus has been on face-to-face workshops, partly as a means of developing a stronger sense of belonging to a research culture in the university (Deem and Brehony 2000; Pilbeam, Lloyd-Jones and Denyer 2012) that is populated and embodied by real-life individuals rather than an abstract or virtual sense of community monitored by a faceless bureaucracy. Some of the side benefits of these sessions are:

- The personal contact means I find out first-hand from participants what is useful to them. This direct feedback is invaluable in modifying and developing workshops as the research environment changes over time.
- Attending sessions provides some structure for those whose own programmes are very unstructured. Having an appointment in the diary can help to break up and organize time, with the effect of using that time more efficiently ('I'll make sure I've finished writing this section before I go'). Of course, the opposite can also be the case if participants use the sessions as a procrastination technique! But, at least they gain something useful in the process.
- The opportunity to meet research students from other parts of their Faculty can instill a sense of belonging to a wider community, and an appreciation of other research that is occurring beyond their own narrow discipline.

The face-to-face workshops are generally well-subscribed. Previous experience of the centralized workshops included a significant percentage of registrants failing to turn up on the day (private conversations with academic developers from many other institutions report similar issues). Those who do attend provide very positive formal feedback, so the quality and usefulness of the sessions does not appear to be the reason for such absences. However, much higher attendance rates at the faculty-based workshops suggest that it is important for students to feel that the 'generic' content is aimed at their specific needs. So far we haven't managed to engage remote candidates in the programme, nor those whose part-time candidature prevents them from attending during standard office hours, and that is clearly an area of need that requires attention.

Thesis writing groups

Most of the workshops listed above are directed towards the needs of the first year of research degree candidature. The introduction of thesis writing groups was aimed at those for whom the initial excitement of embarking on ambitious, long-term research projects had abated (Nesbit 2004). I wanted to find a way to help second- and third-year candidates maintain their momentum and motivation, and avoid the potential isolation of writing up intensely individualized projects (Aitchison 2009; Aitchison and Lee 2010; Conrad 2006a and 2006b; Guerin *et al.* 2012; Leonard 2001).

I intend the first five sessions of the thesis writing groups to establish the 'habit' of meeting and to facilitate discussion on topics such as examination procedures, the overall shape of a thesis (both traditional and by publication), writing exercises applied to examples of participants' own writing, introductions and conclusions, argumentation, and authorial voice. Then, in a bid to encourage independence and the exercise of agency in the move from 'student' to 'researcher,' it is the participants' responsibility to take over running the sessions for themselves. Again, online versions of these groups need to be established to engage those who cannot attend in person.

In feeling my way through what current research students need from me as an academic developer, I have drawn on the published literature, observations of what other universities offer, direct feedback from postgraduates themselves, and what I myself had found rather mystifying as a PhD candidate. There is, of course, much more to be done, but the overarching aim is to provide a coherent range of workshops so that current research students are less reliant on guesswork than I was.

Cally Guerin

Offering generic support within different departments may ultimately prove unsustainable in terms of individual and institutional efficacy. The following sequential pieces by Ian Brailsford and Susan Carter recount the history behind a centralized generic support programme that, driven by the growth in postgraduate enrolments over 20 years, has grown from a single thesis writing workshop into comprehensive, campus-wide skills training for all stages of doctoral study.

Inception of generic doctoral support: the vision

This case study chronicles the evolution of support initiatives for doctoral candidates at the University of Auckland from their inception in the early 1990s. While the specifics are local to the University of Auckland – a large research-led university in New Zealand's largest city – the motives behind the initiatives and their manifestation will resonate with readers either thinking about setting up a generic support programme for doctoral students or reviewing their existing provision. The outlines of the University of Auckland journey can be detected from the changes in nomenclature:

1993 PhD Study Group
1997 PhD Network
2003 Doctoral Skills Development Programme
and finally, since 2007, Doctoral Skills Programme.

From the early informal cohort of students offering mutual support facilitated by the academic staff development unit, the emphasis has subsequently shifted to the centralized delivery of skills within a structured format.

Generic support for doctoral students is provided by student learning advisors, librarians, computer skills trainers, career guidance counselors, alumni, professional book editors and publishers and academics. At our university, this support has seen four distinct organizational phases: initially under the auspices of the academic staff development unit in the 1990s (in the early 1990s known as the Higher Education Research Office [HERO] and subsequently the Centre for Professional Development [CPD] from 1996); then transferred over to the Student Learning Centre (SLC) at the beginning of the millennium; from 2007–2012 organized through collaboration between the School of Graduate Studies, SLC/Centre for Academic Development, and the Library and Careers Service, and, since the latest restructure, it is now relocated under the Library's governance.

While the moves in the mid-2000s to instigate a fully-fledged Doctoral Skills Programme followed high-level discussions involving the Dean, the Board of Graduate Studies and the University Quality and Planning Office, the initial 1990s' 'PhD Study Group' was the brainchild of two staff developers, Adele Graham and Barbara Grant, who were primarily interested in the pedagogy of postgraduate supervision. Workshops for new academic staff in the 'Art of Graduate Supervision' had been offered in the late 1980s, and in 1990 the Faculty of Arts requested workshops for its postgraduate students as well. In 1992, HERO ran five sessions to Masters and PhD students on negotiating supervision and managing the thesis. In the same year, Graham and Grant interviewed thesis students in the Department of Mechanical Engineering 'to elicit their attitudes towards the postgraduate supervision procedures they experienced.' Various conference papers resulted from this research along with a set of guidelines for supervisors and graduate students and, in May 1992, Estelle Phillips, co-author of the seminal *How to get a PhD,* delivered a full-day workshop on 'Managing a PhD' to 31 University of Auckland PhD students.

Doctoral enrolments at the university grew steadily; in 1990 there were 371 candidates, increasing to 618 by 1995, 929 in 1999, and over 2,000 by 2013. Growth was recognized as consistent: 'heavy demand from students and supervisors for programmes aimed at postgraduate teaching. This is likely to generate more activity as the proportion of postgraduate students climbs' (*HERO Annual Report* 1993: n.p.). Within this context, the first PhD 'Study Group' under HERO's umbrella emerged in May 1993, with a full-day workshop entitled 'Getting Started on your PhD – Humanities and Social Sciences.' The morning dealt with writing research proposals while the blurb for the afternoon session entitled 'Setting up a Support Group' dangled this carrot:

> Meeting regularly with a group of your peers can be fruitful and motivating.
> In this session we will discuss the mechanics of establishing such a group plus some processes you can use in the group.

The PhD Study Group that was subsequently established met the first Friday of the month for the rest of the year; students suggested the topics and HERO provided the facilities and organization. The first five workshops dealt with scholarships and awards; working with your supervisor; making your research happen; giving conference papers; and, intriguingly, should a PhD be a series of projects or a big bang? Attendance levels were robust with between 25 and 35 students per session, while 70 candidates were on the group's mailing lists. From this point, doctoral students were treated as a distinct sub-species of postgraduates.

The PhD Study Group grew organically, mostly through word-of-mouth advertising and notices on departmental notice-boards; no systematic attempt was made to contact all 500 of the early 1990s' doctoral students at the university. By 1995 the programme was rebranded as a 'PhD Network,' offering 20 fortnightly sessions and, by 1996, HERO's successor, the CPD, was also offering one-to-one consultations with PhD students. The 1997 PhD Network was designed following a survey-based needs analysis with PhD students, resulting in a stripped-down programme: getting published as you go; giving conference papers and seminars; organizing references to avoid chaos; and project management and time management. In September 1998, doctoral education took centre stage at the University of Auckland with a Vice-Chancellor's Symposium entitled 'Policy and Practice to Enhance the Quality of the PhD Experience.' The event brought together candidates, supervisors and heads of department to explore the 'doctoral supervision experience from different angles.' At the same time, topics for the PhD Network sessions were extended to include 'using the internet for research' and 'thinking ahead to a career.'

Ian Brailsford

Brailsford's history reveals how a generic doctoral support programme arose from the awareness that doctoral students occupy an ambivalent space: emerging researchers who are both students and academics. In their first year, doctoral candidates are novices making a sometimes difficult transition; yet, by the end of the process, they will be virtually peers alongside early career academics. For this reason, generic support often focuses on the transition into research, and from there, into a professional future. In the late 1990s of Brailsford's case study, discussions took place between the CPD and the SLC to review 'the boundaries for the provision of services to graduate students', with the result that CPD would focus on supervision and SLC on the production of Masters and PhD theses, a tale picked up by Susan Carter in the following section. Carter notes that the role of generic support for students in general at the University of Auckland – as at many other institutions – emerged from recognition of the psychological challenges of a long arduous process that often seems to offer few completion points for affirmation. As such, the story of generic support extends from its pragmatic purely skills-based beginnings, to a more collaborative and holistic focus.

Growth of the vision: the Doctoral Skills Programme

Alongside academic staff development, the SLC at the University of Auckland emerged in the 1980s from counseling services' recognition that there were increasing numbers of students who needed help with the discourses of academia. The university recognized its social responsibility to ensure that traditionally under-represented groups such as Māori, Pacific Island, low socio-economic, mature and female students had equitable access to tertiary education. It also recognized the fiscal common sense of retaining these students rather than leaving them to fail through lack of literacy on entry.

Once it was established, SLC staff recognized that there were other transitions that required attention, including those from the learning achieved in undergraduate taught courses to learning as an independent researcher. Keen to develop its research prowess, the institution set its sights on increasing the ratio of research students to undergraduates, and increasing annual doctoral completions. Amongst a raft of other initiatives, a full-time academic position was established in 2003 for a lecturer who would develop a generic doctoral programme teaching some of the meta-skills of research.

The full Monty: a stand-alone doctoral programme

The next shift was prompted by recognition that support for doctoral students came from a variety of sources, primarily the Library and Careers Office as well as SLC. It would be less confusing for students if there was one cohesive programme incorporating support from different providers. The School of Graduate Studies oversaw several years benchmarking against Australian and Universitas 21 universities and planning, resulting in the launch, in March 2007, of the Doctoral Skills Programme (DSP), a cohesive programme combining support from the various providers. The DSP is benchmarked to international standards and responsive to literature on the doctorate (including that of Sharon Parry, Gina Wisker, Terry Evans and Carey Denholm, Barbara Lovitt, Chris Park, C.M. Golde, Brian Paltridge and Sue Starfield, Patrick Dunleavy, Chris Hart, Vernon Trafford and Shosh Leshem, and Lyn Pearce, amongst many others). Core work aligns with the University of Auckland's Strategic Plan of the time and with graduate profile description. This careful alignment seems crucial for buy-in from the wider institution. One of the critical aspects of generic support is that it has genuine backing, ensuring funding, but also ensuring that academic staff will warmly recommend students to take up the optional courses on offer. We learned that we had to pay attention to marketing.

A notable DSP feature is the compulsory Induction Day, which students must attend as part of their requirements to move from provisional to full doctoral registration. The Induction Day has become a central teaching activity. At 2012, the DSP offered 39 optional sessions in addition to the compulsory Induction Day. The sessions are designated as early, mid or late phase, and further, as core and additional, with core sessions being suitable for all students and additional being of use to different groups of students (for example, there were some on quantitative and qualitative methodology and applying for ethics committee approval). The division into phases caters for the quite different needs of early and completing students, and for those in the middle distance range who often need re-inspiration as well as practical support (with writing, getting to conferences, and creating posters, etc.).

The DSP hosted a one-day annual forum with panels, guest speakers and lunch provided. For about eight years there was a regular fortnightly writing group for students whose first language is not English, where for two hours English-first-language volunteers from the community worked carefully with them on their writing. The volunteers were gleaned initially from the University of the Third Age, a group for retired people still interested in thinking and learning, and often former academics (Carter 2009b). In 2011, an Academic Careers Skills module was launched with a series of workshops inculcating students into the processes of academic work. We also provided workshops for departmental and faculty writing retreats, and support individual groups of postgraduate students wishing to set up peer review groups, or to have our input to some event they are organizing.

Now sturdily developed and with fresh fine-tuning under a new structure, the DSP needs to continually look for ways to demonstrate effectiveness. Given the doctorate's lengthy duration, it is challenging to find ways to measure generic work convincingly and claim that speed of completion, pleasure in the process or excellence of the product can be attributed specifically to the provision of strong generic support (Brailsford, Carter and Kelly 2010). Financial strain has raised storms of change, with a trimming of sails, but the ship sails on.

Susan Carter

The University of Auckland's history shows the rise and development of generic support within a single institution. In the UK, postgraduate skills training is a national requirement, with universities mandated to equip students with the requisite skills both for study and future careers. Jean Webb accounts for the relatively new University of Worcester's decision to introduce a formal qualification in research skills, while highlighting the tensions imposed by the auditing requirements upon which funding depends.

Postgraduate skills certification: a case study from the New University sector (UK)

The following is a case study drawing on my experiences and observations as an academic in the position of developing research student training programmes in the early days of such movements in the UK prompted by the highly influential Roberts' Report (National Archives 2002). Motivation came from the concern about the nation's position internationally in relation to development and research in science and technology, which had considerable implications for its economic and financial standing.

The findings of the Roberts' Report emphasized the benefits of training for research students, not only in matters of research, but also in skills that are transferable to industry, the workplace and career development. This led to funding being provided for support. The impact of the decision to institute research training as part of the student experience was twofold: firstly the Research Councils' funding of research students was tied to the provision of a suitable programme. Secondly, the Quality Assurance Agency, which safeguards practice in Higher Education in the UK, incorporated the recommendations into their Postgraduate Code of Practice (QAA 2004) that governs all institutions. These recommendations enable flexibility within a diverse sector.

Not every university in the UK has funded research students. Moreover, in the past four years the Research Councils have shifted from an open access, student-led competition for places to allocation of studentships to universities with an established track record in successful research grant applications. The result is a cycle of exclusion, which becomes increasingly difficult for the new university sector to break in to. The potential danger is of a two-tier higher education sector which splits institutions into those which are research-led and those which are principally engaged in teaching, thus diluting the quality of experience for students overall, and the potential effectiveness of universities as places of challenge to accepted knowledge and the creation of new knowledge and thinking.

Role of institution in relation to national requirements

The University of Worcester, where I have been an academic for over 20 years, has a thriving research student population, which is small but nonetheless significant – 10,000 students in 2010–2011, of whom 20 percent were engaged in postgraduate research (University of Worcester, 2011). In 1991, a small unit at Worcester was set up to foster research degree students. This was a secure and positive beginning with most students on bursaries fully funded by the university. The then Director of the unit, Dr Frank Crompton, initiated a highly innovative research student training and support programme at a time when such programmes were certainly not the norm in the UK. In 1999, Worcester expanded and set up a Graduate School (now the Graduate Research School) for which I was Associate Head. One of my central tasks was to develop a more formal research student training programme, which was somewhat ahead of the Roberts' Report. The programme had to be generic and interdisciplinary from the outset, since a small institution with circa 120 research students had neither the capital to invest in subject-specific training, nor sufficient student mass within individual cohorts to always make this viable. Furthermore, a good deal of research is increasingly interdisciplinary, which influences the teaching approach as well as content and structure in designing the programme.

The programme consists of a Postgraduate Certificate in Research Methods, comprising three modules at postgraduate level. The first compulsory module is skills-based, ensuring that the students fully understand research processes, ethical matters, etc., and provides a base for the development of the research proposal. As in other universities, the full proposal represents a research process in itself, in order to evidence originality, knowledge of the context, methodology, theory, ethical considerations, timescale, etc., which takes a full-time student up to six months and a part-time student up to a year to complete, depending upon their starting place. The second module is a subject-based research methods course, which forms part of the master's programme, and may be offered external to Worcester. The third module, 'The Professionalization of the Researcher', is optional for those who wish to achieve the PG Certificate and addresses such matters as responding to a call for conference papers; making a conference presentation; and developing a presentation or paper for publication. Further areas are writing for publication, editing, making funding applications, teaching, organizing and running a conference, etc. etc., in other words, the kinds of areas which academics are supposed to 'know' by osmosis, yet really only learn by hard experience.

The teaching approach adopted in these generic modules at Worcester draws on student knowledge and experience and also that of academic colleagues. It is impossible for one individual to have the requisite specialist knowledge to teach across the sciences, humanities, social sciences, education, and health psychology. It is therefore essential to think around the positioning of the tutor/lecturer as the fount of all knowledge. Instead, generic skills trainers act as facilitators, enabling research students from all areas to learn from each other and apply interdisciplinary or specialist approaches according to their own particular needs and concerns. The demands of such approaches to teaching are considerable, yet very rewarding. The skills required are those of listening, problem solving outside one's subject specialism, and encouraging students to build an understanding of their work that they can interrogate and deeply understand. The whole approach is, at all times, student centred with a deep appreciation of process and problem solving: its goal is to take forward the next generation of thinkers who will shape our world.

Jean Webb

Each of these narratives from institutions in Australia, New Zealand and the UK share common themes in the design of programmes to support doctoral candidates' research, writing and personal development: recognition of need, a foundational basis on experience, and the emergence of doctoral students as a distinct cohort with the potential to work together on the various challenges of doing a doctorate.

Such positioning of generic support needs to be established and maintained within an institution's existing political framework. Acting as 'agents of organizational change' (Percy 2011: 33) may be hard: we need to discern the boundary between what really is generic, and what lies outside our scope. The more we can ensure that supervisors, departmental heads and deans understand what we do, the better, a message that may be less easy to convey if generic advisors are located within service units rather than within research-active academic programmes. We need to be shrewd with our marketing, aware that generic support must not be seen as remedial, primarily for weak students, or as inferior to discipline-specific supervisory advice. Doctoral students can benefit from an impartial sounding board at stages throughout their research journey; nonetheless, we need the trust of supervisors as we broker advice. Some of our work will be academic, some pastoral; there may well be demarcation boundaries to negotiate with counseling services as well as supervisors.

At some universities, generic learning advisors provide individualized support for students throughout their doctoral journey. This complements supervision; however, it also resembles it closely. The generic perspective affords unique insight into expectations across the institution, but also demands clear articulation of roles and responsibilities, as shown by the following piece from Deborah Laurs, who works with doctoral students at Victoria University of Wellington, New Zealand.

One-to-one generic support

The importance of providing learning support for undergraduates is well-recognized, with tertiary learning centres routinely offering academic skills workshops, one-to-one consultations, customized programmes within core first-year courses, and targeted programmes for international and other equity groups (Chanock 2002; Craswell and Bartlett 2001; Loads 2007; Samuelowicz 1990). Less well-known, however, is the individual support we offer to postgraduates. Handbooks such as *Doctorates Downunder: Keys to Successful Doctoral Study* (Denholm and Evans 2006) make no mention of non-supervisory support avenues other than fellow students and library staff, and a survey at my university (Laurs 2010) revealed that only 40 percent of doctoral supervisors knew about the research skills seminar series, thesis writing workshops and one-to-one postgraduate consultations offered by our Student Learning Support Service (SLSS).

One reason for this lack of awareness is the tendency to regard learning support as a remedial service (Clerehan 2007; Percy 2011). Frequently aligned with student services such as finance and counseling rather than with academic units, learning centres are often seen

> as a form of crash repair shop where welding, panel-beating and polishing can be carried out on students' texts – an idea that makes sense only if you regard the text as a vehicle for the writer's thoughts, and separable from the thoughts themselves.
>
> (Chanock 2007: 273)

On the other hand, as Kamler and Thomson (2006) affirm, academic writing entails much more than mechanical skills. Once postgraduate students and supervisors appreciate the complex processes associated with co-creating knowledge, learning and applying the discursive rules of the discipline and developing authorial identity, the contribution that generic support can make becomes clear. Rather than merely fixing problems, learning advisors develop considerable expertise in the genre of thesis writing (frequently more so than individual supervisors), given the breadth of our 'perspective across the disciplines, across the various phases of higher education, and across the cultures from which our students come' (Chanock 2007: 275). For example, amongst other one-to one appointments, my colleagues and I saw 77 PhD students during a 20-month period (March 2008–Oct 2009), some of them consulting us regularly throughout their candidature. In each case, all sought advice that was far from remedial.

We find that postgraduate students may feel inhibited about expressing unformed thoughts to their supervisor, and often perceive learning advisors as a less threatening audience, particularly in the initial stages. In this regard, generic advisors have the advantage of not being part of the formal supervisory relationship, a complex power hierarchy (Grant 2003, 2005; Symons 2001; Wisker *et al.* 2003) that, at times, might benefit from third-party input.

As intelligent readers and disinterested sounding boards, generic advisors help students find their voice and refine expression of ideas. While in no way purporting to be a counseling service, I find many of the sessions with doctoral candidates involve exactly this – with no input on my part other than allowing the student to talk. Although often criticized as 'an expensive luxury' (Wilson, Li and Collins 2011: A139) by insitutions seeking to economize, one-to-one appointments afford doctoral candidates an invaluable 'safe space' in which to share their uncertainties, vent their frustrations, and clarify their thoughts, in order to shift from a concept of writing for oneself to writing for an audience (Flower 1981).

Working one-on-one, learning advisors are ideally placed to complement the formal supervisory relationship, irrespective of whether they are employed as academics or general staff. Undoubtedly, good research under the auspices of the subject-specific supervisor is the key to doctoral success, but thesis production is an integral part of this journey (Kearns, Gardiner and Marshall 2008). Supervisory feedback on written drafts often focuses on aspects that need improving, without necessarily providing guidance on how to do so. As one graduate student interviewed by Yeh (2010: A-8) commented, 'the typical scenario [is that] we submit a topic and we are told, "This does not do. Try again."' This is where our generic understanding of the structure of the thesis and the moves it must demonstrate, come in. A domestic PhD student (in Religious Studies) at my institution characterized such support as follows:

> Through the...techniques I learned at SLSS...I have been able to take my research analysis to a higher level – a kind of spiral effect of writing and analysis development.
>
> (Laurs 2010: 26)

Generic advisors not only help to develop and refine postgraduates' skills in reading and writing (possibly in other than the student's first language), they also offer assistance in the related areas of critical thinking, academic integrity, argumentation and written expression, thereby leaving supervisors free to concentrate on content-related advice.

Although many postgraduates access generic advice independently (the student–learning advisor relationship remaining confidential), the best results arise when student, learning advisor and supervisor work together. Such three-way collaboration has the potential to create an efficient synergy, although the relationship requires clear parameters – and willingness on the part of all concerned, as revealed by the following supervisor's response:

> I would react with suspicion if a learning advisor attempted to insert him or herself as a partner in the supervision of a graduate degree....Somebody skilled in the pedagogy of learning, or of education, but not in a specific discipline, might just as well do harm rather than good if attempting to provide help to students writing an advanced thesis.
>
> (Laurs 2010: 27)

Collaboration always risks exposing one's practice to scrutiny, and delicate care is needed to ensure that generic advisors do not presume to intervene in discipline-related issues. However, lack of subject knowledge is a particular complementary strength, as revealed by an International PhD candidate in Law:

> Although the advisor had no special training in my field I found that the questions she asked helped me to clarify my own thinking and even to think about aspects of the topic which I had not considered before.
>
> (Laurs 2010: 26)

Writing a doctoral thesis is a complex and challenging undertaking over and above the other requisite research skills. Some students receive all the guidance they need from their supervisors; others are sufficiently adept at managing the process so as not to require extra support. On the other hand, many more students

– and their supervisors – appreciate generic support as a valuable complement to traditional discipline-specific supervision.

Deborah Laurs

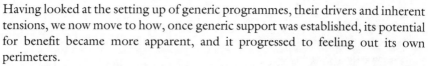

Having looked at the setting up of generic programmes, their drivers and inherent tensions, we now move to how, once generic support was established, its potential for benefit became more apparent, and it progressed to feeling out its own perimeters.

Part II begins with a chapter showing how generic programmes develop as learning advisors find their route, responding to the potential of the place they occupy within the institutional framework. It's a space often referred to as being 'central' that can nonetheless feel marginalized to those working in generic support (Alexander 2005; Rowland 2006: 75). It occurs in the borderlands between disciplines, another spatial metaphor that captures its risks and potentials, the perils of cross-cultural misunderstanding and the considerable benefits of trading.

PART II
Developing generic support's potential

Chapter 3

Responding to cross-campus student requirements

> the practice of doctoral work could be seen as a taking up and utilization of the affordances provided by the programs in which the candidates operate, the research environment in which they are embedded, the people they encounter and, in turn, the practices they develop from these opportunities.
>
> (Alison Lee and David Boud 2009b: 16)

Chapter 3 opens Part II's investigation of the development afforded by the generic perspective. Susan Carter begins in the first person to bring alive the typical episodes that lead to recognition of doctoral student need. Those of us working in doctoral support see such need with sharp clarity.

A threshold moment for a generic advisor

At the end of a motivation session for doctoral students, a doubtful-looking woman stays behind to talk. She studies at home because she has two small children. She lives on the fringes of the city where rent is cheaper, so it is hard for her to organize coming in to department events. She feels outside of the collegial circle, a different species from the other doctoral students who share a friendly office in the department. Recently her annual departmental presentation was, she felt, torn to shreds by faculty members. What was probably intended to be helpfully rigorous feedback came across as a rejection of her research project and of her herself. The final nail in her researcher's coffin was the throw-away comment that 'all doctoral students need to spend eight hours each day on their thesis to get anywhere.' She would never be able to do this. In fact, she felt reproved for having children and domestic responsibilities.

Individual consultations with students often direct generic support. The woman above prompted me to recognize that I could do more about the problem she described. A couple of other students mentioned seemingly negative feedback at their oral presentations. None made their appointment to discuss that particular grievance, but it came up as a cause of tension exacerbating other insecurities.

Crucially, these students came from different departments and my position outside of departmental cultures and power hierarchies has given me an insight into another skill that students need to develop as emerging academics: in this case, the ability to negotiate and control public feedback from those higher up the academic power structure and, indeed, to develop strategies for manoeuvring efficaciously within research communities. I factor strategies into my session on conference presentations on ways of handling the social dimensions unleashed by the open invitation for 'questions' that often end up as stern interrogation. Similarly, my writing workshops stress that all academics receive rigorous criticism because they operate within a dialogic working environment, and there is a need to toughen up about feedback, control the emotions as part of researcher development, and take on self-control as a conscious project.

Susan Carter

In this chapter, advisors who have developed their teaching, expanding their repertoire and honing material in response to recognized needs, tell their stories. Generic sessions allow for a space outside of departmental politics (and perhaps judgment) where students can talk about the challenges safely, as Susan Carter and Catherine Cook show. There is also potential to work holistically, developing a range of skills with one international cohort, as Gina Wisker and Gill Robinson have successfully done. Theoretical discussion across disciplines allows for dynamic discussion, with Mary Roberts suggesting that foregrounding the epistemological boundaries, the borderlands where academic cultures meet, enables individual students to see their own discipline's logic more clearly. It's possible to teach how to be attentive to detail at different levels; Linda Evans ends this chapter with an example of how to sharpen definition.

Addressing the psychological challenges of doctoral study is arguably a significant part of all generic sessions: students may feel ashamed of and secretive about their shrivelled enthusiasm or lack of progress, and unwilling to declare it to those in their own department. Importantly, generic sessions can broach such issues explicitly.

Motivation: collaboration between counselling and academic advising

The two-hour motivation session for doctoral students at the University of Auckland emerged initially from counselling experience. During the first half of the session, a counsellor identifies common emotional, social and identity-change challenges that can de-rail the doctoral progress, based on literature and on her own decade-long counselling of doctoral students. Her observations have both authority and authenticity. In an interactive second half, a learning advisor provides nine different strategies for overcoming inertia, writer's block or disinterest, again based on literature and on individual work with students.

Some specific tensions beset doctoral candidates. Family and friends' failure to recognize the work involved or the project's importance can demotivate. Identity changes during the process of the doctorate, which, for some, raise pressures elsewhere (for example, in relationships or within other circles, including church groups) that might not have been problematic previously. Completion itself can seem frightening, closing down the possibilities for the thesis and raising the spectre of job hunting.

Tensions may also relate to gender. Males may have friends earning good money who cause them to feel inadequate. Marriage can raise the possibility of starting a family or buying a house, with a wife growing impatient. Financial support from a female partner runs against the traditional heterosexual model of the man as bread-winner. Working in a subordinate position within the supervisory relationship goes against masculine gender stereotypes.

Women have different challenges. The equality that females experience early in education can run out at the doctoral level. Cook, in her role as counsellor, finds some families are happy to have a daughter with a Master's degree, especially if she has a well-paying job, but they become less sure when their doctoral daughter is growing older, failing to produce children, and remaining relatively poor. In Cook's experience, families and friends advise women but not men to quit when it gets tough. Women with an abuse history can find that supervisory 'rigour' stunningly disempowers them. Such women may also find it hard to claim an authoritative voice as an expert in the field when historically they have relied on keeping a low profile to avoid trouble. Women may also find that, as their identity shifts and they do become more confident, male partners complain that they are less attractive because they are less feminine.

As well, gender role expectations tend to make it more likely that families regard the female doctoral student (who does not have a 'real' job) as the obvious caregiver, available for babysitting or care of elderly family members. Doctoral women with children may feel judged as inadequate, both at home and within the university (Carter, Blumenstein and Cook 2013).

In the session, Cook proposed five strategies from research that will cultivate motivation and 'grit,' that Wild West characteristic of stamina, perseverance and sheer endurance. 'Grit' evokes crawling across a rocky landscape while bleeding from gunshot wounds. Her recommendations for doctoral grit include balancing and prioritizing, sorting the crucial from what is able to be sacrificed, and communicating more constructively. Our session also advertises that doctoral students can have free counselling sessions with her – usually, immediately afterwards, several of those who attended would discretely take up this offer.

Carter's learning advisor half of the session includes advice that is common in guides to thesis writers, and some that emerges from her own experience. At this point the session moves from advice about emotional stress to strategies for handling the work when interest has waned. Students share their own tips and experience.

This session achieves several outcomes. First, it acknowledges and normalizes the stresses that some students feel, advertising the counselling available, attracting and catering for students at risk of bailing out. Then, putting practical strategies for overcoming writer's block, or disinterest, into collegial discussion suggests routes to re-engagement. Collaboration on a student need recognized from two generic perspectives, counsellor and learning advisor, drives this generic session.

Susan Carter and Catherine Cook

In the following piece, Gill Robinson and Gina Wisker from the United Kingdom report on a programme that not only succeeded in building effective relationships among learning advisors, supervisors and students, but also recognized its own Scholarship of Teaching and Learning potential, by engaging in action research from the outset. The opportunity for two-way cross-fertilization between teaching and research opens exciting possibilities for energetic, passionate teachers.

Building international research communities

Although doctoral development and support programmes are relatively common now, they were unusual in 1996 when the programme for Israeli PhD candidates was put together at Anglia Ruskin University in Chelmsford, UK. The programme developed because the reliable agents who had brought MA and BA students to Anglia Ruskin decided there was overwhelming need for a PhD programme, and an enterprising Dean of Education agreed, put together two equally enterprising staff members, one of whom led the programme throughout from 1996–2006, and let them engage with the process. There was a felt need for a way of supporting a cohort-based PhD programme, consisting of part time, mid-career professionals, many of whom sought to carry out research related to their professional practice. All spoke English as a second, third or fourth language and each came from the variety of origins that make up modern Israel, e.g. Romania, Afghanistan, Poland, Czech Republic, Morocco. The programme nonetheless needed the same rigorous requirements as a similar programme for UK candidates. Once the programme was underway the student group was always about one third Arab and one third Jewish, and 60 percent or more female. These part time mid-career professionals needed to gain qualifications for their personal and work development, and in Israel at the time this opportunity did not exist.

The programme pre-dated the Roberts' (2002) and Metcalfe (Metcalfe, Thomson and Green 2002) reports. The Metcalfe report found many universities lacked supervisory and student development programmes, which the Roberts' funding helped establish, although the majority of money went to the more established, traditional, older UK universities, as they had the largest number of PhDs.

Our programme, then, was highly original and initially developed as the students developed. It began with the programme leader, Gill Robinson, meeting all the candidates before entry to explain the programme and the PhD process prior to any development of proposals. Different stages of the development programme evolved:

we provided workshops on methodology and proposal writing; getting started after proposal acceptance; navigating the PhD/confirmation of candidature process, seminars and some thesis writing; and viva preparation.

There are several features unique to this innovative and successful programme: the commitment of the agents and their local support in pastoral and intellectual terms and in community building; the cohort nature of the programme that built sustainable research communities; the guardian supervisors who supported all the students, above and beyond their own supervisory teams, stepping in should a student lose their supervisor. The programme generated action research, which fed directly back into its improvement, and reflective self-awareness of the students in terms of their own learning as researchers.

We accompanied the doctoral learning journeys with action research right from the start. The intention behind this was to involve students as co-researchers so that they were inside a research process that focused on their own development, and to directly feed back into the programme their discoveries about learning and its implications for any changes in supervision, the programme and their own behaviours in order to support their likelihood of success.

Our action research initially used Meyer and Boulton-Lewis' (1997) reflections on learning inventory to explore the intentions, outcomes, motivations and awareness of learning, which produced fascinating insights into the dissonance between students' intended outcomes, which were frequently transformative, and their approaches to research, which were often accumulative, quantitative-based, i.e. fact collecting yet aiming to make a change in the practice (unaware of the gap that presented in the middle of the process). We also explored and encouraged meta-learning (Flavell 1979), and built much research around the positive benefits of communities of practice (Lave and Wenger 1991), which the students were fast building through the local communities and group work we encouraged during the initial and ongoing stages of the programme. Participants then took over, extended and sustained this research and support throughout and beyond the programme into professional capacities. Three of the graduates became co-researchers with the course developers and have delivered at international conferences and co-published with us since 2005.

The structure of the course is described below. It aimed to enable students to have a supportive staged development, from identification of the question through to the proposal, and also at the procedural and developmental stages in their work through to a final workshop on viva completion, which some students attended more than once as their studies took a little longer than the three years on which the programme was initially developed. The research development programme was unique in its day because it helped foster communities and sustainable research development practices and collaborations between students, not on shared topics, but on the processes and journey of the research. The accompaniment with action research helped develop reflective learners and improved the programme throughout. It also added credibility to decisions made about elements of content and delivery because these were research informed.

The learning processes involved a range of workshops led by the programme team and guest experts on methodology and methods, interactive sessions in which students worked in groups: explaining their question, conceptual framework, achievement to date and re-questioning ongoing work and justifications at appropriate stages. This exploration used the action learning model of groups of five or six taking turns to explore these issues then being questioned by the others, leading to clarification, analysis and the sharing of good practices.

Through the process the whole cohort have been supported by the agents, who are a focus for information, care and communication, and who accompanied the students throughout the workshops. The agents have been very much part of the overall team and their wives also participated in the programme to successful completion. We all never became so close that we couldn't say difficult things about people's work, yet we were all extremely professionally friendly and have remained so even with graduates.

The programme intended to build communities and life skills for the journey, and it not only did that but also helped develop insights into and some early research informed practice on, methodology and methods, and the work and writing expected at different stages in the PhD process. The materials the team members developed have been turned into guidance work papers for programme delivery and also into several books (Trafford and Leshem 2009; Wisker 2001, 2005, 2008, 2010).

The Anglia Ruskin University (UK) PhD programme for Israeli students

A particular strength of the programme was that it is cohort based, a form of professional and social support so often missing from the traditional PhD experience. We were provided with excellent prospective candidates, recruited by the agents in Israel through rigorous selection. The UK core team consisted of Professors and Readers who each possessed extensive experience of supervision and examination at the doctoral level. In the final stages the team also included three Israeli graduates from the programme, who worked with the UK core team during the workshops.

Throughout their doctoral studies, candidates had a Director of Studies and a second supervisor. In support of this process, the University provides regular workshops on 'good practice' in supervision. Recently, mindful of the demands of distance supervision, an on-line support programme for supervisors was developed. For those based locally, a Supervisors' Away Day, a gathering involving discussion and workshopping to update skills, is held each year. Candidates are also encouraged to visit their supervisors in the UK early in the process and thereafter at critical moments in the research and writing-up stages.

All candidates are required to defend their thesis in front of two examiners, one of whom is external to the University. Candidates defend their thesis in English, but a translator is also present during the examination if required.

The workshops

The students receive a three-phase compulsory input in line with the University requirements as follows:

PHASE 1: AN INTRODUCTION TO RESEARCH DEGREES

This is a series of workshops held over three days, normally in Turkey. This stage has been designed so that each member will have personal time with a tutor and also take part in group discussions. This arrangement allows advice and guidance to be given on everyone's proposed research areas.

The purpose of the workshop is to:

- Introduce the nature and personal demands or undertaking study for a PhD
- Explain the process of registration for a PhD at our University
- Offer advice and guidance on the production of a research proposal
- Provide personal tutorial time for each member to discuss their possible research topic(s) with one of the tutors
- Outline the next stage of the research process – and the arrangements for the Summer School on Research Methodologies for Doctoral Candidates.

PHASE 2: RESEARCH METHODOLOGIES FOR DOCTORAL CANDIDATES

This is a ten-day Summer School during which the candidates are resident in the UK at the Chelmsford campus. The Summer School programme takes into account the students' existing expertise in research methodology. In designing this Summer School the team has been concerned to balance the provision of 'new' ideas about research, the opportunity for each candidate to discuss their own proposal with a tutor, and the reinforcement of existing views. The programme achieves a balance through presentations by tutors who have each undertaken extensive doctoral level research.

The formal sessions are supported by scheduled time when the students discuss their proposal with colleagues and then present those ideas to experienced research supervisors. Thus, candidates will be encouraged to accept responsibility for their own academic intentions and engage in scholastic discussion about their proposals.

The purpose of the Summer School is to:

- Explore the philosophical issues that influence the design and conduct of doctoral study
- Consider the respective contribution of different methodologies to the design and conduct of doctoral research
- Explain the main characteristics that constitute 'doctoral worthiness,' and which are used by external examiners as the criteria to judge the quality of theses

- Assist all candidates to refine methodologies, and text, of their respective research proposals prior to submission to the University for registration
- Explain the process of registration for doctoral studies at Anglia Polytechnic University
- Provide tutorial time for each candidate to discuss and clarify their research proposal with an experienced research supervisor
- Enable all candidates to make use of appropriate text and electronic sources that have relevance to their research area(s).

The programme contains formal lectures, specific tasks, group discussions, plenary sessions, individual study and personal tutorials. The structure of the programme is cumulative and developmental.

PHASE 3: FINAL WRITING AND VIVA PREPARATION

The final phase, which is compulsory, is attended by candidates normally in their third year of study. It contains formal lectures, workshops and role play. The purpose of this phase is to:

- Enable candidates to critically reflect on the coherence and rigour of their research
- Consider the effectiveness of their written thesis in communicating research questions, method, methodology, findings and conclusions
- Enable the candidate to refine the text of the thesis
- Assist them in understanding the importance of knowing their research thoroughly
- Offer them opportunities to explore and experience strategies for defending their thesis in the viva
- To prepare the candidate for a successful outcome.

Additional workshops

We were aware that the distance nature of the programme calls for special vigilance. In response to perceived need we have introduced two additional workshops, Confirmation of Candidature and Getting Started, both of which have been well received.

CONFIRMATION OF CANDIDATURE

This is an additional compulsory two-day workshop that gives students the opportunity to confirm their candidature through working with tutors to audit their progress. One issue addressed in the workshop is scholastic cohesion and understanding within the thesis. The other issue is an emphasis on the role and contribution of conceptualization within the process. The Confirmation of

Candidature Workshop runs parallel with the Viva Preparation Workshop, enabling candidates who are part way through their research to dialogue with others nearing completion.

GETTING STARTED

This workshop initially reflected the ideas and concerns of the 2003 Cohort regarding strategies for getting started. It runs parallel with the Phase 1 Workshop, thus allowing an exchange of ideas between those just entering the programme and those who have already had their proposal accepted.

For the final iterations of the research development programme all five stages ran. Students were supported throughout the programme by their 'guardian supervisors,' the agents and the programme leader, who acted as a form of personal tutor, making the links among individuals, supervisors and institutional demands, and sometimes dealing with hundreds of emails a week from the candidates. By responding to student needs in this way, we continue to give serious attention to how the quality of doctoral research can be improved and supported.

Gina Wisker and Gillian Robinson

This UK programme bridged cultures and distance. Bringing students into what is effectively a Scholarship of Teaching and Learning research project, invited them to learn more about their own research projects by observing their own learning, a circular development. The healthy link between teaching and research pulled doctoral candidates into explicit observation of their own learning.

Perceptions enabled by generic doctoral support include a better understanding of theory and methodology, two cornerstones of every thesis that might, on first appearance, seem difficult to teach across campus, because they are so specific to disciplines. In particular, theory seems so closely linked to epistemology as to be irretrievable from discipline context. However, arguably it is the theoretical and methodological discipline differences that chart some of the generic requirements of a doctorate. Barry White explains how he came to write a detailed book on thesis production:

> The book had its origins five years ago while I was presenting seminars for thesis writers from diverse disciplinary backgrounds and with equally diverse theoretic approaches. That each could be expected to write and structure their thesis differently had been long established. Less clear were the choices involved and the decisions that explained those choices. The subsequent journey to seek clarification resulted in moulding and remoulding an evolving manuscript [i.e. his book].
>
> (White 2011: 339–340)

White's book is fully contextualized in a history of the development of new knowledge and its acceptance in different disciplines. His journey beats a path from Plato and Aristotle through Descartes and Newton and on to Barthes, Derrida, Nietsche and Rorty, with 279 works cited joining some of the gaps in between. White's mapping of the thesis makes an excellent contribution to the thesis guide genre by merit of its grounding in generic practice, including when it comes to the theoretical signalling of thesis structure. Classroom discussion across disciplines can be revealing: explaining to a fellow doctoral student in another field why something works in your discipline may enable both of you to better discuss theory in your own theses. O'Connor and Petch (2012: 85) throw down the gauntlet: 'the task of the teacher is to embed the invention of new intellectual tools in order to create the context in which imaginative variation and creative contribution can flourish.' The next two contributions show academics at work in the invention of intellectual tools to help doctoral students imagine and create their research. The first description of how such a session might work comes from Mary Roberts.

Generic critical thinking workshops

There has been much discussion, ably canvassed by Jones (2009) as to whether 'generic skills and attributes' can really be taught generically or whether they must be embedded in a discipline. Jones (2009: 85) herself 'challenges the assumption that generic attributes transcend disciplinary knowledge.' Admittedly, each academic discipline has its own requirements shaping otherwise 'generic' skills and attributes. However, these skills and attributes, although conditioned by their disciplinary framework, share enough common ground that it is not only possible but beneficial to teach/discuss them across disciplinary boundaries. A series of generic workshops on critical thinking for postgraduate students makes a case study.

In my role as a learning advisor I saw a need for students to develop a clearer understanding of critical thinking, one of my university's four graduate attributes. A conference paper by Melville Jones (1996) led me to decide to run three two-hour workshops and to focus on analysing the structure of an argument, identifying and critiquing the assumptions on which an argument is built, and developing an inquiring habit of mind.

The first trial workshops in 2009 were open to both undergraduates and postgraduates. In 2010, the level of demand led to separate postgraduate sessions being run. About half the students have been PhD students and the rest have been mainly Master's students (with honours students). Interest suggests that many postgraduate students are keen to further develop their critical thinking skills.

Brief description of programme

- In session one, the students fill out a questionnaire on *Critical Thinking: Knowledge, Skills and Attitude*. There is a general discussion about critical

thinking, and then the students do some exercises that focus on specific critical thinking skills such as identifying assumptions, causality, false premises, and necessary and sufficient conditions. I am indebted to Stella Cottrell's book on critical thinking skills (Cottrell 2005) for much of the material used in this session.
- In session two, students put these skills into practice while analysing an article.
- Session three is left open for response to student requests and needs. For example, students have requested exploration of barriers to critical thinking or ways to incorporate and display critical thinking in their writing.

In all three sessions I note crucial discussion points and feedback from small group sessions on an electronic whiteboard. These notes are printed off, typed up and emailed out to the students after each session.

Session three also allows time for formal student evaluation. The students are asked what they hoped to learn from the workshop and their answers have tended to cluster around the following themes.

- How to do some specific aspect of critical thinking (analyse a question, write critically, structure an argument, etc.)
- How to think critically about 'grey' or 'dirty' source material
- How to become confident in their own ability to think critically
- How to address cultural conditioning that makes critical thinking difficult or distasteful (this question is consistently raised by some international students)
- How to address notions of 'truth' and 'fact'

However, many students simply say that they want to understand critical thinking or to know how to 'do' it. Their lack of specificity is, in itself, interesting as it seems to demonstrate that although students are aware of a gap in their academic literacy, they have not given the precise nature of that gap much thought. Asked whether they think critical thinking is discipline specific, students tend to answer that in general it is not, but that there may be some aspects of it which are conditioned by discipline.

The evaluation form that the students fill out is simple and very open-ended; they are asked to identify three things they liked about the workshops and three things that could be improved or changed. Because this programme has only just started, the numbers involved are small, but indicative. Out of 13 students, 15 cited the discussions as one of the three aspects that they liked, commenting on how much they appreciated the diversity of opinions that were expressed. Over half of the students also liked the skills exercises that they did. A third of the students commented positively on the summary of discussions that they received by email, finding it very helpful to receive 'consolidated' material.

Observations

The generic workshop environment provides a space where students can reflect on the skills they have already mastered, identify areas that they still need to explore, and learn from the experiences of their peers in this area. For many students, this may be the first time that they have been asked to think and talk explicitly about the particular academic skills they have mastered and are mastering. The 'apprenticeship' model of supervision means that such skills are often not explicitly taught or discussed.

The cross-disciplinary, generic approach of the workshop appears to offer some benefits. It can be hard for students to disentangle the concepts of critical analysis and critical thought from the discipline-specific context in which they first encountered these concepts. The process of identifying, isolating and analysing the concepts appears to lead to greater clarity about the nature of critical thought in the context of the academic endeavour. At some point in the discussion the differing epistemological and ontological frameworks of the different disciplines represented in the room are introduced, usually by one of the students. This discussion always appears to be interesting and enlightening to the students. Some of them have never considered that there may be more than one epistemological or ontological viewpoint; others have considered it but have not necessarily thought about it in relation to their own critical thinking.

Cultural issues are also raised by students in this workshop. About half the students in the workshop come from a variety of backgrounds. For some of the international students, the cultural constraints surrounding critical thinking are a considerable issue. The workshop doesn't directly address these issues, but simply being able to raise them in an environment that acknowledges the existence of more than one academic paradigm seems helpful.

Overall, to date I have come to the following conclusions. Doctoral skills development often needs to be more explicit and more focused than it currently is. The 'apprenticeship' model may be less suited to non-traditional students who lack the cultural capital to identify what is being modelled for them. Even if disciplinary skills are explicitly taught and practised, many students still benefit from the cross-disciplinary insights that are available to them in a generic teaching context where they can be linked to the larger academic endeavour. Students benefit from the opportunity to learn how others, including those from other cultures and disciplines, define, assess, deploy and value critical thinking.

Mary Roberts

The following account from Linda Evans adds a concrete example of how you might teach sharp conceptual awareness, in this case, with an exercise on academic definition. It is seldom the case that supervisors have the time to direct students through specific detailed tasks that establish authorial acumen; generically, it's possible.

The building blocks of theory generation

Conceptual clarity, I always tell doctoral students, is a key ingredient of theory generation; as Freidson (1994: 15) points out, 'we cannot develop theory if we are not certain what we are talking about.' So it is absolutely essential that students clarify their understanding of the key concepts that are the foci of their research. Then, in order to communicate clearly their conceptualizations, as well as remain focused themselves, they need to define these concepts. Definitional precision is therefore equally important – not least for maximizing construct validity. Yet students do not find it easy to define concepts. Ask them to do so, and they will almost certainly come back with what I call a conceptual interpretation, rather than a stipulative definition – *describing* the concept rather than *defining* it. I therefore teach – often in classes, and sometimes one-to-one with some of my supervisees – what I consider a key advanced research skill: how to formulate a stipulative definition. Below I explain the way I go about this.

Promoting conceptual clarity, definitional precision and critical analysis

The teaching process

I typically follow a four-step process that involves teaching students how to maximize construct validity by: *identifying the key concepts for clarification; conceptualizing; communicating and matching constructs;* and *disseminating with conceptual clarity* (see Chapter 3 of Evans 2002). Here, to cut to the chase, I focus only on the component of conceptualization that involves formulating stipulative definitions.

Teaching students how to formulate stipulative definitions

Since students seem genetically wired to take the easiest option, where possible, I begin by explaining to them the difference between stipulative definitions and interpretations of concepts, suggesting that, given the chance, they will always opt for creating the latter since it is effortless. A stipulative definition, I tell them, is a precise, unambiguous explanation that stipulates what something is and that is exclusive in applicability. To illustrate my distinction between what I refer to as 'definitions' and 'interpretations' I present them with a little exercise. I ask them to consider which of the following is a definition – as I interpret it – of a chair.

- A chair is a piece of furniture intended for sitting on.
- A chair is a seat.
- A chair has four legs, a seat and a back and is sometimes padded. It is usually made of wood or plastic but other materials can be used.
- A chair is intended to seat people.
- A chair is a piece of furniture that people may sit on.

I remind them that a definition should explain precisely what the thing being defined is, and it should be so precise and unambiguous that it excludes applicability to anything else.

At this point, if I am teaching a group or class I typically receive a diverse range of responses. The point is, of course, that none of the above is a stipulative definition of a chair, yet never have I taught a class in which more than a small minority of students – if any – recognize this. So I then introduce them to a technique: 'take each of the five statements above,' I tell them, 'and, in relation to each, ask yourself':

a) Does the statement stipulate what a chair *is* – what category of phenomena it lies within; that is, whether a chair is, for example, an article of clothing, an animal, an item of food, etc.?

and

b) Could the statement be applicable to anything other than a chair? In other words, could the word 'chair' in the statement be replaced with anything else and would the statement still make sense?

Once they have done this (and understood that the answer to the first question should be 'yes' and the answer to the second should be 'no' in the case of any statement that is a stipulative definition) most students see the light and revise their earlier responses. At this point we usually establish fairly easily that none of the statements is a stipulative definition of a chair, rather, they are interpretations. Depending on the statement, I point out, 'settee,' 'stool,' or 'bench,' for example, could replace the word 'chair.' Moreover, of the five statements, the third and fourth statements do not explain precisely what a chair is. They are distinct from the other three statements – which do stipulate what a chair is – because they do not begin with 'A chair is *a*...'

I should emphasize that I go to great lengths to point out to students that any form of conceptual clarity – interpretation or definition – is to be commended. I also tell them squarely that formulating good stipulative definitions is neither quick nor easy and that they should not expect to get it right at the first attempt. Most of my stipulative definitions, I point out, involved many re-drafts over many months – and may yet be revised. It is also worth mentioning that I always precede my teaching with an exercise devised for the purpose of leading them to discover for themselves the confusion and ambiguity that can arise when conceptual clarity is eschewed. Space restrictions prevent my detailing this here.

Giving guidelines for formulating stipulative definitions

To teach the process of formulating definitions I draw upon my scant knowledge of philosophy and I always point out – as I do here – that since my background is not in philosophy, those whose expertise is in this area may find it easy to pick holes in my suggestions. Specifically, I show students how to use the necessary conditions of the concept that they wish to define, and use these as the skeleton upon which to flesh out stipulative definitions. I present the example of the necessary conditions of punishment. According to the philosopher, Flew (1954), punishment must be:

- unpleasant
- for an offence or a supposed offence
- of an offender or of a supposed offender
- carried out intentionally
- carried out by those with authority to do so.

A list of necessary conditions such as these, without adding anything more, I point out, constitutes one form of conceptual interpretation. If we wish to formulate a definition – as I interpret it – we need to develop the list further.

I ask students to try formulating a stipulative definition of punishment based upon acceptance of Flew's necessary conditions. I remind them that it is necessary to stipulate precisely what punishment is: that is, what category of phenomena it falls within. This is often the most difficult stage in formulating definitions. In some cases it is complicated because it involves a choice between different levels of categories of phenomena: categories have sub-categories and one needs to decide which level is best used in the definition. In other cases it is complicated by the need to ascertain precisely what something is. Decisions often have to be made, for example, about whether something is a process or a product, whether it is to be defined as an action or as a form of behaviour, or whether it should be called an ideology or a belief.

Having formulated a stipulative definition of punishment, such as: *a deliberate action carried out by someone with authority to carry it out, and causing unpleasantness to an offender or a supposed offender for an offence or a supposed offence*, we then return to the task of defining a chair. First, students must list what they consider something must have in order for it to be a chair (paralleling the listing of necessary conditions). What features must it have, they must consider: legs? (if so, how many); a back?; a seat?; etc. At this point it is not unusual to have heated discussions relating to furniture design and style, but the best definition of a chair that I have, so far, been able to formulate is: *a chair is a piece of furniture with a back and is designed to seat one person at a time.* I use this definition to point out the importance of choosing every single word in a definition with great care.

The use of the words 'designed to,' I point out, are deliberately chosen to incorporate recognition that although more than one person may simultaneously sit on a chair this is not consistent with one of the key design features of a chair – that it is *intended* to seat only one person at a time. Had I used the word 'seats' instead of 'is designed to seat' my definition would have been flawed. In definitions, I tell my students, choices between words such as: 'does,' 'may,' 'could,' and so on need to be made with great care. The way in which verbs are used – the tense and any qualifying terms that are used – is particularly important: whether, for example, you write 'seats,' 'may seat,' 'could seat,' 'is intended to seat,' or 'may be considered to seat' needs careful consideration if the definition is to match the precise meaning intended. Finally, students test their definitions by asking themselves the two questions listed above. Alternatively, I may introduce a game whereby each student formulates a definition of a concept and presents it to the class – minus the name of the concept being defined. If anyone can think of an alternative word that fits within the definition and it still makes sense, the definition is flawed.

All good fun! But by giving students the tools and the technique to formulate their own stipulative definitions, we are also giving them the tools and techniques to critique other people's definitions and thereby to inject an element of critical analysis into their work. But that's another story.

Linda Evans

The first two stories of this chapter described how generic sessions might emerge from recognition of student need across campus (the need for motivation, and the need for holistic support). The third showed how a need for a better understanding of critical theory could be addressed, and the fourth honed in with close detail on how students might be taught to define terms accurately, and to sharpen their analytical thinking. Overall, we are hoping that the chapter scopes out the potential of *generic* contribution to doctoral learning.

The next chapter considers the ways that this extends to fulfilling institutional responsibilities in terms of individual identity and of equity.

Chapter 4

Acknowledging values, identity and equity

> Your way objective analytic
> Always doubting the truth
> Until proof comes
> Slowly quietly
> And it hurts
>
> My way subjective gut-feeling
> Like always sure of the truth
> The proof is there
> Waiting
> And it hurts.
>
> (Konai Helu Thaman 2008: 461)

A common theme throughout this book is that learning advisors negotiate between the institutional drivers of the university as a business and the blue skies view that universities guard the deep level values of their societies. Two benefits run concurrently, sometimes happily and sometimes in tension:

- more new knowledge = more income; and
- more equity of doctoral success = more chance of equitable societies.

This chapter highlights the second to underscore that generic support should support those who are historically under-represented or whose journey through the doctorate is made difficult by their strong sense of embodied identity.

Some students find the formation of an academic identity taxing because of one (or several) factors of what they bring with them into the doctorate, those factors Finke (1992: 13) terms the 'inflections' of identity – 'race, class, gender, ethnicity, age, and any number of other related "accents."' Generic doctoral workshops can address the troublesomeness of emerging academic identity, enabling students who share characteristics important to their academic identity to develop interdependently. Alongside concern with graduate skills, attributes and employability, this chapter adds another significant dimension of generic doctoral support: the fostering of a strong community of colleagues that makes the identity transition possible, and even pleasurable.

Universities are obliged to ensure equity of access to education. Nevertheless, statistics provide evidence that some groups of people remain under-represented within academia, which is historically an elite male preserve within a Western culture. Kreber (2013: 857) notes that 'the scholarship of teaching has not adequately taken up the bigger questions of social justice and equality in and through education.' Equal success opportunity can be best achieved by ensuring that the university is a homely place for previously under-represented groups of people who may find it alien and impenetrable on entry. When one generation from a subset has success, it tends to take that group into further success. Success in equity is a measuring rod for the value of tertiary institutions.

The label 'equity' white-washes over different histories of contestation, each of which is foundational to some identity formations. Although essentialism hovers as a theoretical spectre to be avoided, in practice, many doctoral students feel a dimension of their identity is so crucial that they work best when they are supported in specifically this aspect. McCaffery, for example, highlights the challenges faced by American Indian doctoral students in 'maintaining cultural integrity in a predominantly White elite educational institution' (2012: 92). Around the world, different institutions have different groups that they need to sustain into full agency.

However, support for minority or under-represented groups is dependent on learning advisor interest (and perhaps credentials with and within that group), and on senior management priority – large considerations that cannot be overlooked. Learning advisors who are outsiders will need to gain support and assistance from insiders. Even when senior management is committed to backing rhetoric about equity with action, such support has historically experienced additional scrutiny. For example, when women-only gatherings exclude males, there may be suspicion of a feminist plot cooked up by the coven to allow for the privilege of a junket. Additional care must be taken with auditing and reporting on such work. Increasingly, though, institutions recognize the desire for research from diverse groups to come through strongly. Both equity and excellence are at stake.

It is possible, with the right combinations of support, to develop strongholds conducive to robust research from groups who are under-represented in national statistics for doctoral completion. Generic sessions, where the development of researcher identity is discussed as it is lived by those grappling with the experience, provide a space where differences can be broached. This chapter addresses generic support's potential for sustaining diverse values, marginalized peoples and academic identity development.

The first inset author, Vicky Gunn, establishes a platform for work with specific groups by insisting that *embodied identity* affects the transition of doctoral students through the fraught borderlands between theory and practice. Academic identity is best when it feels authentic, comfortable, and defensible in terms of lived experience and belief systems. Gunn anatomizes doctoral identity and learning in terms of sexual orientation. She is alert to the body's entanglement with theory (see too Hopwood and Paulson 2012, for a reinstatement of the body in terms of doctoral study, and Carter 2011a and 2011d, for the relationship of body, theory and thesis voice). By queering doctoral learning (one response to Kreber 2013), Gunn stakes out the experience of difference, emphasizing that doctoral scaffolding, like all teaching, needs to consider multiple student positions. In particular, Gunn pinpoints what is troublesome about having to negotiate a lived identity that differs from the mainstream when actual experience problematizes critical theory.

Gunn finds that, even when doctoral research has an underpinning theory that relates to experience, there may be unsettlement between theoretical construct and lived reality of being, say, a LGBT researcher using gay theory: some aspects of lived experience may diverge from theory. Life is seldom clearly cut to theoretical patterns: as Melinda Webber, speaking as a Māori researcher, puts it: 'any theory or ideology…can be liberating and it can be constricting' (Webber 2009: 3). Any framework may be, at times, apt and even salvational (Hooks 1994: 59), yet sometimes at odds with personal beliefs and feelings; researchers may be driven to draw on multiple theories in order to capture their own position accurately. We suggest that it is often easier for generic groups rather than individual supervisory relationships to mitigate the lived experience of becoming a researcher, embodied, enfolded in multiple communities of practice and influenced by potentially conflicting positions. In talking with others, just as in ante-natal classes, shared experience makes the research journey possible and doable.

Managing 'straight' PhDs from queer places: generic support for Lesbian, Gay, Bisexual and Transgender (LGBT) students

Sexual desires and sexual orientation tend to be overlooked in doctoral pedagogy discourses. In a Westernized higher education system, it is probably assumed by supervisors that these slightly troublesome phenomena are best dealt with elsewhere, through the hallmarks of an inclusive institutional setting: campus climate initiatives, student associations, and health and well-being centres. The silence around the role sexual desire plays in academic identity is loud and particularly deafening in an environment where close relationships between supervisors and students are likely. I do not mean the attraction of PhD students to their supervisors and vice versa (though this topic is worthy of at least some professional levels of awareness). Rather, I mean how one's personal experience of research interacts with one's ideas about one's self and the way research methodologies can value or challenge that self. If we accept that the development of sexual identity is 'fundamentally tied to the construction of a personal narrative that integrates desire and behaviour into a meaningful and workable configuration'

(Hammack, Thompson and Pilecki 2009: 868), this is important to researcher experience. How dominant research narratives and paradigms interplay with this configuration, either positively or negatively, is an issue worthy of consideration in generic doctoral support. Arguably, the nexus of intellectual meaning-making, attachment to and rejection of beliefs, and one's identity autobiography is where conflicts may need to be clarified or reconciled. This process is central to the generation of the creative energy necessary to both sustain an individual through a PhD and allow new knowledge to emerge.

I start from two contentious observations:

1   Doctoral processes can embody heteronormativity.
2   The categorization of sexual identities in research (as in politics) has a tendency to essentialize experience (including that of heterosexuals).

These observations suggest that research is a lived, bodily experience, in which orientations play an invisible yet in other ways palpable role. The impact of this role in terms of the quality of the doctoral experience and output is worthy of identification. Generic sessions looking, in particular, at the dissonances associated with insider and outsider status within one's researcher community should be included as part of any doctoral programme.

Heteronormativity embodied in the PhD?

If, as post-colonialist approaches to research indicate, research methods can embody Western attitudes and cultural assumptions through knowledge production (Asmar, Mercier and Page 2009; Smith 1999; Webber 2009), they are more than likely to also embody heteronormativity too. Though this sounds far-fetched, it is not so outlandish if research methodologies 'universalize from a specific bodily dwelling' (Ahmed 2006: 4). Arguably, that bodily dwelling tends to have a sexual orientation (even if it is asexuality). Dominant methodologies and their subsequent materialization are thus oriented towards the dominant normative group's desire, in this case towards the heterosexual body, its dimensions and sensations. In my case, this played out most clearly in terms of what was considered both acceptable to cover in a PhD and as having most symbolic capital within the discipline. This meant that my original disciplinary enculturation occurred in a place of the abstracted body, one with which I was familiar but was not mine. Mine felt absent. In such a context, PhD research and the structures from which it is cultivated could thus be considered straight, even when the student isn't.

Essentialization and insider researcher status

Additionally, the recent historical evolution from gay and lesbian, to lesbian, gay and bi, to LGBT, and on to queer studies is illustrative of the development of and investment in a single research category around sexual orientation. This categorization makes a commonality of very diverse insider group experiences, which risks inscribing them as 'essential.' If research methods and the methodologies that underpin them have a tendency to essentialize the subjects of their studies, this has a consequence: insider LGBT scholars quickly find themselves walking the liminal line between being an insider and being an other within their own insider community. Discordances between lived experience and theoretical approaches to that lived experience can abound, with PhD students forced to either ignore or work through their own identity configurations to make sense of intellectual unease or contradiction.

In illustration, I'll use one example. Dissonance can arise when the dominant narrative around sexual orientation shifts within the methodological community into which one entered. To clarify, it is clear that the master narrative concerning same-sex desire has tended to be expressed in terms of overcoming struggle to be confident in one's own identity as gay, lesbian, bi, trans (Savin-Williams 1998). Most of the research on Higher Education LGBT student development tends to be located within this narrative (see Marine 2011). A newer narrative with growing currency, however, is that fluidity rather than stability in the orientation of one's desire is emancipatory and, drawing heavily on a scholarly discourse influenced by the work of Judith Butler, liberating from binaries (see Butler 1990; Cohler and Hammack 2007). This new narrative challenges any fixed notion of the compositors of 'LGB or T,' effectively queering all sexual desires and inherently linking them with gender.

This newer narrative, however, is also a location of significant potential contradiction between the lived experience of members of the LGBT communities and the theory upon which the researcher is encouraged to base his or her research. While for some the emancipatory narrative affords permission to both feel and be liberated in terms of desire's orientation and the gender expression attached to it, for others it is an oppressive intrusion that questions the certainties of their sexual identity (see too Webber 2009, who notes the same dilemma in the context of Māori researcher identity). In the later situation, a PhD candidate might feel threatened by queer theory enough to avoid or delay engaging in the intellectual activity that could help him/her unlock the research question. If this student then does go on to incorporate the theory, it can have a deeper significance too, leading the researcher out of insider status within his/her own community (and its apparent commitment to stability of forms) and into a scholarly space in which fluidity is privileged. At this point, the PhD student can experience the challenges associated with exile.

In this illustration, it is clear that PhD student support across disciplinary boundaries is something that can be offered proactively through generic sessions; discussing the links between theory and lived experience provides an opportunity for students to anatomize the nature of insider researcher status for LGBT and queer researchers. Without wishing to consolidate all sexual orientation identity groups into a single category, it is clear that our insider researcher experience of sexual diversity and identity has the capacity to disrupt intellectual norms and received wisdom. If this disruption happens in the PhD period, however, it is mixed with the ingredients of personal, psychological, and career development.

In effect, research produced here, while core to the continued criticality that keeps the disciplines alive, is also a full-on, lived-bodily encounter.

Vicky Gunn

Generic sessions primarily attend to what is problematic about the doctoral experience, at multiple levels, including the way that embodiment – the challenges of the quotidian body, its entanglement with theory – can impinge on the transitioning of identity. This dimension of doctoral support makes important contributions from academe to societies. The longstanding social responsibility of academia towards good citizenship underpins doctoral 'massification.' Most expressions of graduate attributes list good citizenship qualities such as tolerance and respect (although Clanchy and Ballard [1995] challenge their realization in practice). For some students, building an authentic and viable academic identity in a niche historically troubled by bias is challenging. Yet once resolved, such psychological challenges of identity construction may render cutting edge results of value to others.

Next, Sally Knowles describes segregated writing retreats for women, some of whom face specific challenges relating to their gendered roles. Statistics show that women remain relative under-achievers in the higher levels of education, including doctoral level (Bell 2010; Mastekaasa 2005; Universities Australia 2010). Becoming a wife and mother makes doctoral work more difficult for women (Brown and Watson 2010). Many have internalized the social understanding that women ought to be child-focused mothers, accessible and caring homemakers. Such attitudes may make it seem inappropriate to focus 'selfishly' on research (Carter, Blumenstein and Cook 2013). Yet, even when family demands compete, research deadlines must be met and that thesis written. Pointing out that some assumptions of academic work are arguably masculinist, Knowles's piece shows how women might be accommodated more fittingly and productively.

Hives of collectivity, inspiration and intellectual generosity: generic writing support for women

> 'A vital release from other commitments – the domestic front is an unsuitable place for my writing due to frequent gusty prevailing winds!'
> 'A wonderful, pared-back space for nourishing and expressing our writing selves.'
>
> (Retreat attendees' feedback)

For many female doctoral candidates, isolation, self-doubt, and performance pressures are the concomitants of their dissertation writing experiences. They may grapple, too, with a system that places high value on individual choice and autonomy, and the associated qualities of self-responsibility and stoicism. Furthermore, postgraduates must contend with their own personal expectations regarding the 'proper' nature and meaning of community, autonomy, productivity and disciplinary support. I discuss an approach for supporting a community of women – one that stretches disciplinary boundaries, particularises the generic, and challenges gender norms (also see Grant 2006).

Call to the hive

Female desire for a community to buffer intellectual and social isolation may draw them away from their writing. Going to a women's writing retreat prioritizes their writing and gives them community. The small ongoing community of women writers I have organized and participated in since 2003 meet seasonally for a five-day residential writing retreat in a restorative bush setting. This community welcomes women doctoral candidates and exposes them to different disciplinary expertise and experiences. Such a unique environment complements the supervisory and disciplinary supports. The structured interactions embed generic support that draws on the strengths of different others. When this support is conceived of 'ecosocially, as a total environment within which research activity ("study") is realised' (Green 2005: 153), mutual bonds of understanding are created.

Doctoral writing can entail pain – for example, of unlearning, involving renouncing a safe position – (Simon 1995) and can be comfortable or pleasurable, a discovery involving new learning and investigation. Whatever the balance, relationships in supervision will sometimes fail to live up to a 'wholesome mentoring relationship' (Bargar and Duncan 1982: 30). Solutions for some women may lie within structures that can engender a mutually-supportive writing culture and community of peers (Grant and Knowles 2000; Grant 2006; Grant 2008). Such measures are necessary not only because many women wrestle with the realization that they don't fit the norm of the 'ideal' candidate, but also because they carry the burden for changing and adapting to these dominant norms. Conrad and Phillips (1995) contend that such groups 'may be especially important for women' (p. 316) where isolation is known to occur due to their different social responsibilities, an isolation Leonard (2001) attributes this to the chilly climate of higher education.

Emerging writers who struggle to write may feel imposters and frauds. A widespread sense of fraudulence or imposter syndrome (Brems *et al.* 1994) is true particularly for women with liminal status in the academy (Salmon 1992).

Collectivity in the hive

Our women's writing experience is enhanced by the presence of other women writers. Alone, women may 'feel as if we lack courage or commitment, we find writing lonely and hard, we can't get to it' (Grant 2006: 494). The community aspects of retreats, practical and emotional support, coexist with the solitary aspects; with collective obligation to support each other's writing, a deep level of mutuality is achieved. Rhythms of solitude and togetherness support each participant's writing goal(s).

Generic support during retreats is offered collectively through comment and discussion, tailored to each woman's writing topic, and crafted to improve arguments. We set goals before the retreat, announce them in the opening session, then discuss our progress and plans for completion. Examples of retreat activities include:

- 'social' writing activities
- small group sessions for work-in-progress
- peer editing in pairs/small groups
- group workshops on titles/first sentences etc.
- discussion of aspects of writing, such as: style, voice, rhetorical moves, and
- guided self-reflection.

Interdependence – cross-pollination through peer feedback

Interdependence is encouraged to lessen feelings of isolation. Each participant presents her work-in-progress to make maximum use of the expertise and diverse knowledge of the group, promoting cross-disciplinary alliances as well as non-hierarchical mentoring (Grant 2006). While the feedback to the author is specific, it is generic in the sense that we speak from the position of generalist rather than disciplinary specialist. Furthermore, when focusing on the processes of the doctorate itself through identification of the structural features of the thesis genre and the thinking through the development of ideas, participants gain awareness of writing processes.

For women, the masculinist notion of autonomy intrinsic to scholarship can be experienced as isolation, and female candidates may assume that they should already understand writing processes and protocols. Generic writing support can displace this cultural script of negative individualism.

Busy in the hive – improved writing productivity

Because doctoral students work in accountability-driven environments in which efficiency, 'throughput' and 'fast' timely completions are expected, the stakes are high. Confidence in writing is imbricated in notions of authority and mechanisms of power, investment and identification, suggesting a related concept of 'imaginative space' (Grant and Knowles 2000). In being a writer, by regularly doing the practice of writing, we become writers in our own and each other's imaginations. In this sense, the act of writing has significance far greater than the immediate output (Knowles and Grant forthcoming).

Hives of intellectual generosity

Disciplinarity refers to disciplinary conventions, behaviours, actions and beliefs that constitute a discourse community of scholars who police and are policed by regimes of truth. Doctoral students are required to abide by disciplinary conventions that circumscribe what counts as intelligible and proper, demonstrating allegiance to 'sharply delineated intellectual enclaves' (Zerubavel 1995: 1095). While disciplinary conventions are best taught within the discipline, others aspects or research writing can readily be taught generically. It is not surprising, then, that generic writing groups are an emerging trend in universities (Galligan *et al.* 2003). Staged and structured, fluid and organic, these veritable hives of collective industry have contributed to the production of many doctoral outputs. In 'a culture of performativity...at a time when equity considerations are receding from institutional discourse' (Devos 2008: 196; Sinclair 2000), a women's writing group can affirm individual writing identities, providing imaginative space for women to be central as writing subjects (Grant and Knowles 2000).

Sally Knowles

Knowles spells out the multiple factors that make retreats for women valuable. Her emphasis on the need for interdependency to build networks of trust also holds true for specific cultural groups: retreats for targeted cohorts are usually productive places as well as safe ones.

Now, we move to look at generic support for indigenous students, using New Zealand as a case study. It troubles countries such as Canada, Australia and New Zealand that their indigenous peoples are under-represented in doctoral success. Aileen Moreton-Robinson (interviewed by Conversation 2013) reports that only 164 indigenous Australians have PhDs – where, in 2011 alone, there were 6,780 PhDs awarded in total (Group of Eight 2013). In New Zealand, the 2006 census showed only 387 Māori PhDs among the 16,770 doctoral graduates residing in New Zealand (2.3 percent); at a time when some 14 percent (565,329) identified as Māori from a total population of 4,027,947 (Statistics New Zealand 2006). Governments and institutions seek ways to understand why such discrepancies exist in order to better ensure that indigenous students make ground within academia.

In New Zealand, our case study here, institutions have a legal responsibility to the tangata whenua (people of the land), Māori, because the country's history as a nation is built on the 1840 *Te Tiriti o Waitangi*, The Treaty of Waitangi. The fact that this document was signed in an English language version but discussed among Māori in a Māori language translation gives rise to contention as to what the wording of the agreement actually meant: nuances of meaning have significant impact on contractual rights and obligations. Abstract terms can be points of contestation as to what exactly was intended. Nor was the Treaty signed by all *iwi* (tribes), raising the question of who is bound by it. Nonetheless, it is largely accepted in New Zealand that the Treaty is a legally binding contract, which, along with later Acts, means the government and, thus, higher education institutions, are obliged to fulfil responsibilities to Māori success.

We are indebted to Adreanne Ormond for gently pointing out that, although, from a White perspective, equal Māori representation at university is about equity, for Māori it is about *rangatiratanga*, a term that means sovereignty and holds some of the connotations of the terms 'leadership and self-determination.' Funding often comes from 'equity' sourcing, but for indigenous people, such as Māori, this is an insultingly patronizing framework – and we also thank Lisa Chant for her more detailed explanation of the tension around these issues. Like other indigenous peoples, Māori also have a valuable perspective to contribute: their emergence as successful researchers matters. *Tino Rangatiratanga* (independence) is about Māori reclaiming ownership and agency as indigenous people.

The Western history of development underpinning academic values is not shared by Māori. Two strongly held belief systems are at risk of talking past each other. In the words of Evelyn Stokes (1985: 19), 'What needs to be explored now are ways in which other cultural frameworks can be admitted and given appropriate status.' The foundational Māori academic Mason Durie (2009: 4) reiterates the indigenous view of the academy:

> typically [indigenous] meaning comes from understanding connections and associations rather than focusing on an analysis of component parts studied in relative isolation from a wider perspective. Universities frequently have different starting points.

Addressing the gaps between differing worldviews is not an easy task, suggesting that a generic approach may be the most appropriate for supporting those with non-Western frameworks.

Here, Lisa Chant, a recent doctoral graduate, and Susan Carter describe the New Zealand Aotearoa example.

Indigenous scholarship: the Māori doctorate example

In response to the desire to support Māori research students, the Tertiary Education Committee of New Zealand provides funding for Ngā Pae o te Maramatanga (NPM) ('horizons of insight'), a nationwide support for Māori hosted by the University of Auckland. Excellent people are involved in this programme, as the website (http://www.maramatanga.co.nz/) testifies. Driving its inception in 2002 was the desire to promote 'the transformation of New Zealand society such that Māori participate fully in all aspects of society and the economy' ('Ngā Pae o te Maramatanga' 2013: n.p.). NPM goals include the commitment to achieve the following through excellent research:

- Seek an understanding of the contribution of Māori peoples to new frontiers of knowledge, economic development, environmental sustainability, health and social well-being and educational achievement
- Build relevant research capacity and capability – create and maintain pathways to research excellence
- Share knowledge effectively with a variety of communities (locally, nationally, internationally)…to bring about positive change and transformation
- Give meaningful expression to indigenous knowledge/mātauranga Māori to address issues, needs and opportunities
- Advance our profile as a leader in indigenous development by increasing our profile internationally.

The 'Ngā Pae Strategic Plan' (2010–2014: n.p.) evocatively directs:

> Pursue the horizons of understanding and love,
> The near horizon, the distant horizon,
> So that one may emerge into The World of Light.

Their sights have expanded to the recognition that much of what they do is relevant to all indigenous peoples. Les Tumoana Williams (2007: 18), an early activist in Māori education, saw NPM as a 'transformative model for indigenous advancement.' Indeed, the academic journal that emerged, *MAI Review* (2012), is for Māori *and* Indigenous, and is now recognized as a leading journal for this discourse.

The national network crossed disciplines and institutions, thus enabling Māori scholars from across the country to pool their enthusiasm and energy. Loyalty was focused on the drive to support Māori researchers *per se* rather than in relation to their disciplines. Lisa Chant next recounts her own experience of the PhD process in first person, a first person who is Māori. She had excellent supervision, but describes how support specifically for Māori catered for some of the culturally related challenges of the doctorate, including anxiety.

Adapting to the requirements of the academy

Drawing on my own experience and colleagues', I cannot emphasize here enough how profound indigenous doctoral candidate despair can be due to fear of failure to achieve the expectations and aspirations of the global nation of indigenous communities for PhDs by indigenous peoples. As novice academics, we fear having our indigeneity and engagement with indigenous knowledge in the PhD process negated; we fear failing to uphold responsibilities to our own peoples' knowledge as we meet academic requirements; and we fear losing self-confidence through our lack of traction in university systems and processes. These fears haunt most indigenous scholars, new, emerging or highly experienced.

Partaking in the Māori and Indigenous programme Ngā Pae o te Maramatanga meant benefit from writing retreats and guest speakers. I had individual assistance from Prof Williams, a wise and intellectually exceptional scholar who is also Māori, and who was a foundational leader in establishing this programme. At the point where my study was a jumble of ideas, knowledge, experiences, unexpected findings, and in need of substantive reorganizing and reframing, I arrived in Prof William's office through the urging of many of my colleagues who were fellow PhD candidates on the MAI programme.

He asked me to draw a picture that explained my thesis. I looked around his study, filled with the artwork of leading artists, and explained my complete lack of artistic talent. Nevertheless he insisted, saying that art was the way he chose to see the world, which I took to mean he wanted me to be able to communicate with him in his own world. This provided a wrong assumption: the true lesson was that drawing my whole thesis on one page made it clear which bits were extraneous to the final part of the journey. Aspects that had seemed so important became visible as an overwhelming morass of information that was impeding my momentum. It wasn't just the picture that told the story. As I verbally interpreted the picture to Prof Williams, I simplified my own understanding of a mass of complex knowledge and ideas, while extracting the key ideas, which of course dominated my picture. Explaining my thesis to someone other than my supervisors, someone both wise and Māori, let me clear the way for further progress.

At the time I was overwhelmed by the 180,000 odd words I had produced. Prof Williams as an expert at supporting doctoral students perhaps instinctively knew that trying to get me to refine the words I had produced using the medium I had used (words), would not be as focusing as using a completely different medium. He had found that using a picture on one page was a useful way of getting a student to express the core of their thesis, particularly as Māori culture was historically oral, with an ancient and substantive tradition of the use of art to communicate knowledge. Art is a sound basis for traditional Māori teaching and learning.

The other thing Prof Williams taught me was to be confident that I was the master of the *mātauranga* (Māori knowledge) of my study and that I was the only one who could decide what to write, when to write, and how to write it all up. At a certain point I had to stop being a student and become the teacher, and a master of the *mātauranga* I had chosen to engage with. His own firm vision of the potential of Māori scholarship, something he donated an enormous amount of time and energy to, along with others, gave me confidence in myself as a Māori scholar.

Universal values

Stepping back from Lisa's individual account, we also want to emphasize what Māori scholarship offers to the broader world of academia, to non-Māori scholars. Firstly, it holds core values central to this project. Acknowledging Linda Smith for her guidelines model, Fiona Cram spells out the guidelines that she has personally developed as a Māori researcher, showing how Smith's guidelines work in practice (Cram 2001: 42–50). These include many of the criteria already demanded by ethics approval committees, but in addition Cram emphasizes the need for collaborative approaches to research, research training and reciprocity: in essence, research should relate to the community itself. Researchers are in effect caretakers, *kaitiaki* (guardians), better able to serve because of their academic achievement – and often the first generation in their families to find that success.

Ensuring first generation Māori cross this divide can be uncomfortable for both non-Māori and Māori. Alison Jones (2012) has eloquently talked about the 'dangerous liaison' of working as a Pākehā (non-Māori) within a Kaupapa Māori framework that espouses the principle of 'for Māori, by Māori.' She suggests that 'the question of what Māori aspirations for self-determination mean for Pākehā or non-Māori educational researchers...simply generates Pākehā confusion and avoidance' (p. 101). And, in a careful positioning piece, Melinda Webber (2009: 5) questions what it means to be accepted as a 'real Māori' and who has the right to define authenticity or realness. Similarly, Native American scholar Vine Deloria Jr. (1998: 25) questions the privileging of academic approaches over learning from elders, challenging that

> *Self-determination, sovereignty, hegemony,* and *empowerment* are nice big words...but what do they really mean? I feel sometimes they assist us in creating a set of artificial problems, wholly abstract in nature...and thereby avoiding solving them.

He emphasizes that real knowledge about people resides in the people themselves, and advises those who want to learn about indigenous frames to stay closely in touch with the elders. Webber (2012) explained that working within a Māori framework means being accountable to two systems of authority: academia and tribal elders. The time taken to apply for formal ethics approval is matched by visits to senior members of the community, observing time-consuming protocol to gain their approval for the project. Such research is not only part of the academy: it is also firmly grounded in the real world, belonging and held accountable, there.

Theoretically, indigenous people have firm ground beneath their feet. Linda Tuhiwai Smith (1999: 185) has established Kaupapa Māori as a decolonizing methodology that embodies 'the notions of critique, resistance, struggle, and emancipation.' It is strongly anti-positivist, and strongly performative, establishing a 'counter-hegemonic approach to Western assumptions' (Smith 1999: 189). Kaupapa Māori gifts a surge of energy to oncoming Māori and to other indigenous researchers. It's a model that makes use of cultural values, a model that could be adapted by researchers in any projects where culture and community are significant. This is not to say that good theory is powerful enough to overwrite historical contestation or live tensions.

Nevertheless, it is promising that Māori research is currently so energized, with some of the government compensation for past injustices from Treaty settlements being put into scholarships by Māori communities. This new energy is closing a gap. It is also giving much that is valuable to the academy: in the face of neoliberalism, we need reminding that the benefit of the doctorate importantly relates to social benefit. Kaupapa Māori gives sureness of community anchorstones to the academic community at large.

Lisa Chant and Susan Carter

Supporting indigenous researchers is vital for the well-being of society. Individuals matter; communities matter. At the same time, the research community transcends ethnic and cultural boundaries, with students embarking on doctoral programmes world-wide.

To emphasize that this work is significant because it serves important ethical values, Alison Phipps next shows how generic doctoral teaching can use them as navigation beacons. Her use of the simple terms 'good, just and beautiful' are reminders that educational jargon, generated from research into good practice, should not distract us individually or institutionally from the historic task of serving society. A firm articulation of core values underpins the need to work towards equity and fairness for all, the 'good' and 'just' criteria that Phipps stakes out.

Good, just, beautiful: deepening dispositions for dealing with difficulty

Over the last ten years it has been my task to develop two distinctive Graduate Schools at the University of Glasgow: the first for graduate students in the arts and humanities, the second for graduate students of education. This has always been rewarding work, for postgraduate education sits on the cusp of so much potential and means engaging with students full of ambition for the possibilities of the academic world. It offers a window into future worlds of ideas as the themes that are emerging for researchers to tackle are displayed in proposals for study, in graduate conference presentations, in upgrade and progress review sessions and then finally through examination, as they come to fruition.

Throughout my tenure I have found it helpful to have some generic working principles for graduate education. While these should be contextualized across the arts, humanities, social sciences and education, they are, I firmly believe, solid principles for generic doctoral engagement. I might describe these as follows:

1 Ensure funds are as close as possible to the students.
2 Ensure power to determine the nature of student experience is as close as possible to students.
3 Let students' ideas flourish – say 'yes' more than 'no' to all that aspires to create space for thought.

4   Relish the quirkiness of collective and cooperative student activity: it is implicitly critical of all that is wrong with the academic status quo and therefore of considerable value.
5   Ensure that what you try and do with others is good, very, very good, as good as it can possibly be under your circumstances; that it is just and has an integrity; and that it is beautiful – whatever that may mean under different disciplinary and interdisciplinary circumstances.

What you will notice from this rather vague list is that there is no mention of strategy, no reference to targets, key performances indicators, aims or objectives. There is no mention of e-learning, reflective practice or any of the other normative ways of codifying education and therefore also doctoral education in the context of higher education. This is no accident. Graduate students are engaging with difficult questions in the arts, humanities and social sciences, as in the physical and life sciences. These are questions to which there is no immediate or obvious answer, which require exploration, patience, tenacity, risk. They are often questions that change, fractally, through the course of study and for the student to be able to grasp their nature requires a process of deepening dispositions to enable questions, which are difficult, often too difficult, to be engaged with increasing confidence and distinction. Long-term engagement with such matters requires the cultivation of dispositions that cultivate patience, tenacity, exploration and an adventurous spirit. To show how these principles work themselves out in practice I'd like to describe briefly just one initiative that I was privileged to see grow and flourish during my time stewarding graduate education in these venues.

eSharp

eSharp (http://www.gla.ac.uk/esharp/) is an international online journal for postgraduate research in the arts, humanities, social sciences and education. Based at the University of Glasgow and run entirely by graduate students, it aims to provide a critical but supportive entry into the realm of academic publishing for emerging academics, including postgraduates and recent postdoctoral fellows. One of *eSharp*'s aims is to encourage the publication of high quality postgraduate research; therefore, all submitted articles are anonymously double-blind peer reviewed as part of the acceptance and feedback process. This rigorous and constructive process is designed to enhance the worth of postgraduate and postdoctoral work. *eSharp* also engages in training postgraduate students in the various tasks that running an academic journal requires. Enhancing both employability and the graduate experience is a key aspect of its aims and objectives.

Ensure it is good

The students are celebrating again. This time we are standing in the Human Anatomy museum at this ancient Scottish University, surrounded by body parts, strange objects in jars, and I've been asked to speak about what the theme of this latest issue, issue 15 of Summer 2010, might be telling us. The theme is Uniting Nations: Risks and Opportunities. *eSharp* are at it again. How many times have I done this, I wonder, awed once again by the ability of this ever changing team, churning over annually, to sustain a presence of the highest quality, as a publisher of fascinating work on important themes. *eSharp*, are not just good, they are very good at what they do, and with their own business model, plan, training arm, governance structure and high quality online journal articles they have developed an enviable reputation. I never set the bar this high; it was the students' own passion for producing something that was different, difficult and very good that got us here, again, in another quirky, relatively rarely frequented corner of the university, to toast the next issue with a glass of wine and a speech from a humbled academic.

Ensure it is just

Committees, governance, transparency all matter if education and its experience is to be experienced as just. Obviously there are many different and competing understandings of justice, and graduate students of the arts, humanities, social sciences and education know this intellectually and also in practice. *eSharp* has governed itself, in its own way, according to both the demands of a neo-liberal university – let's not pretend here, there was little that could be done to change those conditions of accountability – but it has done so through touch rotations of General Editorships, training editors, through the development of new spin-off projects and regular, nerve-racing [wracking?], high stakes presentations to the Vice Principal, among others. It has been important to those involved that they work to demonstrate justice and accountability in their working relationships and this has meant engaging in the serious committed work of committee involvement.

Ensure it is beautiful

> The willingness continually to revise one's own location in order to place oneself in the path of beauty is the basic impulse underlying education.
> (Scarry 2001: 7)

What is beautiful is so often a matter of personal taste. Beauty, as Scarry teaches in her work, is a basic element in education. Ensuring that *eSharp* have enough resources to make what they do beautiful, in their terms, has meant we have seen issues launched with balloons, jazz bands, flowers and even sleight-of-hand magicians. Space for beauty to emerge seems to mean that there is space for ideas to find appropriate form. If you browse the backlist of articles – and I'd certainly recommend you do this – you will find a feast of thoughts and images, carefully held in an aesthetic form which has emerged through successive generations of editors and reviewers.

'*Ajunt da flat ært a'da boondries a'sens/Beyond the flat earth of the boundaries of sense:*' doctoral candidate Silke Reeploeg cites the contemporary Shetland poet Robert Jamieson (2007: 113) in her paper in *eSharp*'s issue 15, concluding that part of the challenge of her work is that 'not everyone's voice has the same power – with imagination and narrative always enveloped by the forceful global ocean of institutional, political and economic forces' (Reeploeg 2010: 121).

Giving graduate voices some power so that their imagination may find narrative opportunities has been the task of stewardship entrusted to me by the University of Glasgow for ten years. The more the dispositions have deepened, the more I too have found myself 'Ajunt da flat ært a'da boondries a'sens.'

Jamieson's poem *SIEVÆGIN* (2007: 113) continues:

Du spits ati'da oshin,	If you spit in the ocean,
a drap myght rekk Æshnis.	that drop might reach Eshaness
	[the westernmost tip of the Shetland Isles].
Bit hoiest du a sæl,	But hoist a sail,
du gjings quhaar du will,	and you go where you please,
ta njoo-fun laand.	to new found land.

'But hoist a sail'…perhaps that is all the wisdom we need, no more, after all the technology and technocracy of educating is done: a sail, a fair wind and a sense of adventure.

Alison Phipps

We co-editors come from New Zealand, a set of islands in the South Pacific where the image of sail, fair wind and adventure has a resonant uplift as a metaphor for our academic work and its contribution in terms of ethic and identity. The identity of international students and those for whom English is an additional language (EAL), often also strongly influences their doctoral experience – 'thinking about themselves [as an academic], performing [as an academic], and being thought of' as such (Tonso 2006: 273–274) in a language other than their mother tongue. Although the politics of alienation are very different, they too need to find their feet in a place that is likely initially to feel alien. Academics have responsibility as hosts to help these students to acquire insider status to academia and to feel equally as accepted as those whose first language is English. The next chapter moves to generic support for this group.

Chapter 5

Generic support for English as an Additional Language (EAL) students

> Suturing with languages is a political act of power, liberating and potentially terrifying, but always transforming – a creative act of the power to form and shape anew. Culture and interculture take form and shape through this process... Languages are shifting agents along frontiers of the self.
>
> (Alison Phipps 2003: 13, 15)

Often the first image of generic doctoral support that comes to mind is grammar and linguistic workshops for students for whom English is an additional language. Yet, there is more to it than this. That these students and their supervisors have a need for additional support is obvious, as noted by Braine (2002: 59):

> The acquisition of academic literacy by non-native speaker graduate students...extends beyond the ability to read and write...Graduate students not only need to build interactive relationships with their teachers, thesis supervisors, and peers, and develop effective research strategies and good writing skills, they also need to adapt smoothly to the linguistic and social milieu of their host environment and to the culture of their academic departments and institutions.

As Stacy (1999) observes, the ability to manage postgraduate study takes on added complexity when 'filtered through different linguistic and cultural expectations' (Melles 2001: 9). Bromley (2013: 179) also points out the need to understand the often complex human dimensions of doctoral innovations in terms of cultures and personalities. EAL students frequently discover the environment they find themselves in quite alarmingly different to what they expected due to different cultures of teaching and learning (Wu 2013). Already successful within their home academic environment (Cadman 2000), they must now strategize how they will manage to squeeze the identity they bring with them so that it fits the shape of the new community. Chameleon cultural changes must be broached with expectation of discomfort. Yet in reality it is often hard to foresee how that might feel, and students sometimes arrive optimistically envisioning that total immersion in an English-speaking environment would mean seamless absorption of language (see Fotovatian 2013). Instead, it adds linguistic dislocation to other challenges.

International doctoral students leave their families and friends to step into an alien community where they often find themselves on the outskirts of social warmth (Ali and Kohun 2007; Aspland 1999; Nagata 1999). The crossings they must make traverse language and cultural boundaries (Holmes and Riddiford 2010). Life in their new environment will be 'embedded in the local culture,' and fitting in comfortably as an accepted insider is 'a potentially complex and conflictual process of negotiation rather than a predictable, unidirectional process of enculturalization' (Morita 2000: 278). This entails a nest of challenges, including the ability to fit in by communicating 'freely and easily with supervisors and others' (Cryer 2005: 32). As Cryer maintains, 'students who have English as a mother tongue have a head start on those who do not' (2005: 32).

Added to cultural difference is the obvious hurdle of producing 80–100,000 words in formal English academic prose while also displaying critical analysis and theoretical savvy. Paltridge and Starfield (2007: 2) note with some understatement that EAL research students 'often have difficulty meeting the demands of the kind of writing required of them in this particular genre.' Strauss (2012) also documents supervisor/student frustrations in relation to the production of the English language thesis.

EAL students may feel that they and their writing are somehow marginalized (Ali and Kohun 2007; Zamel 1995): 'Speakers of English as an additional language…still appear to be less empowered and more disabled in the institution' (Hutchings 2006: 248); moreover, 'international students [may be] treated as second class citizens' (Morley, Leonard and David 2002: 271). They frequently pay higher fees than local students (although this is not the case currently in New Zealand, where they merely have limitations on how long they can leave the country before losing their student visa). At the same time, they can find themselves treated with exasperation by supervisors who lack understanding of their academic and cultural backgrounds, and driven to feeling under more intense criticism than locals. Similarly, they face the oral examination with additional anxiety: will they be able to process questions in English, read the nuances, and give clearly formulated responses fast enough? Might language hesitancy be seen as lack of expertise? Thesis examination may raise challenges when cultural lenses are incorporated within it (Carter, 2011e). Although, in fact, linguistic anxiety proves not to affect the outcome or the experience according to one small research example (Carter 2011b), it nevertheless raises questions about equitability of assessment for the increasing number of international EAL students.

Furthermore, despite education's increasing internationalization, resources for EAL students are seldom adequate (Strauss, Sachfleben and Turner 2006). Generic advisors offer a safe environment away from the potentially face-threatening discipline-specific setting of supervision. In neutral space, international students may (re)gain confidence and be overtly introduced to the implicit rules. Most learning advisors regard international, particularly EAL, students as a prime responsibility, and often work with them and their writing.

Although formal academic writing is arguably no one's first language, it is more difficult for those whose first languages don't use articles, or whose cultural preference is for long sentences that happily synthesize complex ideas in ways that seem impenetrable to English language readers. The structure and overall aesthetics of a written text reflect its writer's thinking processes (Kaplan 1966), meaning that 'Anglo-Saxon' academic writing's insistence on linear structure and reader-centric foreshadowing' (Siepmann 2006: 143–144) may prove unfamiliar territory for students whose discursive backgrounds favour more digressive forms of expression. It has been suggested that at postgraduate level the difference between native and non-native speakers' writing skills is greatest at the level 'of punctuation/spelling, accuracy of grammar, appropriateness of grammar…[and] smallest at the discourse level (quality of content, development of ideas and adequate treatment of topic)' (Casanave and Hubbard 1992: 38). However, we find it hard to untangle language mechanics from other discourse levels: often from a reader's perspective, syntax, grammar and punctuation carry meaning that inflects the argument, revealing or masking critical analysis. A loss of confidence as the complexity of thesis writing becomes apparent can cripple the writing of it. For these reasons, 'support, encouragement and motivation are key benefits of writing interventions' (McGrail, Rickard and Jones 2006: 30), with successful thesis-completion relying on more than mere linguistic competency. Indeed, Melles (2001: 6) coins the term 'academic acculturation' whereby learning advisors act as interpreters and/or mediators between student and university cultures.

Catherine Manathunga begins this chapter by theorizing the EAL student experience as 'transculturation' within 'unhomeliness.' Her insights are complemented by Sara Cotterall's research on the student experience, which explores the dangers of allowing international students' estrangement to remain unchallenged. Xiaodan Gao and Karen Commons demonstrate how intercultural workshops can help students – both local and international – to identify cultural assumptions that might otherwise create misunderstandings between different groups. Only when EAL students are successfully acclimatized to the institution – *and* vice versa – can generic support begin to address the specific challenges highlighted by Meeta Chatterjee-Padmanabhan in mastering the diverse 'languages' required by doctoral-level reading and writing. We begin with Catherine Manathunga's experience with EAL students, viewed from the dual perspectives of supervisor and researcher.

Reflections on working with doctoral students across and between cultures and languages

Supporting doctoral students for whom English is an additional language is a rewarding and challenging task. This reflection summarizes some of my thinking and practice as both an academic with more EAL students and as a researcher who has been investigating intercultural doctoral pedagogy for some years now. I am often struck by how difficult it can be to put the pedagogical strategies that I espouse as a researcher into active practice as a supervisor and teacher. I am always concerned about the gap between theory and practice; between my pedagogical philosophies and what I actually do. Being a post-structuralist and a post-colonial theorist, I am hyper-aware of the realities of power and truth-claims and the inherent contradictions and positionings present in any discourse that I may adopt. I am constantly reminded of T.S. Eliot's poem 'The Hollow Men' (1974: 81):

> Between the idea
> And the reality
> Between the motion
> And the act
> Falls the Shadow.

The other issue I am often contemplating is my sheer admiration for anyone who undertakes the task of writing a doctoral thesis – a highly challenging endeavour already – in a language other than their own first language. I remember vividly the struggles I had as a doctoral student in shaping and refining my thesis and have watched at close quarters my students, colleagues and friends engaged in this huge task. Yet I performed this task in my own language. How much more difficult it must be to write at this high level of sophisticated analysis in a second or third or even fourth language. I therefore have a great deal of respect and admiration for EAL doctoral students. It is with all of this in mind that I reflect on four key ways in which it is possible to support EAL doctoral students. These include respecting students' cultural knowledge, supporting students' reading and writing skills in English, situating students in an inclusive research culture and supporting students in coping with 'unhomeliness.'

Respecting students' cultural knowledge

EAL doctoral students bring with them a wealth of cultural knowledge and very often a great deal of professional and academic knowledge. They are also likely to be studying research topics that are directly related to their own cultural contexts either in other countries or within their own communities locally. In this regard, they are often more expert about these cultural practices, discourses and contexts than their supervisors. As a result, it is vital to acknowledge what Michael Singh (2009: 198) calls our 'cross-cultural ignorance' and position students as the authority figures on these issues. Not only does this involve learning from doctoral students and creating spaces within the still largely Western Academy for this cultural knowledge, but it can also involve encouraging students to use their own cultural and linguistic terms, phrases and metaphors within their research. For example, Michael Singh and Xiafang Chen (2012) describe how Chen used translations of Chinese characters to provide new understandings of pedagogy. It can also involve assisting students to develop transcultural knowledge, where they blend relevant Western understandings of key phenomena and their own cultural knowledge to create unique and highly innovative knowledge. I have written about this as 'transculturation' (Pratt 1992), drawing on post-colonial theoretical perspectives about this concept (Manathunga 2007a, 2011).

Supporting students' reading and writing skills in English

Providing adequate support to develop and enhance EAL doctoral students' abilities to read and write in English is also a core part of effective doctoral pedagogy. One of the most useful strategies supervisors can adopt is to set reading and writing tasks for each meeting, particularly early in candidature. It is also useful for students to work closely with language learning advisors throughout candidature. Individual appointments with learning advisors can help students make progress with the complexity of formal academic English. It is possible to explain how critical analysis and synthesis are clearly demonstrated in the cultural expectations of a Western language system. Through the use of critical questions, suggestions for further readings and extra discussion during meetings, generic advisors can support students' gradual mastery of literature reviewing, research design and later data analysis.

An important part of this development and feedback process is to focus early comments on ideas and issues rather than spelling and grammar. This builds student confidence and allows you both to focus on substantive aspects of research rather than on technicalities. Advisors can always ask for clarification if the grammar and spelling is obscuring the student's meaning to such an extent that it is difficult to grasp the central concept they are exploring. When generic courses allow for work on students' own writing or reading difficulties they are enormously useful. Early writing activities help identify those students who would benefit from working with language learning advisors from the beginning of their candidature. Then there will be other students who require support in refining their use of English over time.

Situating students in an inclusive research culture

It is also vital to ensure that students feel part of a vibrant and inclusive research culture, where they have opportunities to interact academically and socially (Lovitts 2001) with other academics, peers and students at various levels of study. Research, especially in the Humanities and Social Sciences, can be a lonely experience for all students but this is compounded for EAL students because they may be far away from family, friendship and community networks and may be grappling with unfamiliar cultures and contexts. The quasi-informal atmosphere of generic classrooms helps to ensure that students are part of the university.

Making sure that for group work, groups are mixed so that students meet others, providing tea breaks and suggesting the advantages of exchanging contacts for future mutual support are all significant contributions that generic courses can make. Supervisors may find that they can facilitate introducing students who share some similarities in topic, methods, theory, or interests to each other, actively prompting networking. I have made a point of dedicating as much time as I possibly can to attend the sessions of the annual Postgraduate Research Colloquium that our Faculty hosts and have tried to meet most of the research students in our Faculty so that I can link students with each other. It is also useful to share your national and international contacts with students and to introduce them to other researchers at events.

Supporting students coping with 'unhomeliness'

Finally, it is important to provide students with emotional and personal support and encouragement as they grapple not only with the challenges involved in conducting research but also with the different cultural, political, social and environmental context they are trying to operate within. Sometimes an EAL student knows virtually no one on campus other than their supervisor when they start their studies. Although it is important to maintain professional boundaries as an academic, personal issues and challenges (especially those involving homesickness, cultural alienation, difficulties in understanding local rules and practices etc.) are likely to impact students' research. Adopting a friendly, accessible style of communication, showing the student respect and trust and being open to discussing problems or issues are very important. I also use stories about my experiences or those of other students or colleagues to demonstrate the challenges and uncertainties research brings. Having recently moved from sub-tropical Brisbane to cold, windy Wellington and having to leave my family behind for periods of time has increased my understanding of how displaced you can feel in new locations (although Australian and Aotearoa New Zealand cultures and language are very similar). 'Unhomeliness' (Bhabha 2004: 13) is a concept I have borrowed from post-colonial theory that captures the ambiguity, uncertainty and difficulties that are involved in working across and between cultures (Manathunga 2007b, 2011).

Therefore, I think that if we show respect for students' cultural knowledge, actively support students' reading and writing skills in English, situate students in an inclusive research culture and support students in coping with the 'unhomeliness' that is part of researching across and between cultures and languages we can assist EAL students to enjoy their doctoral studies and build ongoing research collaborations and networks with us and with other researchers and students.

Catherine Manathunga

Manathunga highlights how the alienation of independent inquiry is further exacerbated by working in a second, third or even fourth language. The shadow between theory and practice is especially dark when it falls between institutional rhetoric and expectations of how this plays out in practice. The following piece by Cotterall further investigates the darkness of that particular shadow.

The mythical community of practice

This contribution draws on the findings of a longitudinal narrative study of the doctoral learning experiences of six international PhD students enrolled at a metropolitan Australian university between 2008 and 2011 (Cotterall 2011). The study investigated the nature and quality of the participants' learning experiences, the support they received and their opportunities to engage in the academic practices of their departments. I focus here on three salient issues which generic support programmes might seek to address: community, communication and chance.

Community? What community?

All six doctoral researchers in my study complained that they lacked opportunities to interact with other researchers (students and staff) within their university community. Ryan and Viete report that many international graduate students in Australia feel 'excluded, ignored, isolated, marginalized, or simply distanced' (2009: 309). One of my participants travelled to a neighbouring university to take part in regular seminars; another tried unsuccessfully to network on his campus with other researchers using similar theories. None had local friends but instead operated within an entirely international student community. Such experiences reflect a profoundly 'one-way flow[s] of knowledge' (Ryan and Viete 2009: 304), despite the rhetoric of internationalization that pervades Australian higher education.

International doctoral researchers who lack opportunities to engage with the wider research community often find that their learning experiences are limited to interactions with their supervisors. This is a far cry from Wenger's (1998) ideal 'community of practice.' Furthermore, when relations with supervisors are strained, doctoral candidates feel isolated and anxious. Senior colleagues could remedy this by creating opportunities for doctoral researchers to showcase their work in departmental seminars or reports and inviting them to collaborate in research or review activities, or serve on departmental committees. Too often, the rich experience international researchers bring with them is shared only with their supervisors, if at all. However, for such initiatives to succeed, productive social relationships need first to be formed as evidence of the research community's willingness to engage with the international doctoral researchers they have recruited.

Researchers have recommended a range of peer-based interventions to enhance doctoral candidates' experience of the research community. These include establishing student writing groups (Aitchison 2009), study groups (Devenish *et al.* 2009) or journal editing projects (Hopwood 2010b). None of the participants in my study had access to such opportunities. Generic doctoral support programmes are well placed to assist with establishing these kinds of networks and activities.

Communication – a deafening silence

The second theme in my participants' narratives was the way they colluded in the prevailing 'culture of silence' when they experienced frustration in their doctoral work. Despite experiencing significant tensions, ranging from bullying to racism, the participants chose not to make formal complaints or seek redress. For instance, commenting on the tension he experienced with his supervisor, Jack explained:

> I just got to do whatever he wanted me to do...because, you know, when you're arguing with a professor anyway, the truth is you really have a lot to lose.

This experience highlights a systemic difficulty for doctoral researchers. Whereas anecdotal evidence of tensions with supervisors abounds, reluctance to voice concerns beyond one's peer group remains the norm. Although this reluctance is understandable given the high stakes of doctoral work and the supervisor's dual role of pedagogue and gatekeeper, the situation is clearly unacceptable and represents a crucial opportunity for generic doctoral support programmes.

It would help if doctoral researchers had somewhere to go when their supervisors fail to provide support. While Manathunga (2005) recommends that supervisors adopt a more proactive approach to monitoring their candidates' well-being, such advice will only ever be heeded by the minority. Indeed the research literature is rich with proposals for enhancing the researcher–supervisor relationship. So perhaps it is time to acknowledge that problems will always occur and to focus on establishing support strategies for the hapless victims. Doctoral researchers may find it easier to raise sensitive issues outside their supervisory team; perhaps generic doctoral support programmes could offer a forum for expressing such concerns and seeking advice.

Doctoral researchers themselves might also be encouraged to adopt a more proactive approach to their academic identity trajectories. However, the narratives developed through my study indicate that a sense of agency is supported by feelings of confidence, which are often linked to positive supervision practices. Where candidates fail to enjoy one, they cannot benefit from the other. Generic programmes could help by informing doctoral researchers of their rights (Morris 2011), providing a network of role models, resources and mentors and supporting researchers as they take action to address their problems.

Chance

The third important theme emerging from my participants' narratives was that significant differences existed in the quantity and quality of the participants' learning opportunities. While no conclusions can be drawn as to the *cause* of these differences, this is an issue of major concern. Important discrepancies were observed in the quality of the participants' supervision experiences, the timing and frequency of their access to conference funding, the quality of their writing-focused support and the academic networks they were introduced to. These differences suggest, as Starfield (2010) argues, that there is an element of 'chance' associated with the outcomes of doctoral research. Generic support programmes might attempt to establish some benchmarks of the practices within the institution and assist new doctoral candidates in lobbying for the resources, training and opportunities they required.

Ultimately, doctoral trajectories are idiosyncratic and unpredictable. Nevertheless, universities need to monitor the quality of the supervision, resourcing and opportunities for participation, which they provide. My interactions with the study participants suggest that doctoral researchers may well benefit from discussing their research with individuals beyond their supervisory team. Such opportunities could even be seen as useful chances to 'rehearse' ideas in the less charged atmosphere of a community of peers. There is much that could be done to enhance international doctoral researchers' learning experiences. Given that research students contribute approximately 65 percent of university research output in Australia (Siddle 1997, cited in Pearson, Evans and Macauley 2004: 348), surely such investment is warranted.

Sara Cotterall

The generic support Cotterall advocates provides an ideal platform for the sort of interdisciplinary, cross-cultural interactions that make the international student experience worthwhile. Tackling issues of (mis-)communication, interpersonal relations and identity head-on, Xiaodan Gao and Karen Commons describe a programme specifically designed to raise the intercultural awareness of both international and local students.

Developing international students' intercultural competencies

Doctoral study is on the increase – an increase that is particularly significant in Asian countries, but also prevalent in Europe and Australasia partly as a result of the rapid internationalization of tertiary education (Nerad 2010). In New Zealand, for example, between 2003 and 2010, numbers of international PhD enrolments increased by 507 percent (personal communication, New Zealand Ministry of Education, 20 September 2012). Both the increase in PhD numbers and the changing dynamic in terms of student backgrounds have implications for tertiary institutions. Until now, many tertiary institutions have focused on financial gains from the internationalization of higher education, but they seem to have paid little attention to 'interculturality issues' (Bash 2009: 476). If the increased numbers of international doctoral students are to succeed in our institutions, we need to meet their particular needs. Otherwise, we risk increased incompletion on the part of international doctoral students – as well as unrewarded investment of time and expertise on the part of academics. A brief analysis of the socio-cultural needs of these students suggests that generic support in the form of an intercultural training programme might be useful. Such a programme can provide a platform for international doctoral students to understand and develop skills to overcome the challenges of intercultural communication and negotiation.

Research shows that international PhD students often find it difficult to adjust to their new environment. Myburgh, Niehaus and Poggenpoel (2002: 128) in their explorative study found that, although international doctoral student participants reported their experience to be rewarding in terms of learning and personal development, an overriding concern was their difficulty in adjusting to the new environment. They observed that such difficulty left them feeling 'confused, inhibited, lonely, discouraged, and insecure.' Denholm (2006: 123) states that all doctoral candidates can at times experience 'introspection and self-doubt.' For international candidates, such feelings can be exacerbated due to cultural expectations – among other factors.

To be successful in doctoral study, learners need to be independent negotiators of their environment. According to Krone (2006), doctoral candidates should be independent learners who are actively responsible around their study and active participants in their research community. Conrad (2006) states that belonging to a research community involves developing peer relationships and participating in departmental or university activities. She maintains that such involvement increases enjoyment and reduces stress. However, as Morita (2009) points out, the sub-cultures within a discipline or academic department can be complex and multi-dimensional. If students come from very different cultures and educational environments, it is possible they will lack the appropriate communication skills to successfully negotiate these sub-cultures. Morita (2009: 457) suggests that international doctoral students need assistance to gain access to their peer community – both inside and outside the classroom.

A related challenge that international doctoral students often face is dealing with the supervisor relationship. Although candidates are usually expected to have the confidence and competence of academics, in reality they are still apprentices. Bash points out that international doctoral students 'may need to negotiate their way through the web of ambiguities and intercultural subtleties which characterize this blurred boundary between the worlds of the student and the academic' (2009: 482). Laurs (2010) notes the definite existence of a power distance between supervisor and student, from the perspective of the student, at least. For example, international students, particularly those from cultures with high power distance and hierarchy, may agonize over whether to simply accept a correction or suggestion in order to appease the supervisor – even where they do not agree. In relation to communication with supervisors, Rowarth and Green (2006: 118) stress that 'regular and frank communication is essential.' How, though, does a student from a high power distance culture manage to communicate 'frankly' with superiors, especially those who blithely assume inviting students to address them by their first name will suffice to break down barriers? Considerable training is required in order for the student to understand not only his or her own cultural behaviour, but also the requisite behaviour within the new culture.

It seems that such skill development is better carried out within the generic support framework. Although postgraduate supervisors, like those in New Zealand universities, often receive comprehensive training that includes cultural awareness, their status as perceived by students may still not be conducive to open discussion in a non-threatening environment. Mullen, Fish and Hutinger (2010) recommend non-hierarchical mentoring for increasing the confidence and academic success of doctoral students. They argue that supervisors should not be the only mentor as doctoral students have complex academic, psychological and career needs. Generic socio-cultural skills training can broaden the range and depth of the learning community by taking international candidates outside their departmental network and offering opportunities to meet other peers in the wider university community.

One example of a generic support programme that offers intercultural skills training to international students is ExcelL: *Excellence in Cultural Experiential Learning and Leadership* (Mak et al. 1998). The ExcelL programme covers six key communication skills that are difficult for international students, namely participating in groups, seeking help and information, making social contact, expressing disagreement, refusing a request, and giving feedback. Through discussions and role-play, ExcelL workshops provide a safe platform for students to explore the cultural values underlying different communication expectations and behaviours. Using domestic students as role models, ExcelL introduces participants to the linguistic and non-linguistic skills necessary to carry out successful communication within the local context. Through practising these intercultural skills, students gain the confidence and skills to communicate effectively with their peers and supervisors, and with the wider community within and beyond the university. Informal evaluation results collated over the past five years from Victoria University of Wellington's ExcelL programme demonstrate that ExcelL gives students increased confidence and increased levels of interaction with people from different cultures (Commons and Gao 2011). For example, a comparison of 55 pre- and post-programme questionnaires for the five programmes we ran between March 2009 and September 2010 showed that students' confidence in interacting with people from different ethnic groups increased by 14.6 percent over the course of their programme. Their out-of-class interaction with people from other cultures also increased by 12.4 percent. Student comments reflect these outcomes, as expressed by one PhD student from a 2012 ExcelL programme:

> I am also more brave to talk such as during [my] thesis group. I think I expressed my opinions many times during the [ExcelL] workshop but I

never expressed my opinion during the thesis group...until I had joined the workshop.

Given the increasing numbers of international doctoral students, it is important to consider what will help them achieve timely completion and a quality experience. Generic intercultural skills training is one way of helping these students negotiate their new environment with ease, enjoyment and success.

Xiaodan Gao and Karen Commons

Perhaps an unexpected aspect of this chapter for those unfamiliar with the role of generic advisors is that none of the contributors to this point have identified linguistic or grammatical support as the main areas provided for EAL students. Attaining fluency in academic English (which often also proves a challenge for domestic students) becomes more viable once the holistic aspects of the doctoral experience have been satisfactorily addressed. Only with consideration of emotional and social well-being can advisors such as Meeta Chatterjee-Padmanabhan address the cognitive and linguistic issues facing EAL students seeking to assimilate academic language into their vocabulary.

Transforming texts: challenges experienced by international doctoral thesis writers

A doctoral thesis is a sophisticated artefact that provides evidence of a researcher's expertise to a 'potentially sceptical discourse community' (Hyland 1999: 341). An EAL doctoral writer with limited linguistic 'capital,' to use Bourdieu's term, may find that persuading a discourse community that their study makes an original contribution to their discipline is a daunting task. It entails 'text work-identity work' (Kamler and Thomson 2006). Enriched teaching of transforming sources should enable EAL scholars to write a doctoral thesis so that the foundations for 'identity work' could be laid, as shown by a qualitative study that involved in-depth interviews in which two doctoral students reported on their anxieties about working with texts. My findings suggest that present instructions on reading for doctoral studies may be over-simplified. Insights from the study provide pointers that could enhance generic support for EAL writers.

The two participants in the study, Ahmed and Roshan (names changed to de-identify the participants) were academics in their respective countries. Both had written Master's theses in their first languages. Both had learnt English for three hours a week on average for twelve years throughout their schooling. De-contextualized grammar exercises and translation of short texts were the staple activities in their English language classes. Both had undertaken English for Academic Purposes (EAP) courses in Australia for a year. Given this brief exposure to the English language, it is not surprising that they felt disadvantaged and ill-equipped to write their doctoral theses in English.

Both reported that language proficiency got in the way of dealing with sources. Roshan (Interview 1, January 2006) described the mechanics of summarizing:

> In summarizing I try, I think, I should try to just put different sentence from the text together. From these parts, I must delete something or miss some sentences...I really avoid summarizing.

His description of summarizing completely bypasses the process of understanding the text and distilling out its core. The anxiety of producing meaningful sentences in his writing masks the greater difficulties of reading and engaging thoughtfully with texts. Hood (2008) points out that summarizing is more than retrieving the main ideational component of the message; it needs to include an understanding of the interpersonal message embedded in the text. Recognition of stance and the relatively subtler elements such as evaluation and voice may elude EAL writers. EAP courses often do not provide sufficient instruction on this dimension of reading (see Swain 2007). The strategy Roshan uses is that of minimal transformation, with greater deployment of paraphrases and direct quotes. This strategy often results in patchwriting (Howard 1995) and/or textual awkwardness. There is a risk of losing evidence of analysis. Many EAL writers are likely to use strategies similar to Roshan's to demonstrate a sense of control over their reading.

Ahmed also observed that strategies for reading (skimming, scanning and inferring) were not entirely transferable from one language to another as is assumed in typical EAP courses. Ahmed commented: 'In Arabic, I can understand scanning and skimming. In English I have to read it [the text] completely from beginning to the last line' (Interview 1, 13 February 2006). It disturbed Ahmed greatly that he was unable to ignore words that might not be relevant in a text, a common instruction given to EAP students. Equally disturbing was the inability to read between the lines and make inferences: 'For me there is nothing between the lines. Nothing' (Ahmed, Interview 1, February 2006).

EAL doctoral scholars may only begin to learn to read in their disciplinary areas in English after enrolling for doctoral studies, which means that they have had very little time to develop the tacit understanding of the intertextual terrain of the discipline. Prior's (2001: 71) insightful observation about knowing the 'concrete histories' of texts is relevant:

> [To] engage in meaningful and recognizable forms of literate activity involves living through concrete histories of reading, writing, talking about and using texts in the heterogeneous domains of a social practice (e.g. in class and out, in talk and text, in formal and informal settings) and then drawing on and transforming those histories to act with others in the present and project some desired future.

Prior's (2001) prerequisites for 'meaningful recognized forms of literate activity' – the frequent multiple levels in reading, writing, talking about and using texts

– are so much more demanding when engagement occurs in an additional language. A lack of the knowledge of the way texts have evolved in a specific context can, indeed, be a hindrance to engaging actively with them, as Prior (2001) suggests. In most cases, international students using EAL rarely have inbuilt opportunities within their doctoral programmes to gain adequate understanding of the 'concrete history' of texts through social engagement with others. At the end of the doctorate, though, their primary reader will be critical of their performance of engagement.

Interdisciplinary or multidisciplinary study, in which at least one discipline may be relatively new to the student, further complicates the act of engaging with other texts. Manathunga, Lant and Mellick (2006) have pointed out that doctoral candidates (and their supervisors) take intellectual and emotional risks when undertaking interdisciplinary studies. Without support, the efficacy of multidisciplinary research tends to suffer. Roshan (Interview 1, January 2006), who was writing a thesis in financial accounting but drawing on theories in organizational management, reported:

> It was like learning two foreign languages at the same time...It was so difficult. I couldn't find meanings of some words even in dictionaries. I had to read something else on the topic to understand what was written.

Mastering knowledge and technical language in two or more areas is challenging within the time frame that doctoral studies afford for international doctoral writers.

The anxieties raised in this report deserve to be investigated further and addressed through appropriate pedagogy. Generic support for EAL doctoral writers would benefit from a pedagogy that enables discussions on the complexities of reading, by getting students to notice how interpersonal elements work in texts in English, providing opportunities to talk about research and theories, and offering suggestions for reading texts in different disciplines.

Meeta Chatterjee-Padmanabhan

It's ideal to work with the EAL student's writing in individual or peer mentoring exchanges. That generic advisors are not expert in the discipline may actually help by boosting the student's ownership of expertise:

> While some would question the legitimacy of a role that seems at least partially to emerge from institutional short-comings, there do appear to be positive outcomes that can be identified by the [learning advisor's] 'sounding board' role. These relate to notions of ownership and power.
> (Catterall 2003: 38–39)

Once nations and institutions recognize the benefits of globalization and encourage international students to buy our educational products, they have an ethical responsibility of care. For the ethics of diversity and the complexity of the ethics of globalization, see, among others, Neumann (2007); Ryan and Zuber-Skerritt (1999); Walker (2006); and Weber and Duderstadt (2006). Traditionally, supervisors had virtually sole responsibility for fostering doctoral students, but the pressures on academic staff in today's climate of accountability and increased research student numbers mean that this is neither practicable nor desirable. There is now recognition that 'the onus of responsibility lies not only with the supervisor, but also with the institution in which the student will research' (Knight 1999: 97). Generic support is safe, away from summative evaluation, and more relaxed than some other university spaces. Learning advisors play a crucial role in ensuring institutional responsibilities are met.

Emphasis on language deficit undermines the confidence needed for the long writing project, as well as detracting from the very real need to prioritize thinking and structural organization before addressing micro-level issues. Any work on writing needs to be in depth. Correct terminology is helpful, as is an understanding of the nuances implied by syntax and grammar. Unsurprisingly, given the mobility and increase of international education and the dominance of English language, substantial literature exists on helping EAL students with writing and researching (Belcher and Braine 1995; Biggs 1996; Goode 2007; Kahaney and Liu 2004, to mention but a few), and on the expectations and experience of international students (Fegan 2006; Paltridge and Harbon 2006). However, not all supervisors have time to engage with this literature, nor with the many excellent handbooks on English grammar.

Taking a broader approach, Paltridge and Starfield's (2007) guide to thesis writing in a second language is particularly strong in identifying the *moves* a thesis must make in its various parts. They suggest the kind of language used to make such moves, for example, the shifts in tense when reviewing literature, but more importantly they address some of the issues raised by Prior's (2001: 55) 'literacy activity': most importantly, writing to fulfil readers' (i.e., examiners') assumptions about what the text should deliver. Similarly, Wisker (2008: 294–299) unpacks the various terms that can be applied to writing – descriptive, critical, narrative, summarizing, synthesizing, contrasting, comparing, analyzing, conceptualizing, evaluating, reflective and creative. Her brief anatomization would be helpful to any student unsure how to respond to supervisory criticism and is particularly useful in generic courses.

Using 'unfamiliarity with English' as a catch-all term for international students creates an artificial barrier: effective communication is dependent on an assured sense of self, with the university community as a whole benefiting from the resultant cultural and intellectual exchanges pertinent in today's global economy. Clear explanations about the tools of written expression (language, grammar, syntax) and space to talk about writing in general are crucial. From here, then, we move to consider specific support for writing, something central to all candidates' successful completion.

Chapter 6

Writing: intrinsic to research

> Writing is a physical, emotional and aesthetic labour...Many students carry their scholarship deep in their psyche, bones and muscle.
> (Barbara Kamler and Pat Thomson 2006: 4)

It's the riskiest part of the work when spies or smugglers make contact with their connections. Contact zones are danger zones. Doctoral writing is such a contact zone, the point when the conversations, thought, reading, data collection and analysis are pulled together and their connections made apparent in contact with the readers. In the fears of the doctoral student, you risk being recognized for what you are: maybe an imposter (Henning, Ey and Shaw 1998; King and Cooley 1995), exposed, targeted, gunned down. For this reason, despite the 'still relatively persistent belief that doctoral writing is an unimportant by-product' of research, an aspect done hastily once the real work is completed (Aitchison *et al.* 2012: 446), for many students writing is the most challenging aspect of their research journey.

It seems this problem is not always addressed within faculties. Hardy and Clughen (2012) present a litany of literature that identifies 'confusions and frustrations for both students and staff' with thesis writing (p. 25). In a study encompassing three universities (2012), they found very little course instruction, meaning that 'students struggle with writing transitions at all levels of their studies' (p. 48). They cite Cook and Leckey (1999) who have shown that 'the requirement to move from guided to self-directed study' was problematic for many students (Hardy and Clughen 2012: 49) and conclude that 'academic literacies should be top of the academy's agenda for learning and teaching' (p. 51). Students can struggle with the lateral thinking required for control of thesis structure (Carter 2009a; Carter and Blumenstein 2011; Carter, Kelly and Brailsford 2012). They may find themselves needing to justify their academic identity with higher levels of theoretical awareness (Carter 2011d). Rountree and Laing (1996: vi–vii) expand on a metaphor (thesis as journey) with a vivid inset story:

> As we snaked up Ruapehu [a tall snow covered New Zealand mountain] the guides gave us nifty tips, one of which was to plant your boot in someone

else's bootprint to avoid slipping on the glassy virgin snow. It worked. With a thesis too, if you want to cut down on the risk of slipping off track and losing your way, perhaps permanently, it is safer to take the well-trod path – to examine other theses, choose a methodology, structure and style you admire and think will work, adapting it to suit you and your particular project. This sounds like dull advice, but doing a thesis at all is adventurous enough.

Generic sessions point out those bootprints clearly – they are generic – and also help those who choose to leave them in search of boundaries to push to stay safely from crevasses.

Unsurprisingly, most generic curricula cover aspects of doctoral writing. It is common to provide sessions on the writing of the thesis proposal, the literature review, the abstract; these explicate the generic expectations (of the examiners) and suggest how to meet them in good clear academic prose. Often writing retreats or regular workshop meetings encourage students to write together and make use of peer and tutor support. For many, these are the lifelines that help with exposure aversion, the fear of riskiness that can block writing.

Similarly, the many excellent guides to the doctorate are based on a sense of genericity, and most offer advice on writing the thesis. Guides usually include some reference to structure, voice, demand on emotions, consumption of time, support from peers, and impact on the supervisory relationship (Brause 2000; Meloy 2002; Rudestam and Newton 2001). Interestingly, some include 'writing the thesis/dissertation' in the title, as though writing a thesis is synonymous with the entire research process. The relationship of writing to research is of course rhizomatic; sometimes writing is treated as a synecdoche. Moreover, works covering academic writing in general are also likely to be useful to doctoral students for their specific anatomization of textuality.

Pitched precisely to thesis writers, Murray's (2011) third edition of *How to Write a Thesis* is underpinned by three sound assumptions: 'Learning comes through writing; quality comes through revision; regular writing develops fluidity' (p. 18). Murray regards writing as integral to thinking. She has a pragmatic workerly approach to surmounting writer's block, writing in various styles and media, recognizing barriers as predictable hurdles to be overcome, and building the psychological musculature to be able to write 1,000 words an hour, a skill most doctoral students will be keen to develop. The edited compilation *Writing in the Disciplines* (Clughen and Hardy 2012) includes valuable practical exercises aimed at teaching the recognition of 'narrative logic' (Haas 2012: 143–168), the ability to choose what is central, relevant, and related, and to then write so that the hierarchy of importance is evident (Murray 2012: 211). Wisker (2008: 294–299) provides student examples of difficulties in showing linkages, theorizing, and synthesizing. She also suggests to participants experiencing writing blocks that 'thinking about how to help [other students] in their work might help unblock you in yours' (Wisker 2008:

210–211). Theories of embodiment and writing, social context of writing and spatiality of writing underpin useful tools: much in these books would be of use to generic advisors.

Writing the thesis is an act of self-fashioning. It can be seen as 'a site of performance, a research performance or enactment' (Barnacle and Dall'Alba 2013: 3). Voice, tone and emphasis will establish the academic identity of the author, positioning them in relation to the pressure points of their discipline. In some disciplines, such as Social Science and Humanities, creating an authorial presence that the writer is comfortable inhabiting is extremely demanding.

Two chapters of this book cover generic support for writing. This one focuses on the way writing is interconnected with the research itself: with reading, theoretical and methodological positioning, data collection, and research design, and with the sometimes discomforting journey through the whole process. It's been noted that 'the activity that is most entangled with a student's experience of both the university and the extra-mural environment is writing itself' (O'Connor and Petch 2012: 76); nowhere is this more problematically true than for research students. The next chapter looks at the production of writing, the challenges of writing as 'output' and its close connection to lived experience and to the development of academic researcher identity. We agree with McAlpine and Amundsen (2011: 15) that 'identity-formation is critical in understanding learning in the doctorate and beyond.' Writing testifies the identity that doctoral students construct.

Here, we begin by contextualizing writing within the overall research process, because this is how we believe it needs to be regarded. All aspects of doctoral work, including writing, head doggedly towards the examination process, as Shosh Leshem and Vernon Trafford show. Chris Trevitt then maps the way that writing must follow the thinking process, initially meandering as the topic is explored, before finally settling into the direct route to a passable thesis. Then we bring in practitioner experience. Claire Aitchison captures the development of her own learning advising on writing, which has shifted as her understanding of the doctoral writing process grew. Her practitioner perspective is then matched by Miki Seifert, a recent doctoral graduate who reflects on the holistic influences that shaped her own thesis writing experience. The overviews provided by this handful of authors demonstrate that advising on writing gives a meta-level understanding of its dimensions. Careful generic teaching enables learning advisors to contribute useful models for centring and stabilizing doctoral writing, and mitigating student negotiation of its tension.

First, then, Shosh Leshem and Vernon Trafford establish writing's connection to other research activities, by beginning with the *viva voce* and working backwards from there (see too Trafford and Leshem 2002). Their breakdown helpfully directs thesis writers as to the sort of explanations their introduction and thesis joinery should entail (see for example Glatthorn 1998; Johnston 1997; Tinkler and Jackson 2000 and 2004). In our experience, such generic sessions show how the whole process visibly frames writing and is framed by it.

Leshem and Trafford debunk the myth that one prepares for the viva only after submission – they propose that the entire doctoral process is preparation; to this we would emphasize that the writing should convey explanations that ward off some of the enquiries that examiners frequently make.

The myth of preparing for the viva

> Where have you reached with your thesis?
> I have already submitted it. Now I am ready to start preparing for the viva.

A myth is something that isn't in fact true, but which many people believe. Myths also often have a basis in a real phenomenon, and they are very seductive-convenient, reassuring, or with some kind of aesthetic attraction, which leads us to believe in them (Ur 2003). We argue that the above frequently-heard exhortation is based on a myth.

Preparing for the viva is a process and not an event. The entire doctoral experience should be viewed as preparing for the viva. It actually starts at the moment when candidates formally register and their supervisors are formally appointed. The implication of this is that preparing for the viva is not an activity which occurs only and after the thesis has been submitted. This is a myth, which in Ur's words might be convenient and reassuring to some candidates, but is in fact quite risky.

Once the thesis has been submitted, neither its text nor its presentation can be changed. The significance of this is that examiners assess the scholarship and presentation within a thesis before they meet the candidate at the viva. Thus, preparing for the viva is inherent in how doctoral research is undertaken and the thesis is written – and these two features occur before the thesis is submitted. Our suggestion is that candidates and their supervisors adopt a longer view of preparing for the viva and see it as a *'constant learning and developmental experience'* (Trafford and Leshem 2008: 191) where preparation does not start or end with submission.

If the viva is viewed as the terminal point of a doctoral journey, it is therefore also the intended destination which is served by everything that occurs before the viva. Figure 6.1 portrays this period from registration against the axis of becoming proficient in defending the research that has been conducted.

Initially this involves the acquisition of basic research knowledge, familiarity with the regulatory and administrative protocols, understanding the nature of the doctoral degree and appreciating the function of a thesis. This involves the registration process itself, scheduled induction sessions, becoming familiar with the prevailing doctoral regulations and postgraduate handbooks, initial supervisory meetings and Faculty or University doctoral research workshops (Eley and Murray 2009: 11–26).

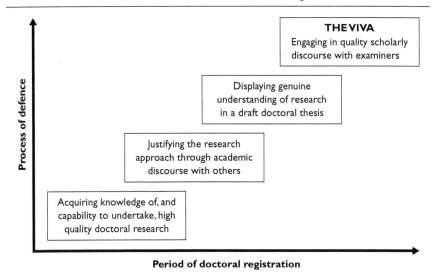

Figure 6.1 Personal development before the viva

The viva involves examiners asking questions of a candidate and engaging in academic dialogue. Preparation for this can clearly be seen as candidates present their work-in-progress at workshops, deliver poster presentations or papers at conferences and, of course, constantly discuss their work with their supervisors. Also, submitting papers for publication and responding to reviewers' comments represents direct personal involvement with the process of 'academic quality assessment' (Dancik 1991). Crucially, each of these activities emphasizes the importance of explaining and then justifying academic positions. Thus, they are preludes to the viva itself.

Before a thesis is submitted, the candidate – and their supervisor(s) – should be satisfied of certain critical areas. Firstly, theses must demonstrate scholarship at the doctoral level of research that will make a contribution to knowledge. Secondly, the thesis should meet all of the stated criteria for submission, and thirdly, the candidate has the potential to successfully defend the thesis. When candidates are able to answer questions confidently in each of these areas they will have defended their 'position' to the satisfaction of their supervisor(s). Demonstration of these criteria must be established within the written thesis. The best defence is done with writing.

These three phases are cumulative ways of developing candidates' ability to engage with their examiners in scholarly dialogue. Examiners expect candidates to be well prepared for their viva since, for many, the viva is 'an exercise in learning and personal development' (Pearce 2005: 95). As a result, their questions normally assume that candidates' development is appropriate. The inability of candidates to engage in such discourse, or be incapable of defending their research, would be interpreted by examiners as evidence of inadequate preparation

90 Developing generic support's potential

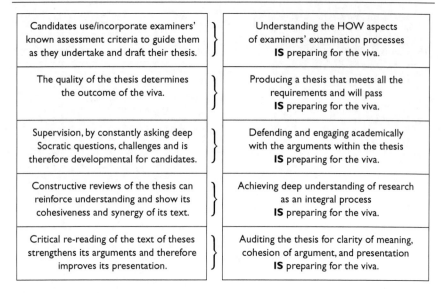

(Source: Trafford and Leshem 2008: 192)

Figure 6.2 The long view of preparing for the viva

for the viva. Figure 6.2 illustrates the HOW of the longer view of preparing for the viva. Knowing what examiners consider to be determinants of a thesis worthy of a doctorate and including them in the thesis from the start, will influence the outcome of the viva. Preparation for the viva commences by integrating arguments and concepts throughout the text of the thesis, and exhibiting in a scholarly and coherent manner an understanding of complex research processes. Employing a writing strategy of 'using the best, most apt form for expressing a particular meaning or idea' (Kress 2004: 17) is a skill that is developed and refined over time. When candidates defend their research and thesis successfully, they are engaging in a scholarly dialogue with philosophical principles and conceptual connections. This is evidence of them thinking like a researcher. Finally, the thesis itself must accord with the protocols of the University, plus being written and presented so that readers can appreciate its arguments, details and scholarship. This is what examiners expect in a thesis and it all contributes to preparing for the viva over the duration of a candidate's registration.

Examples of how candidates actually prepare for their viva include:

- presenting a poster and attending relevant sessions at conferences in their first year, presenting a poster plus a joint paper with their supervisor in their second year and presenting a sole paper in their third year of full-time registration
- collaborating with peer researchers to discuss and collectively review work-in-progress as a community of practice (Wenger 1998)

- seeking out, discussing and learning from the contemporary viva experiences of colleague candidates
- keeping up-to-date with the regulations and handbooks that are prepared and issued by the University for the benefit of doctoral candidates.

University regulations and procedures for doctoral degrees, choosing and working with a supervisor and other associated activities are provided in handbooks which are normally quite explicit (Bentley 2006). If necessary, any aspect of these documents can be explained by supervisors or/and administrators. Thus, candidates are supported by their University throughout their registration so that they can concentrate on their studies and prepare for their viva.

So, is the question of when should we start preparing for the viva valid? Yes, by all means. However, the response to the above exhortation should be that 'preparation' for the viva starts once candidates have embarked on the doctoral journey. This is one of the generic aspects of doing a doctorate despite every doctoral journey being different and proceeding along different routes. However, no matter what route one takes, candidates and supervisors must ensure that it contains those critical features of scholarship which are the foundations of defence within the thesis and in the viva. Thus, a helpful way of shattering the myth of *preparing for the viva* would be to take a *'long view'* of it. Then, both supervisors and candidates should be confident that the thesis complies with examiners' conceptual expectations and holds a defensible story (Trafford and Leshem 2008: 224).

Shosh Leshem and Vernon Trafford

Demystification is one way of teaching independent learning: students have more control of their own progress when they have a clear overview of how the three to four years will unwind. It is also helpful to teach students explicitly how to defend their theses within the thesis itself. Thinking about the viva also means thinking about the social engagement each doctoral thesis makes in its bid for its author to be recognized as an independent researcher and accepted into a discourse community.

Next, Chris Trevitt maps the journey through the thinking and reading processes, showing how these aspects of research provide bearings for writing. Where Trafford and Leshem began at the end of the process to think about its overall goal, Trevitt's vision completes the circle by rolling forward from a definition of the research question. These two approaches contextualize doctoral writing within the thinking, reading, analyzing and talking processes. Trevitt uses a student experience perspective, mapping how the early labyrinthine complexity of research investigation gradually coalesces into a more direct route to thesis submission. In so doing, he allays anxiety for students who find the changes in orientation discombobulating.

Visualizing the development of a PhD research project and thesis

Starting a PhD can be a euphoric time. As a journeyman set to embark on an adventure into the unknown, the PhD student has arranged affairs to make room for this whole new phase in life. An undercurrent of excitement prevails. Unknown and unseen possibilities lie ahead. Shivers of apprehension interleave with bursts of confidence.

While each set of detailed circumstances is unique, one general way to visualize this new beginning is sketched here.

The honeymoon period

Standing at the outset of a PhD, the view opens out ahead in an ever-expanding fashion. The focus is on exploration. The more a student reads, the more they discover there is to read. Each short-term experiment spins off two or three further questions that beg additional experiments. Yet, lucky is the student for whom the starting point is just that: a point. Classically characterized as a question ('The Research Question'), this can be thought of as a vantage point from which to scan the road ahead.

Reality sets in

In reality, of course, most of us take some time to arrive at the final form of 'our question:' the precise focus of our study. Indeed, the whole exploratory process is persistently messy, with 'the road ahead' more akin to an indistinct path crossing a rugged landscape with hidden twists and turns, a complete absence of signposts, and all too little available by way of a map and compass. For illustrative purposes, we can represent this mix of features as per the diagram opposite.

Here, the black star illustrates the initial vantage point – the 'research question.' The spotted bubbles represent discrete tasks or events that you have undertaken which, with experience, are proving helpful, and which contribute in a positive fashion to your overall research agenda. Examples include things like compiling a literature review; designing and carrying out a definitive experiment; locating and meeting the two or three most important researchers in your area, etc. The grey bubbles, on the other hand, represent investments of effort and time (e.g. in the library; trips in the field, etc.) which, with the benefit of hindsight, do not seem to have been helpful at all, and seem quite unlikely to feature as part of the final write-up. For most doctoral students, the capacity to avoid undue exploration of blind alleys of this sort only improves with experience. At the start of a PhD it is perfectly reasonable that perhaps half one's time is 'wasted' in this way (though, of course, it is a moot point if 'wasted' is the appropriate term, assuming students do, indeed, learn from the experience as they progress).

Writing: intrinsic to research 93

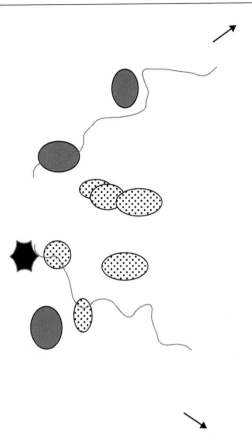

The emerging 'story' – the kernel of an account that will become the final thesis – is then the aggregate of all the spotted bubbles, and the boundary that demarks this 'story' is shown by the two arrows that diverge to the right. As work proceeds, so this boundary expands, opening up new vistas in the research area.

At a broad brush level, a PhD programme will proceed more or less in this fashion for some time, probably half or even three-quarters of the overall lifetime of the project. There comes a point, however, when finishing the thesis becomes the more important objective: tasks geared to generating more data, or unearthing further perspectives from the literature, must come second. This situation can be illustrated as per the diagram on page 94.

In other words, the main focus now changes. The foremost task now is producing a finished thesis in a set amount of time: an exercise in project management. No longer is the focus on exploring new research territory, and experiencing the joys of discovery. The focus now is on determining how best to achieve closure: deciding what is in, and what is out, as suggested by the second pair of arrows which now converge on the lined square – the finished thesis. Easy to say; much more difficult to accomplish in practice.

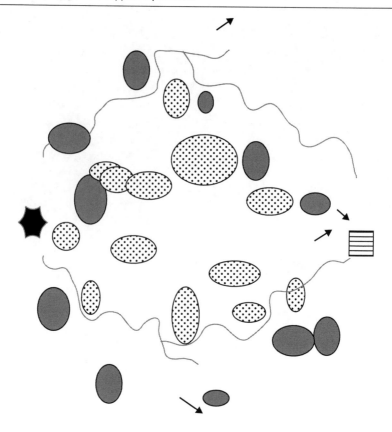

Even so, there will be many discrete activities that get initiated, or even completed, which sit more comfortably in the realm of further discovery and which will be excluded from the final written thesis, as illustrated here by the addition of further grey bubbles. Likewise new and bountiful territory continues to be opened up, as suggested by the continuation of the arrows emanating from the start point.

Navigating the turning point

This is the punch line. The challenge for many students seems to be making the transition successfully between these two main phases in their study programme: what I call 'navigating the turning point.' Meeting the exacting time management demands of closing on a completed draft by a certain date is experienced rather differently compared with the joy of more open-ended exploration, and of widening our perspectives on a given research topic. Some people deal with this challenge better than others: the infamous 'mid-term' blues are often associated with this time. Becoming alert to the need for this sort of strategic change, and the nature of what it is that has to change, along the lines that I illustrate here, has helped a great many of the students I have supervised and advised.

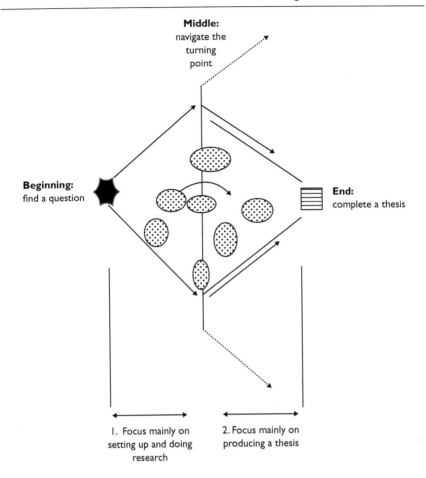

Importantly, all of the activities and tasks represented in grey may not be 'wasted effort' at all, even if they are excluded from the account that ends up being compiled as a thesis. They are illustrative of the continuing open-ended nature of research as exploration. Some will represent the kernel of a future research paper that will get written, others will open up an entirely new avenue for further research which can be pursued later in a career. It is simply that, in order to complete a finished thesis in a timely way, activities such as exploring new leads, working with additional novel ideas, etc. will mostly need to be set to one side over this period. From this perspective, the thesis is really an interim report on progress, though rarely will you ever hear anyone refer to a PhD in this fashion.

Putting it all together

Putting all these ideas together leads to the following visual summary of the entire experience of getting established in a PhD research programme, and then going on successfully to compile a finished thesis in a timely fashion. In my experience, this schema can be very helpful for how it can suggest some of the ways in which the supervisory relationship can change and evolve over the lifetime of the candidature. But that really is another story...

Chris Trevitt

To Trevitt's overview of the student experience, Claire Aitchison adds the backstage story, reflecting on her experience as a learning advisor who is particularly attentive to writing (Aitchison, Kamler and Lee 2010), its psychological dimensions, the importance of language accuracy in theoretical work, and the relationship between writing and epistemology. She has turned academic literary skills into an area of expertise; her development as an expert in this field has kept pace with her heightened awareness of the processes of writing a thesis.

Same, but different: a 20-year evolution of generic provision

I have been supporting literacy development in the same institution since 1991, somehow surviving numerous restructures, revisions and repositionings along with associated name changes and rebrandings. Indeed, for those working on the peripheries of the main game of assessable and subject-orientated teaching in the disciplines, change is one of the few certainties.

Like many Australian universities in the early 1990s, our Learning Centre, as it was then called, was actively uncoupling itself from previous incantations (known as 'study skills') where academic literacy work was generally positioned as an extension of counselling and welfare services (Skillen 2006). It was an exciting time in which our centre was proactively connecting with classroom academics and subject and course coordinators to establish new 'adjunct' and embedded programmes within the disciplines. Our focus was on undergraduate learning. Despite many subsequent restructures, the embedded approach remains the core of our philosophical orientation, which is guided by the pragmatism of academic literacies (Lea and Street 1998) that prioritizes the literacy needs of students in relation to the requirements of their disciplines and subjects. But we have maintained a programme of stand-alone literacy and numeracy workshops spread throughout the year, as well as, large pre-entry and bridging programmes. Our entire literacy workshop programme remains free and voluntary.

Our early work supporting the development of doctoral students was largely limited to pre-entry courses for government sponsored, international aid programme candidates supplemented throughout the year with individual one to one writing consultations. In time we offered writing focused workshops as part of the suite of 'research training' already provided by the research office. These generic three-hour workshops included standard fare such as Writing the research proposal, Writing about the literature, Structuring a thesis, Thesis introductions, Oral presentations, and so on. Over time, we added other workshops such as Writing about qualitative data, Becoming a research writer, Voice in academic writing, and Writing for publication.

Student evaluations have always been very positive as a consequence of both push and pull factors; we do offer quality services – valued even more so because historically there had been limited systematic institutional provision for research students beyond the traditional student–supervisor dyad. In the early days, higher degree research students were grateful for even the smallest crumbs. Apart from the generally positive tenor of evaluations, students regularly requested additional workshop opportunities and ranked 'meeting others' as one of the best aspects. We aimed to build on this.

Our current programme for higher degree research candidates has two components; the popular stand-alone three hour long workshops offered throughout the year which cover the core areas of thesis writing and presentation as indicated above (delivered via face-to-face and online), and a second kind of generic workshop which runs over extended time frames.

In this second series, we currently offer the following:

- **Thesis Writing Circles:** A teacher-directed eight-week programme of weekly meetings with some peer review. Groups are interdisciplinary with a negotiated curriculum focusing on thesis writing.
- **Research Writing Circle Continuers:** Facilitated, ongoing fortnightly meetings of peers sharing and critiquing their research writing. Groups are interdisciplinary and group meetings revolve around the discussion of critiqued participant writing.
- **Writing for Publication Course:** An intensive eight-week programme of weekly meetings to familiarize participants with the practices and processes of writing for publication. Meetings involve instruction, activities and peer review to progress participants' writing towards submission of a manuscript for publication.
- **Writing Retreats:** The form, focus, duration and structure of these retreats vary including, for example, on or off campus, day or residential, highly structured, discipline specific and outcome-focused events to lightly facilitated, participant directed writing production, with or without peer review.

These kinds of ongoing generic workshops are significantly different from single event workshops in a number of ways. In these formulations, participants commit to ongoing participation, and, as such, there is generally a stronger and different sense of commitment to learning, which recognizes the sociality of writing – and that writing takes time. These programmes build community through peer learning especially as authors share their writing together developing communities of practice (Lave and Wenger 1991) around writing, critiquing and rewriting over weeks and even years. In these learning spaces participants feel safe to experiment with their developing disciplinary and writerly identities (Kamler and Thomson 2006). They learn by doing, and from interaction with more senior scholars in what Vygotsky calls a zone of proximal development (1986) under the guidance of a language expert.

These ongoing workshop arrangements acknowledge and accommodate attention to the development not only of the writing (the product or object of the shared endeavor) but also to the writers, through extended engagement in the processes and practices of doing and sharing writing together. In these ongoing workshops the student–teacher relationship is markedly different; less hierarchical, more horizontalized (Aitchison and Lee 2006; Boud and Lee 2005). As participants are encouraged to show and share their expertise, group members develop a healthy respect for each other's disciplinary and research knowledge, disrupting the traditional roles of teacher and learner, as peers and teachers learn together as a community (Lave and Wenger 1991). In fact student evaluations consistently point to how involvement in multi-disciplinary groups enables them to gain a sharper understanding of their own disciplinary norms as well as to develop a knowledge of the shared canons of research and research writing (Aitchison 2010).

In writing this piece, I have found myself reflecting on change and continuity. The traditional generic workshop has stood the test of time. It remains an important and popular aspect of what we do. But times have also required change. For example, I haven't spoken here of our online generic literacy support which has supplemented face-to-face provision. These provide readily accessible, just-in-time information and are favoured by management as a means of addressing large cohorts of students. However, as confirmed again in a recent institution-wide evaluation, doctoral students always prefer face-to-face opportunities to meet together in communities over time. The greatest change for us in our generic work with higher degree research students has been the introduction of over-time support. As the purposes and forms of doctoral education continue to evolve (Lee and Danby 2012), so too will our generic provision – and I suspect that might mean a move to integrated semester-length credit-bearing courses for research writing development.

Claire Aitchison

Aitchison shows how an advisor who is centrally committed to generic writing support develops her own pedagogy, even as she is buffeted by structural changes – her story would be similar to many practitioners'. She is amongst the academic developers whose research advances understanding of the pedagogy of doctoral writing and its implications for identity development.

This overview of thesis writing support as an inherent part of the entire research process is closed by a recent graduate, Miki Seifert, recalling her experience of the challenges of thesis writing. Students' metaphors reflect these challenges: Brause (2000: 11–16) considers images commonly used to describe thesis writing, including 'mountain climbing, running the rapids, running a marathon, coming of age, a war or battle, a hazing experience, a birthing experience, a blind person: an individual stumbling in a room never visited before.' The writing process, for Seifert, a kinesthetic thinker and performer, was very much a reflexive experience, in which freewriting and talking and journaling and drafting contributed to the organic whole. By teasing out the differences between supervisory and learning advisor expertise, in a personal story that emphasizes her own strong supervisory relationships, Seifert confirms Aitchison's certainty of the place of generic support.

Crossing the river of words

Oh-oh! A river!
A deep, cold river.
We can't go over it.
We can't go under it.
Oh, no!
We've got to go through it!

(Rosen and Oxenbury 1989: n.p.)

Starting the second year of my PhD, at a meeting with both my supervisors, I had moved on to talk about the drafting of my first chapter. I was talking – maybe bemoaning is more apt – about how hard it was to write it. My supervisors, being sympathetic women, agreed that it was hard but also agreed there was nothing else but do it. Recently back from maternity leave, one said it reminded her of the children's story she was telling her son about going on a bear hunt. The characters would come to these different obstacles and they would say, 'We can't go over it. We can't go under it. Oh, no! We've got to go through it!'

If writing is hard and there is no magic way of writing a thesis, it then becomes a question of getting through this difficult endeavour. My obstacle at the time was writing about the research methodology I had developed as an artist-activist: a decolonizing epistemological pluralism that requires knowledge production to be performative – that is, something must be done – and transformative – something has to change – and that this process needs to encompass mind, body and spirit. My methodology had grown out of my life; my challenge to capture my mind, body and spirit within the formality of a thesis.

I was rather intimidated and nervous about returning to academic study for my PhD. When I last attended university, I had written my papers using index cards and a manual typewriter. So from the outset, I sought out what resources the university had to offer to postgraduates. One of the most valuable resources was Student Learning Support Service. They not only gave a series of workshops that addressed various aspects of writing a thesis but also provided one-on-one sessions with a learning advisor. I took just about all the workshops that they offered in my first semester. Throughout my time as a PhD student, I continued to take such workshops and seminars. Through them, I learned about writing tools that could enable me to overcome the non-rational fears and blocks that I had around writing.

I found that doing my PhD brought to the surface all my fears and doubts about myself. In order to face and surmount this inner negativity, I needed to nourish myself spiritually. I did this in two ways. One was through building a strong community of support. The other was through my faith as a member of the Nichiren Buddhist organization, Soka Gakkai International. I also had wonderful personal support from my husband and friends, and a great working relationship with my supervisors. Together we vetted my arguments and the structure of my chapters.

In addition to working with my supervisors, I had regular meetings with the postgraduate learning advisor. The difference between working with my supervisors and working with the advisor was the different focus and skills sets they had to offer me. I found that my supervisors were excellent at supporting me in understanding the process of conducting my research and achieving the academic rigour required in a thesis. The learning advisor was able to help me understand the writing process. Since she worked with postgraduates across disciplines, she had a breadth of expertise and knowledge about the thesis writing process. I knew that no matter what obstacle I was facing, she would have a suggestion or two about how to find my way through it. There was another difference. I found that I wanted my supervisors to have confidence in me and my ability to do this research. I wanted to present my best to them and I didn't necessarily disclose the depth of my confusion or fears to them. However, with the learning advisor, I was able to be unguarded. I felt that she had no expectations of me and that I could fully express my confusion, doubts and fears – and that she would help me find my way through them by asking focused questions that got to the crux of the matter and then offering practical suggestions of how to approach the problem.

Nichiren Daishonin, a twelfth century Buddhist priest, writes that, 'The flaws in iron come to the surface when it is forged'(1999: 497), noting, however, that a well-forged sword can also withstand great heat. I viewed the intensity of doing my doctorate as a forging of my spirit. It was bringing forth the inner negativity that lurked inside and that I had to confront and transform if I was going to successfully complete my thesis. I found that my regular Buddhist practice was key to overcoming negativity and it provided me with a deeper and broader perspective on my life as a PhD candidate. Writing a thesis is a daunting journey. To do it, I applied my research methodology to not only the content of my thesis but to the process of writing it as well, and built a community to support me in mind, body and spirit. I had my supervisors to guide and support me through the academic process, and the learning advisor for the writing process. Yes, writing a thesis is much like going on a bear hunt – but I'm not scared.

Miki Seifert

This chapter has shown how the generic perspective can offer a clear overview of writing as iterative cycles of thinking, planning, reading, gathering data, and analyzing: a deconstructive contextualization that may be of value to students otherwise alarmed by the scope of impending task of producing the thesis. Supervisors frequently often have only their own thesis writing experience to go on; generic advisors see hundreds of theses, at all stages of production, across a range of disciplines, and appreciate the thesis genre.

Generic advisors both underscore – and advance – the supervisory input, offering a non-specialist audience that challenges doctoral students to clarify conceptual ideas, while, at the same time, providing the requisite skills to help express them. The next chapter now moves to look more closely at how generic support operates at the level of page-focused teaching and learning talk.

Chapter 7

Writing: process, product and identity development

> Writing involves anxiety, as a researcher is brought into being.
> (Robyn Barnacle and Gloria Dall'Alba 2013: 8)

This chapter zooms in to look at generic writing support's potential to improve student knowledge as well as the finished thesis. In this close focus, we pay attention to the embodied writer as socially contextualized. As Clark (2007: 11–12) explains:

> The thesis or dissertation has a particular function within the academic world; to write one successfully, it is important to understand its "generic" expectations – what it is intended to "do," what it is supposed to "look like," and what the members of the academic community expect it to "be."

At some level, fitting in is a matter of finding the right garments to wear:

> a process of learning to distinguish between the elements of writing that are available for recycling and those which are not – which items of clothing are available from the second-hand rack, and those which must remain in the wardrobes of their original owners.
> (Guerin and Picard 2012: 42)

The 'doctorate as a genre' overview perspective helps doctoral students clarify their understanding of writing conventions (Carter 2011a). It might seem questionable for someone outside the discipline to work individually with students and their writing, but as Trivett, Skillen and James (2001: n.p.) note, few supervisors are 'skilled in teaching students explicitly about the discursive and structural characteristics of writing within their discipline.' Deborah Laurs argues that such expertise not only justifies learning advisors' input, but also provides the kind of support that Seifert found so strengthening in the previous chapter. Strong support is especially needed in small emerging institutions where staff are scrambling to achieve their doctorates: Cath Fraser and Heather Hamerton elaborate on writing retreats designed for busy staff members at a small polytechnic institution. They underscore the point that generic support is likely to occur in both well-established universities and less prestigious tertiary institutions where staff are amongst the doctoral candidates. Susan Carter describes the pedagogy behind a suite of writing sessions at a relatively large research university. Sue Starfield and Brian Paltridge show the strengths of generic support for the 'occluded practice' of writing the research proposal, a significant piece of doctoral writing that is not made public, so that novice students looking for examples usually cannot access a range of models. Finally, Bronwyn James notes that care with word choice and grammar – with the mechanics of revision – sometimes results in significant theoretical consequences, enabling students to over-write discipline terminology to achieve axiologically-based breakthroughs.

First, then, Deborah Laurs considers how generic consultations offer space within the doctoral journey for students to canvass ideas, vent frustrations and grapple with uncertainty as they strive to fulfil the demands of the thesis genre. Anthony Paré's (2011: 62–63) findings show that often even very good supervisors lack 'the linguistic and rhetorical vocabulary' (p. 66) to talk about writing. As a result, they may give 'fuzzy' advice that students are unable to interpret; in a study involving 30 supervisors, 'despite their good intentions and thoughtful efforts, the supervisors...struggled to help students write their dissertations' (Paré 2011: 71). Laurs' definition of the work she does to complement supervision demonstrates the way that a learning advisor with knowledge of the thesis genre – both form and process – and the language to explain its requirements can interpret supervisory comments into advice that can be followed. Moreover, the informality of the student's relationship with the learning advisor – possibly even the fact that it is not bounded by a quasi-contractual obligation – sometimes helps to pull forth (better) student writing.

Close generic work with the thesis writing journey

Students frequently come to our learning centre appointments bearing drafts containing feedback from their supervisors, at the one extreme mortified their written expression has been found wanting, at the other simply keen to learn how to improve beyond what they already have achieved. Sometimes the comments puzzle them, but they are unwilling to trouble the supervisor for further explanation. In many instances, the generic advisor, by using techniques such as the WIRMI *('what I really mean is')* method (see Cadman 1997, and Flower 1981), posing questions such as 'what do you want to say here?' or 'tell me about this bit,' can help unpack the academic jargon and inchoate thoughts that often plague novice writers. Irrespective of whether a particular discipline allows use of the first person within the written text, talking about one's project in an infomal setting gives agency to the student voice. Moreover, a learning advisor can provide the tools and techniques that supervisory comments such as 'needs reworking' or 'meaning unclear' do not: brainstorming the potential of a 'how' research question versus a 'why?'; weighing up one particular thematic arrangement of material versus another, or unpacking the cultural vagaries of the English academic writing in contrast, say, to Continental or Arabic conventions – and suggesting ways (such as the all-powerful topic sentence) to recast. In this way, our role moves beyond mere skills development into the realms of 'academic literacy' (Melles 2001: 6).

It might be argued that such involvement oversteps the bounds, by doing 'things that a supervisor or academic should be doing, such as structuring a dissertation, thinking through the argument of the dissertation, etc.' (Laurs 2010: 26), yet in my experience few students are prepared to ask their supervisor for formative writing guidance. Moreover, students tend to regard supervisors' comments as signs of their own failure. In one instance, for example, a student was frustrated to receive 'just as many comments' on the revised draft as on the original (Laurs 2010), unaware of the ongoing dialogic nature of the supervisory process. Generic advisors can help students view supervisory feedback as constructive – critique rather than criticism. Just as a coach spurs a top athlete to greater heights, learning advisors make the 'implicit explicit, the stuff we don't talk about or that isn't often talked about in an explicit way' (Percy 2011: 115) in order to translate supervisors' feedback into more effective practice.

The informal nature of the generic setting can also help with writer's block. Akin to Kearns' crap writing tool (2010), when a student says 'I don't know what to write,' a learning advisor has the freedom to reply, 'It doesn't matter, just write anything.' Often, all that is needed is a prompt such as 'jot down three things you'd like to say to your supervisor.' Whether the student ever says them is immaterial; the catalyst suffices. Frequently more experienced in the doctoral genre than an individual supervisor, learning advisors variously perform the roles of confidant, cheerleader, coach and critic (Spillett and Moisiewicz 2004), serving the diverse needs of both candidate and supervisor.

As Kearns' (2006) 'roller-coaster' metaphor so aptly illustrates, the doctoral journal is fraught with highs and lows. Life in general has a way of disrupting the best-laid plans, the research proposal's neatly-devised Gantt chart often obsolete before the first month is out. Ideally, students should inform supervisors of matters affecting their progress, but often the immediacy of the situation (ill-health, writer's block, failed experiment, or relationship breakdown – either personal or supervisory) makes it difficult to do so. In many cases, meeting with a learning advisor can place these issues in perspective, as shown by the following comments from a student during one of my sessions:

> I'd just about had enough over the weekend, and even printed off the official form, ready to withdraw. But then I realized – I can't get a job in a call centre because I don't like talking on the phone; I can't be a [supermarket] checkout operator because I'm no good with numbers; I can't even work as a cleaner because I'm allergic to dust...[*sigh, then laughter*]... So I guess I'll just have to carry on [writing the thesis].

In this particular instance, I have shared the student's frustrations – and triumphs – from the very beginning of her candidature. During our occasional 50 minute sessions, we focus on written expression or brainstorm structural and thematic connections; at other times, we simply talk – or more often I listen – as she moves from anger and tears of frustration to 'I *can* do this!' once more. Nevertheless, the imposter syndrome remains a powerful inhibitor. Few students willingly share such anxieties – or even their attempts at brainstorming, journal entries or working notes – with supervisors. The generally-accepted practice is simply to go away and produce another (better?) version of the previous draft, with the emphasis firmly on the end product. For this reason, it is salutory when supervisors share their own works-in-progress and editorial feedback, thereby normalizing writing as a public event.

Support is vital for doctoral students when confronting the unknowns of the research and writing journeys. Such aid comes, in the first instance, from supervisors, fellow students and acquaintances, underpinned by professional learning advisors versed in the ways of the academy. The complementary nature of such support is well-illustrated by my own experience as both postgraduate learning advisor *and* doctoral supervisor (where my pedagogical knowledge complements the primary supervisor's discipline expertise). In fact, I see little difference between my two roles, other than that supervisory meetings tend to be formal occasions where our student presents a more polished rendition of the ideas originally mooted, trialled and honed during learning advisor consultations. Far from undermining the formal relationship, generic advisors are ideally-placed to reinforce supervisors' feedback and, if necessary, to help develop the requisite technical skills and moral encouragement for students' successful completion.

Deborah Laurs

As well as the consultative support that Laurs describes, the conducive environment of a writing retreat allows for emotional and conceptual support as well as providing a quiet uninterupted thinking space. If you are interested in facilitating a retreat, a good place to start is Barbara Grant's *Guide to Writing Retreats* (2008), which carefully details the timeline for organization. Retreats take some time and care with organizing, but can be highly effective. Cath Fraser and Heather Hamerton describe writing retreats run at a small polytechnic; increasingly, at institutions of all sizes, such retreats create oases where writing is somehow made possible.

Doing it together: doctoral writing retreats

Like many other tertiary learning organizations, our institution – Bay of Plenty Polytechnic (BoPP) – has a vested interest in ensuring our staff gain postgraduate qualifications, including doctorates. However, as an organization largely involved in undergraduate teaching and learning, we do not have comprehensive systems in place to support our own staff with their research studies. In actively and deliberately recruiting staff who have research and publication interests, often linked to PhD projects, we have had to improve our internal resources and supports for doctoral candidates and researchers. One successful initiative that we have found useful in fostering motivation, confidence and capability to write is our annual writers' retreat.

The BoPP experience

Writing retreats give participants the time, space and support to embark on or progress formal documentation of their research or practice, either for their thesis, or for journal publication. Writing in a group context allows newcomers to overcome two obstacles to successful completion of a manuscript: lack of momentum and lack of formal structure (McGrail, Rickard and Jones 2006). We were particularly keen to develop retreats that would provide both social and individual opportunities to progress academic writing (Elbow and Sorcinelli 2006). We also decided that we wanted a residential, off-campus experience to break down barriers, reinforce the group nature of the enterprise, and provide relief from day-to-day job requirements. Furthermore, we made a decision that our writers' retreats would be interdisciplinary, providing opportunities for budding writers to exchange ideas across disciplinary boundaries, because we believed this would enhance participants' experience, broaden their thinking and potentially allow for generation of new ideas.

2007: an externally led approach

In our first year, 2007, we booked a number of motel units with a larger conference room for workshop sessions, peer review and lunch and refreshment breaks. We brought in an outside writing expert with experience in facilitating similar retreats. We contacted prospective participants beforehand to gauge their level of preparedness and to begin to establish the relationships necessary to overcome some of the barriers to writing they identified, many of which echoed those reported in the literature. These barriers included self-censorship, and the lack of confidence, time, external motivation, and ability, in particular lack of writing-related skills (McGrail, Rickard and Jones 2006; Moore 2003) and more pressing commitments to teaching, marking or administration (Mercer *et al.* 2006). We also thought a writers' retreat would help to counteract confusion of focus, a relaxed sense of timelines and insufficient feedback, which Belcher (2009) reports can hamper solo writing efforts.

The five-day retreat started with participants sharing their topics and objectives for the week. The facilitator then organized one-on-one sessions with each participant so she could assist with structure, direction, formatting or feedback, depending on the individual's request. People then chose to write either in the workshop room or in their own motel units. Over the week, the facilitator had at least one further personal meeting with each writer, again providing feedback and assisting them to map out their next moves. The facilitator also offered a number of topics for short optional workshops and led two more structured sessions in which we read one another's work and offered comments and impressions.

Evaluations from the 12 writers who attended showed they felt the retreat had offered valuable stimulation and insights. Several had achieved first drafts of papers which were subsequently published, one had made a significant start on a PhD proposal, and another had completely redrafted a chapter of his PhD thesis. Others completed reports for external bodies and articles for industry magazines.

2009 and 2010: internally-facilitated retreats

After talking to the 2007 participants and investigating alternative models (Grant 2008), we made some changes to the second retreat and decided to take on the facilitation role ourselves. Instead of going to a motel, we hired two neighbouring beachside holiday homes for a week and combined outsourced catering with some communal cooking. We invited a journal editor to be a guest speaker and give a session on writing for publication; she was most enthusiastic and asked if she could stay on for two days to complete some of her own writing. While she was there, she also made herself available for some informal discussion and consulting sessions.

Another change we introduced was the routine of 'morning pages' (Cameron 1992), where everyone started each day by covering three pages of a journal with handwritten 'freewriting,' or private writing, which was never intended to produce a public finished product (Elbow and Sorcinelli 2006). This warm-up exercise was a way to free the mind from words and thoughts – about the topic or about anything else that was competing for attention – eschewing any mental rehearsal for a stream-of-consciousness fluency. Otherwise, these retreats followed the format of the first: brief workshop sessions, facilitator feedback, peer review – and lots of personal writing time. Again, this writing retreat was highly successful: 'all participants of the Writers' Retreat reported their progress had exceeded what they might have hoped to achieve at their desks' (Bay of Plenty Polytechnic 2010: 24).

The outcomes – for individuals and for the institution

In written evaluations from our writers' retreats, all participants have expressed a sense of satisfaction and progress, with many reporting an enhanced confidence in writing skills and an appreciation of just what productive habits in research, writing and critical reflection actually look like. They enjoyed the opportunity to exchange ideas with academic writers from other disciplines and subject areas. Several also identified strategies to increase their effectiveness at writing through better preparation beforehand. Support, encouragement and motivation from facilitators and fellow writers have increased knowledge and skills that have remained long after the week was over. These reported benefits are similar to those identified by other writers who noted that working alongside peers and colleagues makes participants aware that they are not the only ones struggling in their endeavour to write (McGrail, Rickard and Jones 2006), allows informal discussion and feedback to improve one another's writing and outcomes (Grant 2008) and, longer-term, can create pan-institutional networks and suggest interdisciplinary collaborations (Fraser and Ayo 2010).

From an institutional point of view, this cost-effective professional development initiative has led to an increase in annual research outputs, including peer-reviewed publications by several participants who had never achieved this previously. The retreats have supported PhD candidates in advancing their work, and demonstrated the way in which a thesis can generate a number of linked articles and establish the framework for a career in academia.

Summing up

The successful outcomes reported by participants and documented through increased publication rates suggest to us that the real value of writers' retreats for participants is twofold. Firstly we have gained an appreciation of the importance of a quiet, comfortable working space conducive to a deep and extended engagement with writing, free from the distractions of office or home. Secondly, the presence of others is important because, as Elbow and Sorcinelli (2006: 18) note, writers 'will be more apt to do the solitary work of writing if they surround themselves with other writers pursuing the same goal.'

The doctoral journey is a long one, but with the opportunity to engage with a community of fellow travellers on occasions such as writers' retreats, there is at least the chance to exchange tips, canvass suggestions and sample new perspectives. The collegial relationships that form through attending these retreats mean that there are plenty of cheerleaders to exhort fellow writers to maintain their momentum and arrive, eventually, at a successful conclusion.

Cath Fraser and Heather Hamerton

As a counterweight to Fraser and Hamerton's account of writing retreats, Susan Carter describes the suite of workshops established in a larger institution, explaining their purpose and pedagogy: what motivated the workshops being provided, how they developed, and what teaching methods were used. She points out that, because classrooms entail talk, students can make sure they work on precisely what helps them most. Such sessions also encourage students to manage their time, their project and themselves.

Thesis writing: a suite of generic sessions

The University of Auckland Student Learning Centre, set up in 2003, slowly developed a suite of different sessions on writing within a university wide doctoral programme. Initially, some writing sessions covered threshold points (Kiley and Wisker 2009) that were obvious from experience – writing a persuasive thesis proposal, ensuring the review of literature was appropriate and that it showed critical analysis. I concur with Rowena Murray (2012: 190): 'writing experiences do not seem to be differentiated solely by…disciplines of study or research… discussing them [the different requirements of different disciplines] in itself can be interesting and helpful': discussing expectations, and how to implement them, is one way of working out what generic requirements mean.

Our engagement with the challenges of writing, both for the thesis and for publication, developed over a decade or so as our own understanding grew. By 2012, the programme included sessions that map onto those suggested by Green and Bowden (2010: 136) comprising, 'seminars and workshops on a range of topics from research higher degree policy and procedures, progress, thesis writing, publication, ethics and intellectual property, research literacies, quantitative approaches, qualitative approaches, career opportunities, stress management, examination and supervision matters.' Some sessions addressed specific parts of the thesis that were significant and thus difficult to write: for example, one, advertised as being for students in their final year, looked at the introduction and conclusion. Other workshops were developed as common obstacles surfaced frequently in individual appointments. For example, one workshop has students identifying the core of their overall project and describing it clearly and persuasively both informally and formally, and included advice on producing the thesis abstract in about 300 words. The informal description meant students relaxed as they got to know each other's work, which seemed to help with the production of a formal abstract. That session was based on how often students describe their projects by mumbling something in discipline jargon that is hard to follow, whereas they must be able to explain their work so that its value is evident to non-experts.

I found too from individual consultations that structuring the thesis seemed troublesome for many students. In my session on structure, I begin by discussing the standard model – introduction, literature, methodology, results, discussion and conclusion – suggesting that if that one will work, it is like a never-fail recipe that safety-focused students might well choose. I encourage others to observe that the model shows the generic moves of a thesis. Somewhere in whatever structure they use they must make these moves along with whatever others come with the discipline. In class discussions, learning advisors can give useful advice to risk-takers who want to explore, push boundaries, blaze trails, and to risk-averse students who just want to finish quickly and safely.

In the structuring session, we look at various content page examples; seeing some together shows the ways that subtitle hierarchies convey a sense of how ideas fit together. Students discuss what works well and what is more opaque, beginning to see the *cognitive overview* that structure implies. Different, the content pages all come from successfully completed theses. We run through a smorgasbord of possible routes to planning structure – including mind-mapping and diagrams that are then shifted around. Most importantly, we discuss the tensions that trouble structuring, for example, between the generic expectations and the epistemology, the topic under investigation and data. Subsequently I surveyed student experience of structure, and results now further inform the session (also see Carter and Blumenstein 2011). One unexpected finding was that the further in to the doctorate, the *less* certain students were about their thesis structure. This flies in the face of expectations that the doctorate entails 'the progressive reduction of uncertainties' (Phillips and Pugh 1994: 84), but makes sense according to increasing awareness of the complexity of a topic. Engaging for some years with students' structuring difficulties led me to believe that often students need to go down to the most meaningful level of their work, their own values and their research axiology, to locate the right structure for their thesis. Then they should explain idiosyncrasy in their introduction at that deepest level. When they do so, they fulfil generic expectations even as they step outside the box a little. Better insights into student experience of difficulty with it enabled us to put out a short book covering suggestions (Carter, Kelly and Brailsford 2012).

A session on style and voice discusses the epistemological implications of these, the way that writing style implies the theoretical frame. Students talk about the context of their own work: their preference, their supervisors', the discipline boundaries. They develop a critical awareness that conventions are not simply mechanical and inert. Another session on grammar looks at not just what is 'right and wrong,' but at the way that syntax and grammar affects emphasis and thus content. Exercises make visible the effect of grammar and syntax in writing expressing complex ideas. And many doctoral students attend the punctuation festivals that we run twice each year, the teaching of which has also led to a short book angled at foundational basic points students need to know (Buxton, Carter and Sturm 2012).

Basic principles behind my sessions include that they all make use of examples, exercises from the guide manuals, and discussion. As much as discipline-based academics read in their field, like other learning advisors, I read in the field of doctoral education, accumulating understanding (including of complexity) and useful exercises and models.

Although our handouts offer solid practical suggestions, classes are open for students to drive. They allow discussion of theory and methodology: 'interactions with others...help motivate a sense of progress...and using these interactions [enables students to] begin to address or work through difficulties' (Jarvac-Martek, Chen and McAlpine 2011: 34). We can swoop in on particular trouble spots that students raise. Often at the beginning students write on a post-it note what they most want from the session, and the session can be tailored accordingly. Additionally, we have peer review writing sessions fortnightly where such work can be done. Another hands-on strand uses volunteer support to assist EAL students with their writing (Carter 2009b).

The workshops are two hours long to make it worthwhile for students to come. We evaluate every session, responding to suggestions; the two hour frame is deemed generally suitable – of the few who comment on time, an equal number say 'too long' and 'not long enough.' A tea and coffee break halfway through attempts to create a homeliness, a degree of informality, and the opportunity to chat and gossip. The writing sessions are all well evaluated, although conspicuously the core sessions of the thesis proposal and literature review get about three times as many students as the others. (This voting-with-their-feet aligns with a survey of departmental graduate advisors who also deemed those two sessions the most needed [Brailsford and Carter 2010].) If we find ourselves short staffed, we pull back on the less well attended sessions. When class size justifies it – we set this at 30 or more attendees based on the size of the two teaching rooms available – we split the group into two, with one half taught by a learning advisor with a science and statistics background, the other by an advisor with a humanities background. Students are divided according to their disciplines. The same handouts are used, but with different examples, and teachers focusing at times on different challenges.

At times, the talk in class will be low genre – 'how do you do all this when you have little kids?' Such crucial back room conversations assure students that any self-doubts are not theirs alone. More often we stay with academic language, sifting the components of good thesis writing: clarity, completeness, appropriateness, depth of theory and adequate defence. Students can raise their individual difficulties, such as the shaping of identity through writing, not an issue for many students, but overwhelming for some. Puzzlement and frustration can be safely dealt with away from the supervisor and department. Importantly, students who fear they might be seen as stupid in contexts where they are known feel free to safely investigate the unfamiliar facets of thesis writing here.

Susan Carter

Thesis writing takes psychological stamina, formal academic language expertise, and insider awareness of discipline convention. The criteria for the thesis must be fully understood and then patently demonstrated in prose. Some of these layers of iterative work are not plainly evident in completed theses. One particularly covert text is the thesis proposal. Here, Sue Starfield and Brian Paltridge show the support framework they use in relation to the thesis proposal, pointing out that students lack ready access to examples of how other students have successfully generated prose that succinctly and accurately sets forth the plan for their doctoral project. They show how they make explicit the theoretical, methodological or interdisciplinary complexity needed for the proposal. The social situatedness of the thesis means that the proposal must perform multiple tasks before a critical audience whose reactions may be coloured by their own concerns about potential future investment and involvement.

Generic support for developing a research proposal

The research proposal for a thesis or dissertation is a classic example of an occluded genre (Swales 1996). What we mean by this is that it is a genre that is not publically available but is 'hidden and out of sight.' Yet it is a high stakes genre in that, in many universities, completion of a successful proposal at the end of the first year of full-time study is the gateway to what is called 'confirmation of candidature' for all doctoral students. On submission and acceptance of the proposal, the student is then confirmed as a higher degree research student and can move on to carry out their research project and write their thesis. At our universities, the proposal is typically read by at most three people who are on the confirmation committee.

Because of its occluded nature and the fact that it is also a kind of transitionary genre, 'en route' to the thesis or dissertation, it is very difficult to obtain examples of successful research proposals to show prospective students. The chapter on writing a research proposal in our book (Paltridge and Starfield 2007) provides guidance for candidates and their supervisors on what to include in a proposal: aims, a literature review, a section on the investigative approach or methodology and considerations of the significance and feasibility of the proposed work. As we know from feedback on our book, this information is very helpful to candidates and supervisors as it explicitly talks about the sections of the proposal and what each should contain.

Our course, *Developing a Research Proposal*, focuses less on the macrostructural components of the proposal and more on offering a set of 'conceptual tools' that students at a very early stage in the thesis process might find helpful. These are perforce generic as, working with a group of students from differing disciplinary backgrounds, what we offer cannot be specific to each student's proposal or discipline. What the course does offer students is a series of tools for thinking about the questions they wish to frame and how they might go about seeking answers to these questions. Over a 12-week semester, usually their first, students meet fortnightly in a group to work through a variety of tasks. All tasks involve thinking and writing and talking. Students are not expected to come with clearly formed ideas of what the thesis is about and then told how to 'pour' these thoughts into a pre-existing mould. The class is rather a site in which they formulate questions through an iterative process of thinking, writing and talking to one another across their different fields of study.

In this next section, we discuss one of our simple tools that on the first day of the course asks the students to think about four questions. The *four questions framework* is the backbone of the course (and we acknowledge Sarah Maddison's initial conceptualization of the tools discussed here), providing a scaffold for all that follows. Students are given a one-page handout with these four questions:

- What is the question I am trying to answer?
- Why is it worth answering?
- How have other people tried to answer it?
- How am I going to go about answering it?

There is enough space on the sheet of paper for the student to write two–three sentences or thoughts in response to each of the prompts. Each question is referring to the different components of the proposal but without using terms such as 'literature review' for example. 'Why is it worth answering?' is of course the 'so what?'/significance question. We find that students tend to respond extremely well to this task. They are challenged to articulate their thinking and write words on a page but not too many words. They often find they know more than they think they know. Talking about what they have thought and written about is a further stage in articulating and clarifying thinking. We make it clear to students that everything is provisional – a work in progress. This week's 'question I am trying to answer' may have changed completely by the time we meet again in a fortnight's time. And if it has, as is quite often the case, that may be no bad thing. As the course proceeds it may be helpful to revisit the four questions framework and ask students to repeat the activity. Of course students may, on their own, repeat it as often as they like, precisely because it is a thinking and writing tool.

We have developed other writing and thinking prompts that we use in other sessions. Visuals can be a very good way to encourage students in the early days of conceptualizing their research. The interlocking Venn diagrams (see Figure 7.1) help students conceptualize their 'research space' by clearly 'seeing' where the niche their topic will occupy is located in relation to key literature in the field. Students are given a handout with three large empty circles, and asked to list key authors for each of the literatures/concepts they are examining. The intersection of all three circles is their research niche.

Working in this way with tools and writing prompts seems to be very helpful to students in the early stages of their research project. While not demanding

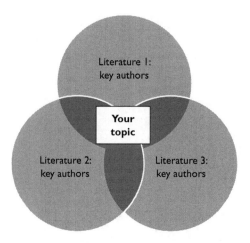

Figure 7.1 Visual prompt for thinking about a literature review

large amounts of writing, students are nevertheless producing text that can be used in the proposal document. At the end of the course, they are expected to produce a draft proposal which is substantially shorter than the final document required six months later. They will however have a draft of several thousand words, which will be the basis of the final document, and they will have received detailed feedback on it from us on it – not on its contents but on its structure, organization, the ways in which the responses to the four questions and other prompts are articulated.

We hope that these generic tools may be helpful to other students and their supervisors as they conceptualize their doctoral theses.

Sue Starfield and Brian Paltridge

We argue that in almost all cases, when a student spends time with someone who has expertise in writing and language, and in discussion with other doctoral peers in different disciplines, they are better able to hone the clarity and accuracy of their ideas. Although the production of formal academic writing and the need for clarity may be the prime objectives of students attending generic advisory sessions, often consideration of the implications of word choice and structure bring what is significant into visibility. We suggest that, in discussion with learning advisors for whom teaching writing is core business, students very often succeed in locating the precise terms they need.

Next, then, Bronwyn James focuses in at the level of language to show that grappling with words is grappling with ideas, often to reach crucial axiological levels. Her piece illuminates the way that students grope deep into the lexicon of their disciplines and theory as they construct academic identities that seem authentic to their own beliefs. In such cases, precision with vocabulary and grammar performs vital changes to meaning: students do substantive work in the process of revision.

Writing and rewriting: students' negotiations with texts and 'selves'

I want to focus on the pedagogical benefits of paying close attention to the written drafts that higher degree research students produce during their candidature, and their own accounts of writing. These drafts and accounts provide insights into the ways in which the student writer not only negotiates the construction of a text that is meaningful within the discipline within which s/he is writing, but also through that writing constructs a subject position or identity for her/himself that is both constrained and enabled by a number of factors. These factors include the genre of the thesis, the social histories of the writer, the disciplinary forms of knowledge and ways of expressing that knowledge that are deemed acceptable within the discipline within which the student is writing, and the student's own internalization or anticipation of these and other norms of higher degree research writing.

My interest in researching and writing about the ways in which writing and drafting are implicated with subjectivity or identity formation came about through my work with research students in workshops, in consultations, and in subjects within discipline-focused degree programmes that are run to support higher degree research students during their candidature. I wanted to know why students make the changes to their writing that they do – sometimes against the advice of their supervisors. In working with this question, I have employed a research methodology that draws on Elizabeth Grosz's work on difference (2005), Judith Butler's performativity work (for example, 1997, 1999, 2004), and Michael Halliday's (1994) Systemic Functional Linguistics. For an extended explanation of this methodology see James (2013).

The view of subjectivity that underpins and gives shape to this methodology is, following Butler's performativity work, fluid, multiple and fragile – conditional on the ongoing recognition by 'Others' who review, critique and assess the writing that a student produces, and vulnerable to misrecognition – those moments when not only the written text but also its writer are called into question through the language used to describe the text. This language-infused, conditional, and relational view of subjectivity fits well with the notion that writing at research level involves writing an academic self into being (Aitchison, Kamler and Lee 2010). Doing this, however, involves the *student who writes* and does a lot of other things besides (James 2011) in complex negotiations with text and with a multiplicity of selves that intrude on, constrain, and enable an acceptable linguistic expression of this academic self.

To take one example, 'Anna,' a doctoral student in Education, researching the communication of her young developmentally delayed son 'Danny,' and using Systemic Functional Linguistics as the framework for this research, drafts and redrafts the headings of a section of her writing. The first draft contains the heading 'Systemic Functional Approaches to Learning Language.' In the second draft, this earlier heading is replaced with 'Systemic Functional Approaches to Language Development – Limitations.' Elsewhere, over three drafts of the results chapter of her thesis, Anna makes use of a footnote where she directly engages the reader. This same footnote remains unchanged with the exception that in drafts 2 and 3 Anna makes one simple but significant change: the wording 'the way typical children his age do' in draft 1 is changed to 'the way speakers do' in drafts 2 and 3.

The text from drafts 2 and 3 is reproduced below with the relevant reworked section highlighted:

> Drafts 2 and 3 footnote
> I can hear the reader ask, at this point, why does the title of the thesis include 'nonverbal' as a classifier of Danny's communication when here I am saying that he has words in his communicative repertoire. By describing Danny as nonverbal, I mean that he does not use speech language as the main form of communication *the way speakers do*. He does not use any of the grammatical resources that speech has to offer.

In light of Anna's accounts of her writing during a series of interviews about the changes to her drafts, these simple textual manoeuvres set in motion a number of significant effects. First, the rewording in the footnote enables a restaging of Danny as a different communicator, rather than dismissing him as the user of a protolanguage. This is a risky bid as it places Anna's work *as a researcher* at odds with the SFL theory as it stands which would position Danny as the user of a protolanguage associated in developmental terms with an infant language. During an interview, Anna provides this account:

> if you plot Danny on a language development continuum he's not very far along, and I'm arguing that he does have a language that's not protolanguage, not pre-adult system. So I guess that's my point there. I, I don't want to locate him on the continuum.

And again, in another interview:

> he's not an infant and I have a real ideological issue which may be a problem for me as researcher is that, I don't want to pitch him at his development. So that's gone out with the bloody dark ages...

As she also indicates in the following interview extract, Anna has internalized or anticipated a potential rejection of her work because of her refusal to pitch Danny as the user of a protolanguage:

> So if they [her supervisors] chose x as a marker I'd would feel like I would have to work so hard to convince her that what I'm doing is right and I don't want, I don't to be writing for that. I want to write for someone who's already got a much broader view of what language is.

Anna's address to the reader at the beginning of the footnote, 'I can hear the reader ask' confronts this possibility of questions about her insistence on interpreting Danny's communication as *language*. She pre-emptively acknowledges, and later, counters a different reading of her data and her argument.

Through these moves in her writing, Anna effectively orchestrates a play of perspectives and 'selves.' Across this series of drafts, Anna engineers language to 'radically resignify' (Butler 2004) Danny as a communicator of significance, and SFL as a theory with limitations. At the same time, she manages a multiplicity of sometimes conflicting 'selves' – *researcher, mother, doctoral candidate, writer*, and more... – through these same changes in text structure and lexicogrammar, and, ultimately, through the limits she draws around potential thesis examiners.

What emerges in Anna's drafts and her accounts is a complexity of factors and risks that impact on both the text that is written and rewritten and the subject positions that Anna negotiates in and through the texts that she produces. More broadly, this account suggests that doctoral student drafting is a site of rich pedagogical possibilities for supervisors, for academic literacy and learning educators and for the students with whom they work. It further suggests that a student's take-up, refusal or sidestepping of the use of particular linguistic resources may be an effect of writing as an embodied, affective *performance* that involves the writer in complex negotiations in the co-production of a text and a social subjectivity that is meaningful within the conventions of genre and disciplinary knowledge.

The question is, of course, how this view of subjectivity and its relationship to writing might inform a generic doctoral writing workshop. In answer, I would say that one of the key things that came out of the research project of which Anna was a participant is that deconstructing text to demonstrate particular genre moves and lexicogrammatical choices (a frequent focus of generic workshops) is only part of the story. Students need to know this but what this research reveals is that students make decisions about what to write based on a lot of things in addition to what we might demonstrate to be good thesis structure, style and so on.

So this piece is a reminder to those of us teaching in generic doctoral writing workshops that simply unpacking the genre etc. isn't the whole story. We could also let students in on Anna's story and the view that writing is intimately linked with identity or subject formation, and with discursive power. When students find themselves stuck in some uncomfortable place in their writing, they might then be able to see this as something to do with a whole lot of competing things going on. It's a reminder to those of us who teach and those of us that write that these stuck places can be very productive places, not some individual pathology at work.

Bronwyn James

Close attention to language can have significant consequences for the novice researcher establishing her/himself as an expert in their field. Chapters six and seven have shown generic expertise develops in theory and in practice, in order to provide a scaffold to thinking and writing.

Part III steps into issues that relate to futurity. The next chapter looks at generic support's adaptation to accommodate the changing nature of doctoral studies. The student profile now reveals an increasing number of part-timers, for whom time restrictions, competing extracurricular commitments and physical isolation pose additional obstacles to completion. Because such students often also work full time, generic support for them may entail the use of digital media, which we also discuss in the next chapter.

PART III

Ensuring generic support's sustainability

Chapter 8

Part-time and digital support

> Social technology is replicating what we see in nature. Cell division and rapid proliferation of genetic material across an organism. Viral reproduction of genetic material between and across organisms. Rhizomatic spread of connections... At the moment though, we are merely scraping the surface of immense, almost infinite potential.
>
> (Steve Wheeler 2012: n.p.)

Many doctoral students are coming mid-career as part-time students, and 'increasing numbers study at a distance' (Kamler and Thomson 2006: 9, citing Evans 2002; see also Evans and Pearson 1999). Hooley *et al.* (2009: 1) reported that about a fifth of all UK doctoral graduates were part-timers, enrolling at an average age of 37.6 years compared to full-timers' average of 27.3 years. Part-timers tend to take longer pro rata to complete: fewer than half were finished within ten years. They described their doctoral experience as '"frustrating," "wretched," "lonely," "tiring," "daunting" and "over-whelming"' (Hooley *et al.* 2009: 1–2). Gardner and Gopaul (2012) capture the pressures from work, family, and university and part-timers' resultant feelings of guilt and demoralization (also see Evans 2006). It's not surprising: these slightly older doctoral students usually have family responsibilities and full-time jobs to maintain them. In comparison to full-time students, part-timers may find friends, family and employers less supportive of their research study (Hooley *et al.* 2009: 6); nevertheless, they are more motivated by interest in their topics (Hooley *et al.* 2009: 7).

So, part-time and distance students often feel keen but isolated. Where full-time campus-based colleagues share offices or work within departmental spaces, attend workshops, collegially discuss their work, and get regular feedback, part-timers can feel outside the pale of an academic community of practice. They are often unable to attend classroom-based generic workshops either. Gardner and Gopaul (2012) demonstrate how full-time doctoral candidature tends to be normative, whereas, especially in professional disciplines, part-time study coupled with full-time work is common, presenting huge challenges in terms of socialization and stress. Learning advisors need to be flexible and inventive in their approaches to supporting part-time and distance students.

Working with part-timers is likely to take place outside usual class times, requiring considerable event management effort to gather the critical mass needed for a lively academic colloquium. It may be optimum to work across institutions to draw together both teachers able to share the load and sufficient students able to make time in their busy lives to attend. One possibility for generic support of part-timers is weekend events, such as Amy Cartwright describes below. Another form of support is online resources for doctoral students: materials that can be accessed 24/7, or informal digital support through electronic media, such as blogs or Twitter's #phdchat strand, to create a collegial network. We don't mean to suggest that digital teaching media resources are solely for part-timers, but, as Terry Evans' experience shows, many such sites are built initially as a way to meet part-timer needs.

However, it needs to be acknowledged that digital support is time-expensive and requires rethinking pedagogy. It's a relatively new medium for teaching; potentially unfamiliar to learning advisors more likely to be 'digital immigrants' than 'digital natives' (Prensky 2001: 2). Going digital represents a cognitive and social shift (Datt and Carter 2011; Carter, Datt and Donald 2012), with changes in styles of learning communication. Learning advisors may already provide support for part-time students by being flexible with their own working hours, but moving into digital support also requires a certain degree of flexibility concerning academic identity.

Notwithstanding, active online conversations are likely to encourage doctoral students to be ethical and equitable. Good academic citizenship is almost compulsory in the sharing of digital dialogics. Wikipedia is an example, albeit one often denigrated by academics, which has opened the possibility of contributing to shared knowledge by actively posting and editing information. Such engagement builds a sense of responsibility to the wider community. At the same time, Wikipedia's shared authorship questions the ownership of knowledge: see too Samuels (2002) for the wittily-expressed suggestion that an over-emphasis on plagiarism misses the point of scholarship. Towards the end of this chapter, Inger Mewburn, well-known as the Thesis Whisperer, declares her philosophy of digital teaching, the ability to make teaching and learning truly democratic, shared, and available to all.

This chapter begins, then, with consideration of classes for part-timers, which must be outside university hours, but also sustainable. Amy Cartwright's account of a UK model suggests how this might be achieved.

Research training/education without borders

> Part-time researchers frequently do not have the time to attend "generic" courses or reading groups and therefore the provision of events – even just

once a semester – which were strictly relevant, and enabled them to meet other researchers in similar positions, would be enormously helpful.

(Hooley *et al.* 2009: 11)

Meeting the needs of full-time research students has been a challenge addressed in the UK since the publication of Sir Gareth Roberts' report *SET for Success* (National Archives: HM Treasury) in 2002. This document, and the outcomes which followed, provided UK HEIs with both a mandate and funding to develop the skills of research students, enabling them to reach their full potential in the workforce.

It was in response to the Roberts' Report that UKGrad was formed as a national champion for researchers, and merged to become Vitae (www.vitae.ac.uk) in 2008. Vitae is a national organization funded by the Research Councils to support researchers to realize their full potential, by supporting staff in HEIs involved in researcher development, influencing policy and dissemination of good practice.

While huge strides have been made in the support for full-time researchers, as evidenced by the Postgraduate Research Experience Survey (Higher Education Academy 2012) results over the three years of survey results, there has been a comparatively low success rate in tackling the specific needs of the part-time cohort of researchers.

Initial work to overcome both the low levels of support for part-time researchers and the lack of data on the researcher experience began in the Vitae Midlands Hub in 2008 where they ran a series of collaborative workshops for part-time researchers to open access to the training to those researchers at any HEI in the region. Alongside this practical support there was an evaluation of PRES data for the part-time experience and participants on the workshops were surveyed on their own perspectives of the PhD as a part-time endeavour. The outcomes from this project were a report on 'Understanding the Part-Time Researcher Experience' and a set of materials to support skills training for part-time research students (Hooley *et al.* 2009).

Inspired by the Midlands experience, the Vitae Scotland and Northern Ireland Hub organized a Practice Sharing event for HEI staff working with researchers, on the topic of the 'Part-Time Researcher' in August 2009. This event enabled participants to share approaches to meeting the needs of this cohort and assess how the Midlands research and materials might help to address the needs of part-time researchers. What quickly became apparent was that HEIs had tried many times and in a variety of ways to engage with their part-time researcher populations but did not feel they had really reached this elusive group.

The group then began to explore ways in which the Hub could facilitate a more collaborative approach to the 'part-time conundrum,' hopefully enabling the establishment of critical mass and a higher profile for part-time researchers in Scotland and Northern Ireland. It was clear from the Vitae report that part-time researchers required training that was specific to them as a group with niche needs and that any intervention was publicized well in advance to allow them to plan their time in order to attend.

With this in mind a sub-group of those who attended the part-time event began to plan for a one-day high profile conference in September 2010 specifically to address the training and development needs of part-time researchers, both students and staff, across Scotland and Northern Ireland.

With financial support from the Hub, and securing match funding from the Scottish Funding Council, the group were able to offer places free of charge to all part-time researchers and an online registration of interest form was launched at the beginning for April 2010 – by the middle of May there had been over 170 registrations of interest.

Most of the funds for the conference were utilized to provide a high-calibre venue in the form of Surgeon's Hall (2012) in Edinburgh, both to highlight the value of part-time researchers and also as a neutral venue for all researchers regardless of HEI.

The truly collaborative part of the whole conference idea was that we intended our workshops to be run by volunteers from HEIs who deliver skills training and career development workshops for researchers and would be willing to contribute to the day – assisting both their own researchers and the researcher community across Scotland and Northern Ireland. Not only were the organizing group pleasantly surprised by the number or researchers registering interest, but also by the numbers of colleagues signing up online to facilitate workshops. This meant that a full and wide-ranging programme of workshops was beginning to emerge.

Attracting 170+ part-time researchers to an event provided the Hub with an excellent opportunity to find out more about the kinds of researchers who made up this unique cohort, and as such evaluation was a key element of the whole process of advertising the conference and the shape of the day itself. Registration of interest was kept fairly brief, with only a few key questions, but what we did ask at this stage was the town/city of residence of the part-time researcher (Vitae 2013c). The information that this simple question provided has been instrumental in our planning for the networking aspect of the conference by allowing us to ask follow-up questions on the booking form to further investigate the needs of this group. Part-time researchers provided information which demonstrated the wide geographical spread of researchers registered at the same HEI – we therefore planned to ask researchers which would be most valuable to them, a network in their HEI or a network near where they lived. This will allow us to make the most of the networking time over lunch by tailoring the networking groups to the needs of the part-time researchers attending. And this is critical to the success of the whole event: not only will it provide a one-stop-shop for the training and development needs of part-time researchers, and allow us to evaluate this group pre- and post-event, but, critically, it will serve to join up the growing numbers of part-time research students across Scotland and Northern Ireland and provide them with a network beyond the one day event itself.

Amy Cartwright

Cartwright shows the momentum possible through collaboration, leading to the possibility of ongoing networks maintained by students themselves. Although part-timers may miss the collegiality available to full-time students on campus, the possibility of sustaining networks outside of their own institution goes some way to compensating, by providing opportunities to build and maintain professional relationships.

Digital support also opens up the potential for networking beyond institutions. The medium allows for participation in the same way as the classroom. Arguably, the enculturation of Facebook and other social networks makes it likely that doctoral students will develop a digital presence that is both academic *and* conversational, allowing 'backroom' talk that might unlock the unwritten codes of academia.

The digital environment can also host workshops. However, if you construct resources yourself, you need to consider your own pedagogic philosophy, in order to translate your classroom practices into a new medium (Carter *et al.* 2012a). While the medium offers increased flexibility in terms of 24/7 access, and enables students to manoeuvre at will rather than being bound by the teacher's curriculum, it requires care to achieve the same sense of immediacy as face-to-face exchanges. Monitoring websites is time-expensive; developing effective online doctoral support is likely to prove both challenging and exhilarating for those lacking electronic-medium savvy.

Pedagogy and practical issues of time, cost and expertise influence what can be provided at each institution. Any shift to the electronic medium is likely to be partly driven by individuals with an interest in, and willingness to undertake, such a project, and partly by the political drivers of each institution in terms of funding choices. Here, Terry Evans describes the logistics of part-time students at his institution, and relates how he and colleagues developed e-learning support for them.

Online doctoral support

Doctoral candidature in Australia and New Zealand is often assumed to be a relatively solitary activity – maybe with the partial exception of those in laboratory or studio work – especially during the substantial reading, thinking, reflecting and writing stages. This solitary activity is often where the most important work is undertaken as candidates 'independently learn' to practise their research craft within its knowledge and traditions. There is no doubt that candidates need support during these periods of independent study, but what to do and when? The answers to these questions are further complicated by the diverse circumstances of candidates and their various possible locations at any given time. This is especially the case now that there are so many part-time candidates (around 40 percent) in Australia and New Zealand, most of whom literally do not study on campus (Evans, Evans and Marsh 2008: 188). It has been commonplace for PhD candidates in some disciplines to spend considerable time away from the campus – for example, in the field or in an archive – sometimes even overseas.

Part-time candidates have often effectively been 'distance students' who undertake their study away from the campus, again even overseas (see Barnacle and Usher 2003; Evans 2002).

The rise of online media and the drive towards ubiquity of internet access produces significant opportunities for universities to provide online support for doctoral candidates in ways that suit their diverse needs, contexts and locations. In 2001 I was involved with colleagues in developing online provision for doctoral candidates in the (then) Faculty of Education at Deakin University (which operates across three campuses). We had about 145 candidates most of whom (about 80 percent) were part-time, off-campus, mid-career professional people. The Faculty of Education was at the forefront of offering PhDs at a distance in the University: its first doctoral graduates occurred in 1984. Many candidates lived overseas, including in North America, Europe, the Middle-East, Asia, Papua New Guinea, New Zealand and Taiwan. Many undertook research within their own workplaces as part of their doctoral studies.

We used typical distance education means to build a doctoral community within the Faculty that involved a blend of face-to-face and off-campus means. For example, for over 30 years we have required doctoral candidates to attend their doctoral confirmation colloquium – this is the only formal attendance requirement during candidature. We estimated that the benefits of attending in person outweighed the difficulties involved for some candidates living far afield. Otherwise, candidates and supervisors were expected and required to have regular contact, whether in person, by phone or email, etc. Furthermore, the Faculty offered an annual four day residential Summer School in February on campus in Geelong and also an annual three day residential Winter School during August in New Zealand to cater for the significant number (20–25) of candidates there and any other students who wished to attend. All candidates, on-campus and off-campus, were encouraged to attend these events, but they were not compulsory.

In 2001 we developed online 'Doctoral Studies in Education' (DSE) 'seminars' and offered them to candidates for the first time in 2002. There had been previous optional online doctoral support, but this new venture was more systematic and substantial. This programme was designed to support candidates – and, indirectly, supervisors – around a sequence of mandatory Core Seminars, which candidates were required to complete, usually in a set sequence. In effect, this produced loose cohorts that studied their online Core Seminars together. Also, optional Research Issues seminars (on methodology, research practices, etc.) and Occasional Seminars (research presentations by guests, staff and candidates) were provided. The Core Seminars focused on the main doctoral skills and knowledge required to complete a PhD successfully, such as identifying and reviewing literature, doctoral proposal writing, ethical research practice, preparing for examination, etc. In addition, they also provided an induction into doctoral study and help to ensure that all doctoral graduates were familiar with online media for study, research and communication. The two key elements of the Core Seminars were that, first, each seminar was based on what candidates need at their particular stage of candidature to complete their doctorates and, second, that seminars were sequenced in the typical order of activities required to complete a doctorate within 3–4 years full-time or 6–7 years part-time. Core Seminars, therefore, were not about 'broadening the mind' or acquiring 'advanced knowledge in the field,' the optional Research Seminars and Occasional Seminars did such things. We were strongly of the view that candidates, especially busy part-time candidates, needed support to keep their work on schedule and at a high standard; we saw it as counter-productive to require candidates to undertake six-week online seminars that were a distraction from their doctorates, however, academically worthy these distractions might be.

The seminars were 'located' within the discussion or tutorial 'spaces' of normal forms of online education software (we have used First Class, WebCT and Moodle). They were asynchronous discussions facilitated by a staff member over a six-week period (Occasional Seminars are usually shorter). There were online resources attached to each seminar in the form of readings, audio, websites, etc. The Core Seminars were closed to the candidates (15 maximum) and the facilitator: no supervisors or lurkers permitted. The Research and Occasional seminars were also restricted to 15 persons, unless the seminar leader agreed to more, but participation was open to all: doctoral candidates *and* supervisors.

In 2007 we moved to encourage all final year doctoral candidates to convene their own seminar on an aspect of their PhD research. This provided an opportunity to present online – a new skill for most and one we believed all doctoral graduates should possess – and to share their ideas and findings with others. The candidates also benefited from having comments from the participants that may help them refine their thesis in some way. Additionally, they provided a role model to new doctoral students participating in the seminar.

The ultimate goal of the doctorate is the candidate's production of an original contribution to knowledge. This individual achievement is predicated, however, on collaboration – particularly online collaboration – to support the candidate's research training and research, and to enable a productive research and dissemination future when they graduate.

Terry Evans

An ability to work collaboratively is likely to be mentioned amongst the positive graduate attributes developed through generic systems, including within the digital medium. Carter, Datt and Donald (2012) spelt out some of the challenges to teachers, however. Although they are continuing to explore teaching in the digital world, they have found in their experience to date that:

- constructing a good digital site is time-expensive and requires assistance from experts
- it is tempting to try for too much and over-reach
- institutions can change software providers so there is risk of losing the resources

- students are likely to be more savvy with the media but still less critical or creative
- students are no more literate in the digital world than in the world of text
- students are just as reluctant to be active participants digitally as they are in person
- and the challenges of getting lively engagement may be the same as ever, only intensified by the relative novice status of the teachers in digital media.

Although younger students tend to be technically extremely savvy (Jonas-Dwyer and Pospisil 2004), not all learning advisors are. Matheos, Daniel and McCalla (2005: 67) research shows that 'blended learning is an emergent concept marked by ambiguity and unclear academic research cluttered with predominantly vague definitions and misinterpretations.' Institutions may push towards e-learning in the belief that it is a cost-cutter, leaving academics out of their depth. Time needs to be allowed for gaining digital dexterity (or at least basic competency) to ensure online pedagogy extends beyond mere transmission of information.

Some are already working effectively (and with enviable confidence) in digital space to provide communities of practice for doctoral students. One such site that has pulled together a worldwide community of doctoral students, supervisors, and generic learning advisors is Inger Mewburn's *The Thesis Whisperer*. She describes the background to her site and its foundation here.

Transforming research training and leadership: modes of engagement in times of transition

The Australian Government introduced a research training agenda as part of the Kemp (1999) Higher Education initiatives in the *New Knowledge and New Opportunities* policy, which followed the West (1998) report into Higher Education in Australia. The policy required Australian universities to provide research training for their students, including additional professional development for research supervisors and students outside the conventional supervision arrangements.

In the intervening years, providing adequate support for students and supervisors engaged in research degree work has become increasingly complex. There has been a growing demand from overseas students and a corresponding drop in local enrolments; a change in students' preparedness for research degree study; continuing casualization of the academic workforce and high workloads. Academics under pressure to publish and get funding also have to cope with an 'audit regime' culture that demands transparency and accountability. This can create perverse incentives, which affect the quality of research student experience.

As research educators we explored the potentials for blogging and social media for providing additional support. The possibilities for extended and collaborative writing and the ability to invite comments from readers is a good way of eliciting participants' tacit knowledge (Williams and Jacobs 2004). Blogging seemed to be a natural extension of the PhD student workshops I ran for RMIT (Royal Melbourne Institute of Technology), and I established *The Thesis Whisperer* in 2010 (Mewburn). To capture the interactive nature of my workshops, the blog is 'newspaper style,' which encourages students and other experts to contribute as 'citizen journalists'. It has become popular around the world with a subscription base of more than 2000 and over 300,000 lifetime visitors.

In 2011, I invited Geof Hill, Coordinator of Professional Development for Research Supervisors at Queensland University of Technology, to write for the blog, and, in the course of being registered as an author for *The Thesis Whisperer*, Geof established *The (Research) Supervisor's Friend* (Hill 2011), a blog for research supervisors. *The (Research) Supervisor's Friend* is still in its early days and, in contrast to *The Thesis Whisperer*, still has a single author. Nevertheless, traffic analysis shows a lower but regular usage of the site and conversations have indicated access to a worldwide network of research supervisors.

We call this practice 'supervision without borders' and argue it is in contrast to the conventional approach to online research education support that perpetuates a 'walled garden' approach through the use of enterprise systems such as Blackboard and Moodle. Our work in digital space suggests that there are untapped potentials for research educators to work with students and supervisors across multiple locations and institutions.

Inger Mewburn

Mewburn found her use of an open access blog has unexpectedly also boosted her academic profile. Yet her enthusiasm for blogging is not based on career advancement strategy, but on the liberation of talking and sharing. Like us, she admires the valiance of doctoral students and value of their work. The principles of open access to doctoral support are ethically and politically promising. This chapter closes with Mewburn's challenge to think about the issues that she raises.

The politics of generic doctoral pedagogy

The other day I attended a workshop on career development for researchers, which was put on by my University. The room was full of people like me – academics who had finished their PhD sometime in the last five years. All of us were wondering how to get hold of money to do more research.

The workshop involved group work and conversation. It was some way into the morning before one of the people on the table turned to me and said 'Oh my god – YOU are @Thesiswhisperer? I love your blog!' I felt like a rock star, a disconcerting, and yet strangely pleasurable, feeling I am slowly getting used to.

I suppose I am famous; at least within a very small circle of people. My blog is a newspaper for PhD students. It invites people to talk about the experience of doing a PhD as a way to share their knowledge with others. I am not interested in PhD topics, but in the people who are doing them and how they manage the process of getting a degree from start to finish and beyond. Through this blogging work I seem to have become a de-facto 'social media expert.' I don't think of myself as such, perhaps because I know people who are doing PhDs on social media and are genuine experts.

However I am visible, so people frequently ask me which software tools they should use to start a blog or what topics they should write about. These people might be surprised that my tools are post structuralist thought and Actor Network Theory and I don't have a topic, just a sensibility. But I understand that many people don't get the importance of this philosophical approach at first, so instead I ask a couple of questions:

- Who are you?
- What stories have you got to tell?
- How do you want to tell these stories?

These questions help me decide what sort of tools, and ways of hooking them together, might be suitable for that person. Let me flesh this out a little, using myself as an example.

We all have multiple identities; all of them together make up who we are. I am a wife, mother, sister, daughter, aunty, academic (teacher and researcher), officemate, knitter, cyclist, citizen, ex-architect... – and more. *The role I play depends on where I am and who I am with.* So the question I posed myself was this: which role do I want to play on the internet? The internet, if we can imagine it as a place, is more like being on television or shouting in a city square. If I ever did get on television I would want to project my best, most composed self – my academic self.

If I am to play my academic self on the internet, I want that self to be *authentic*. To be authentic, all my actions on the internet matter because collectively they tell the story of me. What I say and do, across multiple platforms and in face-to-face situations, combine to create a sense of *presence* others can feel. Therefore the way I run my Twitter account should be consistent with the way I speak on my blog and reflect my academic character.

I like to think I am a thoughtful academic, but not always a brilliant one. I often use humour to get my point across and will always prefer a well-chosen story to a statistic. I'm an idealist. I believe in the university as an abstract concept; as a place where the best part of human instinct can be channelled productively. But I am awake to – even fascinated by – its failings.

I am always happy when *The Thesis Whisperer* is praised; however, I prefer collaboration over competition. I don't want to be the only voice telling the story – I don't have all the answers and all the knowledge to help someone get through a PhD. *The Thesis Whisperer* blog has struck a chord with the audience, I think, because it is full of the kind of information we exchange informally in corridors, in kitchens and while sitting in classrooms waiting for the lecture to start. For example, I have learned most of what I know about writing from books, but I have learned how to put it into practice over coffees with other writers who tell me how they do it. This kind of knowledge is extremely helpful, but hard to find because you have to know the right people. The internet gives you access to these people in an unprecedented way.

I called the blog '*THE Thesis Whisperer*' very deliberately. I always imagined it as a newspaper that myself and other people could write for. I am grateful for the growing number of people who see what I am trying to do and want to write for *The Thesis Whisperer* in that spirit. As academics we are taught to hold on to their intellectual property as an asset. Giving it away seems ludicrous. But if my internet presence is authentic, if it reflects my character, ultimately no one can copy it. I have nothing to fear from imitation if I am not seeking domination.

While I am @thesiswhisperer, I am also not @thesiswhisperer. Hence the sense of pleasure I get when I am recognized by others like the enthusiastic reader in the seminar. @thesiswhisperer is not all of me – just some of the better parts. What are your better parts?

Inger Mewburn

Before moving in the next chapter to consider the increasingly crucial support for career preparation, we endorse the idea that learning advisors, like all academics, are happiest and most useful to others when they work from their better parts. So we leave this chapter with Inger's question hanging in the air.

Chapter 9

Preparation for careers

> [G]raduate employability can be regarded as the always-temporary relationship that arises between an individual graduate and the field of employment opportunities, as the graduate engages with those who are 'gatekeepers.'
> (Leonard Holmes 2013: 550)

Now what? After the elation of completing the doctorate, the summit is attained, yet the view from the lofty heights of graduation success can look daunting. Where is the next funded research opportunity now that the student allowance is cut off? Each graduate looks at available job options when they emerge as independent researchers, with positions not always immediately forthcoming. Then, even though doctoral graduates do have transferable skills, they often have difficulty marketing themselves to potential employers. Skills and desirability as an employee must be evident over and above their academic expertise. Increasingly, finding the first employment opportunity has become challenging. Vitae's (2009) longitudinal study of 2003–2007 new UK graduates' employment destinations found that fewer than half of graduates go on to become academics. This is also the case in Australia, Canada and elsewhere (Neumann and Khim Tan 2011). Doctoral students must begin actively preparing for life beyond the doctorate from the early stages of producing the thesis.

Students' fate after graduation is not always dire. Help with employment may come from supervisors, who can be crucial during that hiatus following graduation. One metaphor posits supervision as a long-term relationship similar to a marriage. (A contributor and colleague, Ian Brailsford, points out in a class on managing supervision that the supervisory relationship often endures longer than whatever celebrity marriage splashed the news at the same time a doctoral student registers.) An ideal happy-ever-after ending to the supervisory marriage would see the new graduate tailgating on their supervisor's credentials, with the senior academic activating their well-established networks to place the graduate within an ongoing research career. This is not always possible, even for an active supervisor with good intentions. The spectre of the graduate still proffering their business cards, looking for any openings long months after they celebrated graduation haunts most institutions.

It is often simpler to direct students towards an *academic* career; those of us who have slowly made sense of academia feel confident to do this. At the same time, we may feel uneasy about how increasingly tough academia is (see Acker and Armenti 2004; Austin 2002). Universities are looking for cheaper academic staff. With the internationalization (and over-supply) of post-doctorates (Cantwell 2011) terms of employment can be tough: short-term contracts may be all that is available to those intent on pursuing an academic career. Some doctoral students will nonetheless be determined enough to find their route through such obstacles.

In addition to academics' own advice on an academic career, there is some excellent literature to use as teaching material – and it gives a good overview of the framework in which doctorates take place. Two books are particularly useful: *An Academic Life* (edited by Cantwell and Scevak 2010) and *The New Academic, a Strategic Handbook* (Debowski 2012). Cantwell and Scevak (2010) open with two accounts from new academics, whose perspective many readers will hold. The book aligns intellectual development with curriculum, instruction and assessment, emphasizing student progression. There's advice on preparing for a researcher career, publishing and supervising, and academic citizenship – negotiating professional relationships, developing close 'critical friends' you can trust, and strategizing for personal development. Finally, the authors sum up in two vertiginous pages the geography of academia, managing to remain impressively neutral in closure to a book that captures some of the gruelling challenges along with the deep satisfactions. After listing pros and cons of an academic career, Debowski (2012) summarizes the many dimensions of academic work, noting that each will be measured. Key indicators of academic success lead to advice on how to be strategic, aware of higher education's multiple purposes and drivers, the nature of its institutions and the impacts of globalization, massification and technological advancements. Current emphasis on outputs and accountability, along with the collapsing of boundaries between institutions and 'stakeholders' within communities, lead to a set of questions about career choice. Topics include successful job application, choosing the type of position, and the application process, which leads to successful teaching, research, engagement, and career advancement. The world of academia – generic doctoral support's context – is thus well anatomized by these two books. Both books provide a good understanding of what an academic career will entail, but neither gives much advice on how to prepare for it during the doctoral journey.

As Bridgstock (2009: 36) notes:

> In the broadest sense, career management involves creating realistic and personally meaningful career goals, identifying and engaging in strategic work decisions and learning opportunities, recognizing work/life balance and appreciating the broader relationship between work, the economy and society. In the most proximal and immediate sense, it also includes the processes involved in obtaining and maintaining work.

In addition to guidance from supervisors, generic sessions show practically how to recognize and document the skills acquired over the doctorate and likely to be desired by employers. Other generic sessions are indirectly helpful, for example, those wherein students learn to be more dynamic in presenting their findings and themselves as researchers. In this chapter, learning advisors discuss strategies applying a generic perspective to the challenge of stepping from the doctorate into a career.

Generic support can oversee the bigger context of choosing work, and the need for understanding in terms of the political set-up of possible employment sites – Jean Rath discusses this here. Within a geography of career options, Natalie Lundsteen approaches employment as requiring awareness of being: the development of 'functioning knowledge' – knowing how to be – rather than 'declarative knowledge' – knowing about (see, for example, Biggs 2003; Ramsden 2003). Such an approach aligns with the idea that the product of the doctorate is the researcher rather than the thesis or research findings, as Park proposes (2007). Institutional statements about their graduates' attributes align with the idea of the researcher-as-doctoral-product (see Gilbert *et al.* 2004 for an investigation as to the feasibility of teaching for such attributes). Finally, Anna Lee outlines strategies for helping students chart their future directions through the geography of career possibilities, with exercises relating to their own lifestyle preferences. The generic perspective makes it possible to build tools for students to use so that they see the wider employment context and the issues of their individual socialization as a valuable researcher. This helps them to make choices and to prepare so that they have work-readiness by the time they complete their doctorate. We begin with Jean Rath's reflection on preparation for life beyond the academy.

Towards fulfilling careers: personal reflections on a developing practice

This account is informed by my experience of designing and delivering development initiatives for doctoral candidates, research-only staff and research-active academics in the United Kingdom, New Zealand and Australia. For the last six years my primary research and practice have focused on supporting those who wish to pursue careers within academe. I endeavour to do so in ways that ensure students' understandings of generic skills will facilitate satisfactory transitions to other career options should those become preferable or more appropriate and realistic. As the numbers of PhD graduates working outside academia continue to increase and the proportion of fixed-term contracts expands within the higher education sector, so the doctorate is no longer solely preparation for a full-time permanent academic position. My practice arises from an understanding of generic skills and attributes as requiring specific contexts to render them meaningful; thus, career preparation ostensibly targeting the academy encompasses broader considerations relevant to all careers. The argument for this approach is strengthened by new ways of understanding contemporary careers. Indeed, Baruch and Hall (2004) have suggested that in recent years corporate careers have changed to resemble the traditional academic model, while the academic profession now serves as a 'role-model' for boundaryless careers, wherein individuals navigate their own paths through intricate, cross-institutional, opportunities.

Whilst we still know relatively little of the ways in which doctoral students perceive and navigate the transition from PhD to initial careers (McAlpine and Turner 2011), a picture does emerge showing that PhD students are often uncertain of their future career paths, and may opt to enter an academic career through a combination of convenience, idealization and happenstance (e.g. Bieber and Worley 2006). Despite gravitating towards academic careers, students' tendencies to idealize academic life mean that many have little awareness of the realities of academic life or the university as workplace. If we are to support doctoral students towards fulfilling careers, we need to equip them with the necessary skills to negotiate their careers with personal and professional agency. I have found the tripartite organizing motif of the intelligent career as proposed by Arthur, Claman and DeFillippi (1995) a useful structure to help students envisage their futures, by strengthening necessary competencies with regard to *knowing why, knowing how* and *knowing whom*. A combination of approaches (e.g. coaching, mentoring, workshops, seminars, portfolio production, advice sessions and work placements) encourages students to explore these three areas in an iterative fashion as they progress through the PhD process. I encourage PhD supervisors to share with students their own understandings of *knowing why, knowing how* and *knowing whom, and to act as guides for students learning to navigate the complexities of academia as workplace.*

During induction sessions I ask students to discuss why they wish to pursue a PhD – and to explain in more detail than simply expressing curiosity about their research topic. Almost inevitably, the question of 'why pursue this particular research and this particular qualification' broadens to questions of life and career motivations. This raises discussions relating to subjective rather than objective careers. I invite students to focus on generating agency by considering perceptions of possible careers and personal, subjective, criteria for success rather than solely external (objective career) measures such as rank and salary. Through 'knowing why' at this early stage students are able to approach their doctoral research in ways that respect their deeper motivations and enable them to engage with research scholarship as an authentic learning experience: aware of, yet not solely determined by, career aspirations.

In the rapidly changing landscape of higher education 'knowing how' to be an academic is a complex, ever evolving process. Initiatives such as the UK's Researcher Development Statement (Vitae 2010a) have highlighted the multifaceted knowledge, behaviours and attributes of effective researchers (and their transferability to other contexts). In my work with PhD students I emphasize that, although the 'casualization' of academic careers means fixed-term contract research positions are likely to be all that is available to emerging researchers in many disciplines, securing an ongoing academic post requires success balanced across the scope of academic practice – albeit that research remains the foundation stone of an academic career. I conceptualize academic practice to encompass inquiry (research in all its guises), teaching, and citizenship or service; with each element to be viewed across time, thus bringing in more personal issues about career and identity. With all early career academics I emphasize the need to gather evidence of their learning and achievements in order to share with prospective employers, and to generate a sense of personal competency. Work-integrated approaches to the doctoral process tend to focus on moving students beyond the academic environment; however, I do encourage doctoral candidates aiming to build academic careers also to engage with non-formal ways of learning the broader aspects of academic practice and to work with their supervisors to identify opportunities to, for example, teach, publish, review and organize seminars or conferences.

In my experience many academics are reluctant to think of themselves as 'networkers,' yet there is evidence that career success relates to positive connection to wider disciplinary networks within and beyond the academy (indeed, in the case of entrepreneurial scientists these latter links may be crucial; e.g. Lam 2007). I present networking to PhD students as a recommendation that they embed themselves in their disciplinary, institutional and relevant practice communities; joining professional societies, attending departmental seminars, collaborating with business, attending conferences, acquiring a senior mentor or peer mentors outside their department, are all ways in which they can meet influential others and build reputation.

Finally, I expand the threefold approach of knowing why, knowing how and knowing whom, by encouraging PhD students to appreciate context, 'knowing where.' Academic practice occurs in the nested contextual spaces of the department within an institution that is situated within the higher education and societal/supra-societal context (McAlpine and Norton 2006). The disciplinary context both sits within and links between these nested elements. These overlapping contexts are dynamic; interacting to produce complementary and conflicting requirements, motivations and processes. Whilst I do not want to encourage 'crystal ball gazing,' students who acquire an appreciation of the ways in which international economic and government pressures shape academic workplaces are better equipped to exercise individual agency in order to plan their careers and take advantage of opportunities as they arise.

Jean Rath

Rath's invitation to identify the why, how and whom of employment questions helps students attune to fit within multiple environments by evaluating themselves and their values as a framework for choice. Next, Natalie Lundsteen focuses on the need for doctoral students to demonstrate their ability as agents of their own future.

Doctoral career paths and 'learning to be'

In becoming successful doctoral researchers, students undergo a transition process in which they orient themselves to their academic institutions, read the cultural landscape, negotiate the unwritten rules and norms, and adapt to their learning environments – assimilating the culture of academia, and 'becoming' PhDs as they establish a view of self in collective activity. Students follow the lead of supervisors, postdoctoral researchers, and others engaged in careers focused on academic research. For a long time, this has been sufficient for those individuals going on to academic careers following completion of the terminal degree. But as the economic landscape continues shifting, and an academic career path is no longer guaranteed, what happens to those students who struggle with 'learning to be' researchers, when all along they know they will never be able to engage with an academic research career opportunity?

Doctoral students experience many instances of learning and understanding in their doctoral study that have little to do with mastery of their intended research subject matter or academic discipline. Running parallel to the development of expertise in a specific academic area, doctoral students also learn to navigate, and make sense of, the learning environment of the institution where they are undertaking their terminal degrees. In this process of cultural sensemaking (Ring and Rands 1989; Weick 1995), new researchers must recognize and read what is known as the 'figured world' of the doctorate. This notion encompasses individual conceptions of a setting's expectations, norms, practices, how things work, what counts as meaningful in a context, and the implicit or explicit routines that form and shape a 'world' (see Holland and Eisenhart 1990; Holland *et al.* 1998), determining the expectations and norms that exist in their doctoral research workplace – be it an office, a lab, a research group, or a department. This Vygotskian process of internalization and externalization is central to how learners engage with the world (Vygotsky 1978; Wertsch 1991) and offers a unique view on understanding how the different practices of academia and doctoral study are interpreted and assimilated by novice researchers.

The workplace culture of academia encompasses a great many unwritten rules, and practices inherent in specific universities, disciplines, and departments may baffle or challenge new doctoral researchers who must, in effect, 'learn to be' doctoral students, especially during the first few years of their research study. This process of learning to be, or trying to be recognized 'as a certain kind of person' (Gee 2000–2001: 99) in a particular context, is usually illustrated in iterations of making sense of and then attempting to fit into the practices of the setting. Some students manage this with ease, but for most the process of 'learning to be' is one of the challenges of the doctorate.

The concept of 'learning to be' is found in Gee's work on educational research on projective identity (Gee 2000–2001), as well as in his work on identity development in playing video games (Gee 2003). This idea of developing identity in a process of negotiation with others within a culture can be applied to novices in any new environment. Entering and succeeding in a workplace is, for many students, an opportunity to try a new persona, to see if who they are fits in an environment, or if they are willing to adapt their sense of self to fit in there (Lundsteen 2011). It is a gradual process of transition; the learning trajectory is not always smooth and forward moving; and not all individuals ultimately decide to make those changes to adapt sense of self and identity to a new work environment.

For doctoral students, the transition into the doctoral study 'workplace,' from whatever previous learning or work environment in which they have been, means entering a new environment and being successful there, through experiencing situations of understanding their surroundings and engaging with the motives that drive workplace practices and behaviours.

The concept of practices in institutional settings is defined as the historical accumulation of interactions where 'the purposes of activities are shaped by the practices in which they are set' (Edwards 2010: 6) and where the objects of activity and the object motives they present to actors in practices 'have the potential to sustain a dynamic which ensures that practitioners engage and re-engage with the knowledge that matters' (Edwards 2012: 174). Doctoral students first have to recognize that the unwritten rules and norms even exist, before they can successfully negotiate and master those practices.

Most professional workplaces expect certain behaviours of employees, but standards of conduct or practices can often be tacit. Consider the university lab with an official 9am start time, but where researchers actually are expected to be at desks by 8am or earlier, because the principle investigator is an early starter. Or the phrase 'casual Friday' clothing, which could mean jeans are acceptable or simply that men don't wear ties. For experienced professionals in any work environment, reading the cues to these norms is almost an unconscious activity. Most academic staff members who support doctoral students are familiar not only with how to operate as a professional, but also have come to understand the norms and practices of their institution, and their work may bridge both the academic and administrative worlds and practices within an institution.

However, for novice researchers, many of whom are accustomed to the explicit cultural mediation of a classroom or tutorial, the process of reading an academic work environment is often erratic. More examples of this reading of the unwritten rules in academia might be learning how to negotiate discussions of first authorship with more-experienced colleagues, discovering which publications or conferences are essential for career-building, or coming to know which departmental seminars and lectures are most politically expedient to be seen attending. If the learning environment of a workplace is one in which motives and values are based on competition, as is true in many business settings and certainly in academic research, a novice such as a doctoral student in academia, or an intern in a business, must quickly become independent as well as resilient in attempting to access the rules which govern a particular workplace.

Once students have become aware of the underlying motives and rules underpinning their doctoral learning environments, they must then decide if they wish to assimilate or not. They may decide to undertake further academic development training in order to learn to be academics and embark on an academic career; alternatively, they may decide to follow other career paths beyond academe. While most universities have excellent resources for preparing future faculty, learning *how* to engage with the world of academia is a type of learning rarely guided by expert others during the experience of the doctoral degree, and even more infrequently is it addressed directly by the faculty or administrative staff from whom the students might expect to provide such guidance. Instead, it is left to the students to manage their own navigation of the practices, expectations, and norms of academia, their specific institution and department, and sometimes their academic field as well.

There is an excellent body of work on how doctoral students develop academic identity and/or skills to become researchers (Hopwood 2010a; McAlpine and Amundsen 2007a and 2007b; McAlpine, Jazvac-Martek and Hopwood 2009). But what about students who discover that what is meaningful and valued in the work of academia is not a match for their own motives? Choosing to follow a non-academic career path has for many years been done furtively – because the motives beyond academia are simply not recognized within the figured world of learning to become an academic. However, as both the economy and the PhD job market have imploded in recent years, we can no longer avoid supporting students who choose a non-academic path. As academic job opportunities shrink, their choice may now be, or will certainly become, more prevalent than that of academic job seekers.

Therein lies a problem for those supporting doctoral students, in providing resources for students in the difficult situation of continuing their trajectory of 'learning to be' a researcher when they know they won't be able to, or choose not to, continue in future academic careers. Many years will be spent developing expertise and mastering the unwritten rules of academia, but it leaves those who leave that figured world of the university woefully unprepared to navigate the next workplace challenge.

Thus, the challenge for institutions is to provide strong learning support resources for those students who will go on to be successful in academic careers, yet also allow doctoral students to glimpse worlds of work and possibilities for careers beyond academe and to begin 'learning to be' in other possible environments. This is of particular importance in those institutions and disciplines continuing to admit large numbers of doctoral students into programmes where an academic career path is uncertain simply due to numbers. For example, a group of humanities scholars at Stanford University have proposed a rethinking of the graduate curriculum at their institution that would prepare students for a multitude of career goals and not just academic jobs (Stanford University 2012). I suggest here that all institutions should provide support for both academic and non-academic careers. It would be wonderful if the norms and practices of academic environments could always reinforce the notion that while much time and energy is spent on learning to become a researcher within academia, the reality is that many students will not actually see this come to fruition. 'Learning to be' a researcher able to read and quickly adapt to other environments besides academia can lead to many fulfilling careers.

Natalie Lundsteen

'Learning to be' a researcher includes developing both the awareness of employment contexts and the adaptability to demonstrate a good fit within whatever niche is available. Basing her work securely on Vitae evidence of what actually happens, Anne Lee next endorses Lundsteen's emphasis on the doctoral researcher as a person, ready to adapt abilities. She provides charts that will enable students to self-evaluate and give good discussion points for conversations around employment.

Professional skills development

How many new doctoral candidates imagine or hope that as they register for their PhD, they are taking the first steps towards an academic career? In my experience it is the minority of students who have a vocation and a clear idea of what they want to do with their careers; most people are trying to work out what the realistic options might include. The UK's Royal Society (2010) pointed out that fewer than 50 percent of PhD graduates stay working in scientific careers, 3.5 percent of whom go on to get permanent research posts, with only 0.45 percent achieving the holy grail of joining the professoriate. The figures are even worse for female scientists. By the end of the doctorate, the necessity to gain employment and make career choices looms large, yet preparation for careers is best done throughout the doctoral process. Although some supervisors believe student career development is an important part of their role, others believe that they should focus only on ensuring that the best possible research is undertaken (see Lee 2012 for some illuminating interviews with supervisors). Many universities' careers services cater predominantly to the needs of undergraduates. Fortunately, there are some sophisticated tools available to careers departments to help doctoral graduates to uncover their talents and motivation and match them to a range of opportunities.

The UK Vitae's 'What Do PhD's Do?' (2004) was a comprehensive guide to the career destinations of PhD graduates in all disciplines designed to help PhD students, their supervisors, careers advisors and employers to understand their options and their transferable skills. Three of their key findings, amongst a wealth of detailed information, were that PhD graduates are more geographically mobile, and have a lower unemployment rate than first degree graduates and less than half were employed in the education sector (Ball *et al.* 2004). Five years later these findings were still relevant. An updated report (retitled 'What Do Researchers Do?') again found that 'half were employed in the education sector: the balance in manufacturing, finance, business and IT, health, public administration and a wide range of other sectors' (Haynes, Metcalfe and Videler 2009: 8). If our doctoral graduates are the creators of original knowledge, many employers will value their abilities to discern what is important, manage complex projects into the unknown and explain difficult material to outsiders.

The researcher development framework (RDF) provides some useful language to identify generic (and therefore probably transferable) skills. Vitae have created a series of different 'lens' through which we can look at the RDF. 'Lens' is their term for different viewpoints that enable the researcher, supervisor and generic support team to all see how the skills, knowledge and behaviours of effective researchers can be translated into skills, knowledge and behaviours required by different types of employment. Currently there are several different 'lenses' and more are being created. (These include engineering, teaching, and a range of enterprise activities including information literacy, intrapreneurship, leadership and public engagement.)

Another key part of this jigsaw is for the early career researcher to understand how they will work best and where to find that kind of environment. Various personality, cognitive and learning style tests have been created (and sold) to assist with this. In spite of the fact that many tests are superficially appealing, most of them are open to the criticisms of coming from an inadequate theoretical base and being used for guidance in fields where they were never originally intended to be applied (Coffield *et al.* 2004; Evans, Cools and Charlesworth 2010; Howie and Bagnall 2012). Users of these tests will need to be aware of the risks of labelling people inappropriately and counter-productively.

Early career researchers will need to carefully analyze their fields of technical competence (e.g. skills of working with people, writing, engineering, science information literacy and/or in the creative arts). For example, they may realize that they are 'reluctant networkers' (Arnold, Cohen and Harpley 2011). They will need to look at their research project from many angles to discern what occupational opportunities it could offer them. Then there is another layer of knowledge to uncover: what kind of environment will they thrive in? This enquiry should be reviewed with some realism about what is possible and acknowledgement that experience changes us, so what we hold dear today may not be the same in a few years' time. The table opposite (Table 9.1) identifies some possible core beliefs and values and is based upon research with doctoral supervisors (Lee 2012). One key difference between the first four columns of skill sets and the fifth (relationship development) is altruism. The graduate's professional skills identified under the first four headings are resources for sale, but the advice they might offer from skills under the fifth heading is freely given as a selfless act. This does not mean that it is unprofessional to operate in the fifth approach. This powerful contribution to society needs to be managed appropriately and within acceptable boundaries.

Table 9.1 Some core values and the skills that link to developing them

	Functional	Enculturation	Critical thinking	Emancipation	Relationship development
Core values	Performativity	Belonging	Rigour	Autonomy	Love Agape (fr. Greek)
What people might be seeking at work (and in other aspects of life)	Certainty Clear signposts Evidence of progress	Belonging A sense of direction Career openings for development Role models	Opportunities to think in new ways Opportunities to analyze and recognize flaws in arguments	Opportunity to set own direction Self actualization	Friendship Empathy
Theoretical base	Organizational development Economics	Sociology Epistemology	Philosophy Scientific logic	Humanistic psychology Critical theory	Social psychology Virtues
Identified by the intent to	Achieve objectives	Include	Analyze	Develop others	Be altruistic
Skills to develop these core values include	Negotiation and project management	Creating and managing groups	Logic Hermeneutics Statistical analysis skills	Counselling Advising Facilitation	Nurturing Contributing to causes

Table 9.2 identifies some of the different ways in which those offering generic support might choose to help a postgraduate who wanted to discuss future career options. If an early career researcher can be encouraged to look at their own career plans in the light of a blend of these different approaches, then they will be able to make more holistic decisions.

Table 9.3 assumes that there is someone who could lead or guide the discussion with the postgraduate; the principles outlined in Table 9.1 can also be adapted to enable the postgraduates themselves to identify different questions to self-assess their own career options. The five approaches prompt different ways of thinking which will help the postgraduate focus on what they should do and when. This type of table can be visited several times during the period of study and discussions about it should begin early in the postgraduate's career so that students are able to think metacognitively about where they are going next. It is especially important that they are encouraged to think about their research as they are pursuing it and what occupational avenues it might open up.

We have seen that early career researchers need to be encouraged to actively explore career options and create networks from an early stage in their work. I am arguing that, by using the five approaches to careers outlined above, any researcher can begin to identify the values that will be important to them in their working lives. Such analytical deliberation allows them to chart their career trajectory and prepare well for it throughout their doctoral studies.

Table 9.2 Approaches to generic careers advice

Functional	Enculturation	Critical thinking	Emancipation	Relationship development
Direct student towards an appropriate careers service where there is specific expertise in supporting postgraduate careers	Help student to identify the most appropriate people to ask for references	Help student to analyze statistics of previous career paths taken and project into the future	Help student to uncover and identify what motivates them	Disclose (appropriately) your own career path and how you now see the strengths and weaknesses of that
Direct student to suitable web advice e.g. UK Vitae	Encourage student to look at and consider modelling the career paths of colleagues they consider successful	Help student to identify current employment opportunities	Encourage student to develop own network	Offer support and encouragement during the application and interview process

Table 9.3 Questions that postgraduates can ask to identify career paths and plan for employment

Functional	Enculturation	Critical thinking	Emancipation	Relationship development
Where is the best careers service and who would be the best person there to talk to? Who would help me with practice interviews?	How many people could I ask to be referees? How should I keep them in touch with my progress? Is there anyone I could work-shadow?	What is the employment market like, where are the best opportunities? What strategies would enable me to increase my chances of reaching my longer-term goals?	When in life have I felt most motivated? Exactly why was that? What are my key values and longer-term goals?	Who will give me honest, impartial feedback about what I am best at?
What timetable (project plan) do I need to set so that I am most likely to get a job offer when I need it?	What contacts will I make through my research? How should I keep in touch with them and how can I learn from them?	What are my transferable skills? What words would different types of employers use to describe them?	What are my weaknesses? How can I overcome them and what do I need to avoid?	Who will give me encouragement when it gets difficult? Can I do anything for them?

Anne Lee

―∽―

Generic support is able to develop doctoral students holistically as they grow into researcher identity, taking into account that fourth dimension, time, and the multiple possibilities of where and how they may be able to contribute after graduation.

The next and final chapter steps back from student support to look at how learning advisors might account for themselves and their programmes. In an accountability-demanding situation, we do not deal in measurable commodities. If we want to avoid the challenges of frequent audits and restructuring, how can we demonstrate the value of generic doctoral advice?

Chapter 10

Evaluation of generic doctoral support

> When you are a Bear of Very Little Brain, and you Think of Things, you find sometimes that a Thing which seemed very Thingish inside you is quite different when it gets out into the open and has other people looking at it.
> (A.A. Milne 1961: 101)

The need to show the value of one's work within an accountability-conscious institutional environment challenges those involved in generic doctoral support. Postgraduate supervisors can use successful completion figures to argue for the success of their teaching at doctoral level. Learning advisors cannot do this. Even were we to show that those who choose to attend our optional classes complete faster or with more satisfaction or have more success with subsequent employment than those who don't, we cannot show causality. Yet finding ways to demonstrate the value of our work is crucial to our survival – when times are tough, learning support centres are vulnerable to senior management's restructuring and disestablishment. We suspect many of our readers will be well aware of the challenges that an audit culture poses – a recent opinion piece suggests that academic developers are an endangered species unless they find ways to measure their work and show its value to the institution (Stefani 2013). So we finish the book by considering the possibilities and limitations of evaluation and assessment of generic support for doctoral students.

First, Tony Bromley translates the extensive nationwide efforts in the UK into suggestions for those operating outside the Roberts' funding context. Tony is lead author of the Rugby Team Impact Framework (Vitae 2008) researcher training and development evaluation model and its 2012 revisitation. He heads the implementation of the RTIF, authoring regular updates on the building of 'impact' evidence across the UK sector. Crucially, he shows that the UK has acknowledged that evaluation of generic doctoral teaching can be done neither quantitatively, nor swiftly, nor cheaply. Therefore, it is more realistic, by applying the legal system's 'beyond reasonable doubt' model, to be satisfied with showing probability rather than proof. Susan Carter and Deborah Laurs present a model constructed from practitioners' descriptors of good generic doctoral support.

Having canvassed learning advisors and others providing such support, we analyzed responses to come up with seven commonly agreed criteria. Together these criteria offer a framework for thinking about quality and assessment. Individuals needing to report on their teaching practice could measure their own work and provide evidence of how it meets the criteria.

Consideration of assessment draws closure to this book's theoretically-informed reflections. These compile an understanding of the boundaries of generic doctoral support, establish its niche in Higher Education, and begin to define its pedagogy. In considering how we might demonstrate the strength of our work in our self-reporting, the chapter sums up the previous chapters' multiple voiced reflections on practice, beginning with Tony Bromley's reflection.

Evaluation and assessment: lessons from the UK experience

The UK has seen significant government investment in the training and development of postgraduate researchers and research staff following the 2002 report of Professor Sir Gareth Roberts. The Roberts' Report particularly highlighted that: 'Currently, PhDs do not prepare people adequately for careers in business or academia. In particular, there is insufficient access to training in interpersonal and communication skills, management and commercial awareness' (National Archive: HM Treasury 2002: 111).

Not inconsiderable Roberts' investment – £120M from 2003–2011 (Hodge 2010) – from the government resulted. This level of investment has raised the question of how to evaluate the impact. An overview of how the impact question was tackled (i.e. the process) outlines the impact framework and impact measurement methodology developed, summarizes the evidence of impact gathered to date (the UK is still measuring impact) and in general seeks to highlight key learning points from the UK experience of the evaluation methodology and the process of implementation. The UK can't claim to have all the answers but we probably have heard just about all the questions and concerns.

The quandary of proof

A few central concerns get raised fairly early in any discussion about evaluating the impact of research training and development:

- How can you prove a training and development activity led to any specific impact, particularly where an impact might be realized a significant time after any training and development intervention?
- Related to attempting to 'prove' something is the more general question of 'How can you assign attribution of an impact to a training and development intervention?'

- What about metrics? The Higher Education sector tends not to favour the collection of a smorgasbord of metrics or Key Performance Indicators leading to the creation of league tables as a solution to an evaluation question (unless of course your Institution does well in the particular league table). A government, however, can favour this approach.
- How can an evaluation methodology make practical sense in terms of useful implementation for a wide range of stakeholders? (The UK experience provided a methodology that worked for a practitioner wishing to evaluate the impact of a workshop or programme of workshops and also worked for stakeholders needing a national perspective).

I will return to these key concerns; however, it is worth tackling the issue of 'proof' straight away. There has to be a realization at the outset in evaluating impact that in all but a very few very specific sets of circumstances (for example, showing somebody a time management technique that they then implement) it is virtually impossible to obtain ultimate proof that an impact has occurred because of a training intervention. Researchers, like anybody else, are exposed to a wide range of experiences during their research and wider lives. When thesis submission is timely, can you really ultimately separate the impact of, for example, the 'Project Managing Your Research Degree' workshop they attended from the influence of good supervision? It is achievable, however, to carry out a well-designed evaluation, with evaluation built in to an activity from the outset. Evaluation should gather a range of information that demonstrates that an impact has been achieved related to a training and development intervention 'beyond reasonable doubt.' This evaluation needs to be premised on a logical understanding of potential impacts from elsewhere, for example, supervision, departmental support etc. And how to undertake such an evaluation is something the methodology described here attempts to do.

Choosing an evaluation methodology: UK national-scale experience

Alongside the investment in research training and development funds to Higher Education Institutions (through the UK Research Councils), investment was also made in a national organization, now known as Vitae, to support the development of postgraduate researchers and research staff (see vitae.ac.uk).

One role of Vitae has been in organizing a national policy forum for the area of researcher training and development. (Another key learning point: have both a national policy forum that has an invited senior university staff and an 'open' conference for anybody working in the sector.) At the Policy Forum of 2005 held in Rugby, discussion turned to evaluating impact in earnest. As a result, a national evaluation group was set up to take the evaluation agenda forward. The group became known in the early years as the 'Rugby Team' because of the initiation of the group in Rugby. It is now known as the Impact and Evaluation Group (IEG)

– for more information, see the website: vitae.ac.uk. The formation of the IEG was an important approach to impact as it brought around the table all key stakeholders including UK Research Council representation, representatives from national organizations and practitioners from higher education institutions. This approach allowed for the development of an evaluation methodology that worked for practitioners at a level of evaluating, for example, a single workshop activity, but also allowed the opportunity to gain the broader national perspective needed by stakeholders such as the UK Research Councils.

An initial success of the group was a realization that metrics alone would not provide evaluation. Metrics are important and have a place, but they must be expressed with an understanding of the limitations of the data. For example, it is useful to know that an investment in researcher training and development has led to wider ranging programmes with a greater number of opportunities for researchers to attend. Attendance increases when sessions are optional may suggest that they are gaining a good reputation. It is good to know that, when people attend, a percentage (hopefully the majority) rate the session as effective. However, none of these figures tell whether anybody actually learnt anything or changed their behaviour and whether this led to any significant impact in terms of improving the quality of their research. Nonetheless, at this point it must be noted that if the major stakeholders in any evaluation of impact is satisfied with a 'bums on seats' figure, this is the most straightforward data to produce. You could acknowledge the limitations set out below in Figure 10.1 and leave it there if they are still happy.

The IEG first presented a draft document 'The Rugby Team Impact Framework' to the sector and stakeholders at the January 2008 Policy Forum and, following a period of national consultation, a final document was presented at the Vitae Conference in September 2008 (Bromley, Metcalfe and Park 2008). The process of having a stakeholder representative group which in turn presented a draft impact framework to the sector for further consultation was an important factor in gathering support, sector ownership and momentum for impact measurement. The UK model has had the benefit of a large combined effort of thought and discussion.

As well as outlining the impact framework, the impact framework document outlined drivers for impact measurement, including the need to:

- demonstrate the appropriateness of the emphasis on skills development of researchers
- provide feedback to funding bodies, such as RCUK and the UK Funding Councils, and to government, who need to evaluate the effectiveness and impact of their investment and on the economy
- inform the enhancement of the quality of the experience for postgraduate researchers (PGRs) and research staff (RS), both within individual HEIs and across the sector in line with initiatives such as the QAA Code of Practice for Postgraduate Research Programmes and the 'Concordat to Support the Career Development of Researchers'

- assess the impact of recent initiatives, particularly the Roberts Funding, on the employability (and perceived employability) of PGR and RS. (Bromley, Metcalfe and Park 2008: 2)

Vitae and the IEG then led the implementation nationally, presenting widely, putting in communication mechanisms, collating emerging examples of impact from HEIs across the sector and providing update reports to the sector at both the National Policy Forum and the National Conference. The 2010 report to the conference provided a summary report and more extensive appendix covering 120 examples of impact studies carried our predominately across the UK by HEIs and national organizations (Bromley 2010). By providing a pool of examples from across the country of identifiable improvements to impact, the UK was able to move forward from mere metrics.

By gathering data from across the UK, the report, although produced only two years after the impact framework was released to the sector, indicates emergent impacts of researcher development of:

- substantial growth in the training and development opportunities for both postgraduate researchers and research staff
- clear demonstration that researcher development is capable of maximizing the investment in research and providing an outstanding return on investment for researcher development
- significant impact on employability, demonstrating direct links between training and development activity and employment of researchers
- significant impact on research practice and outcomes, e.g. direct links with improved doctoral submission rates, increases in grant income, the writing of academic publications, management of research projects and enhancement of research practice
- improvement in the researcher experience
- evidence of cultural change in HE through supervisors' awareness of the need for and value of skills training and development activity
- improvement in employer awareness of the skills offered by researchers, researchers' awareness of skills required by business
- life-changing impact in terms of the personal and professional development of individual researchers.

(adapted from Bromley 2010)

A 2012 report revisited the original document and...

- represents the impact framework illustrated with actual examples of impact evidence, particularly at Impact Level 4 (of the model shown in Figure 10.4)
- reconsiders the drivers for measuring impact in the post-Roberts era and presents key aims for impact measurement in the future

- provides additional insights into the underpinning theory and methodology for the practical application of the impact framework drawn from experience of its use
- illustrates how the impact framework methodology is more broadly applicable beyond researcher development
- explores how identifying outcomes at Impact Level 4 can contribute to our understanding of, and gathering evidence towards, the RCUK 'Pathways to Impact.'

(Bromley and Metcalfe 2012)

An outline of the methodology

The impact framework (and its use as an evaluation methodology) draws from a number of theoretical concepts. For those wishing to read further on theory, the methodology of measuring impact for researcher training and development is covered in more depth in 'Evaluating training and development programmes for postgraduate and newer researchers' (Bromley 2009) and the 2012 IEG Impact Framework document (Bromley and Metcalfe 2012). The main concepts described, drawn together and developed in these two publications, particularly use the work of Kaplan and Norton (1992), Pawson and Tilley (1997) and Kirkpatrick and Kirkpatrick (2006).

As a brief overview, Figure 10.1 represents the complexity of assessing generic doctoral support by mapping some of the possible factors influencing improved impact during the doctorate. This figure establishes that concrete evidence is not easily demonstrated, a fact that has been accepted in the UK after a joint national effort in assessment.

Figure 10.2(a) presents the basic principle of realistic evaluation, a general concept of a mechanism operating in an environment to give an outcome (in the Realistic Evaluation described by Pawson and Tilley (1997) the word 'context' is used; however, the word 'environment' is more appropriate for researcher training and development). Translating this concrete idea to conceptualization of researcher training and development gives a learning mechanism operating in an environment and providing an outcome. Figure 10.2(b) then maps onto 10.2(a)'s simple model the concepts of learning that intends to produce an outcome. Assessment hopes to show how learning leads to an outcome or impact.

The learning mechanism presented in Figure 10.3 is a logic diagram that forms the heart of the impact framework. We now have a series of impact steps from the implementation of a training activity towards an intended outcome. The levels 1–4 are those first suggested by Kirkpatrick and Kirkpatrick (2006). However, importantly a level 0 is added (in line with critiques of Kirkpatrick and Kirkpatrick such as Kearns). The level 0 is important as it relates to understanding the environment in which the learning mechanism is operating. So it represents a first step to assessment, which is to establish a current environment baseline and what impact that environment currently gives. There should be a clear understanding

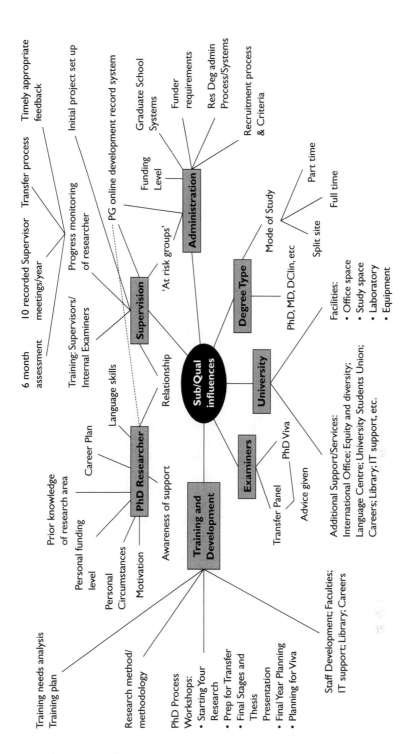

Figure 10.1 Potential influences on time to completion

154 Ensuring generic support's sustainability

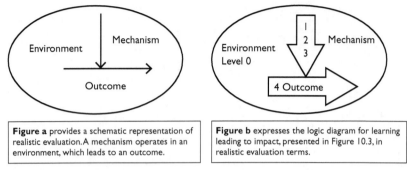

Figure a provides a schematic representation of realistic evaluation. A mechanism operates in an environment, which leads to an outcome.

Figure b expresses the logic diagram for learning leading to impact, presented in Figure 10.3, in realistic evaluation terms.

(Source: Bromley and Metcalfe 2012: 18)

Figure 10.2a and b Realistic evaluation

of what issues a training and development intervention is addressing. We can then think about what we need to do to change the environment to improve the current impact. 'Changing the environment' could be implementing a new programme or session of training and development activity to address the identified issue.

The realistic evaluation concept of mechanisms and outcomes is also affected by the environment of the other factors suggested in Figure 10.1. If a participant joins a workshop from an 'environment' of an unsupportive supervisor, it is likely that the potential for learning in a generic workshop may be affected adversely, for example, or if a supervisor is negative about the student taking advice from anyone other than him or her. Figure 10.1 shows that the impact measurement must be established holistically. For example, if we want to positively influence the time to submission for PhD researchers, we need to think about all the potential influences on the time to submission and take forward a strategy that involves all stakeholders. Generic doctoral learning advisors could show that they have fitted their course reasonably into an appropriate aspect of the doctorate, with consideration for which teaching and learning should stay in the supervisory domain, and what is best situated in the generic workshop sphere.

Figure 10.1 illustrates potential influencing factors on time to submission. Researcher training and development and attendance at a workshop (for example, on time management or project management) are not the whole picture. A 'project' in this area should involve all stakeholders with each adding in their respective component. Those who provide generic support will be aware that their work contributes one piece to the full picture of the support for the doctorate's smooth progression. Generic support figures alone do not necessarily show the cause of improved progress: a big impact on time to submission might have come about from a change in an administrative process, for example, rather than a training intervention.

However, by approaching an issue of improving time to submission from the beginning, embedding the impact evaluation, acknowledging all stakeholders, and where appropriate, working in collaboration with others to think about the logic behind it all, generic learning advisors may be able to produce a clearer impact evaluation. To the metrics, including student evaluations, one can add the collaborations and discussions that make it likely that generic work is engaged with teaching and learning at useful levels and in appropriate topics. It may be possible and ideal to work collaboratively with supervisors, administrators, careers and library consultants; showing that time has been given to the overview gives another proof that generic doctoral support is of high quality.

Level 4 in the Figure 10.3 logic diagram was also treated differently in the impact framework from previous level 4 considerations. There are different measurements of successful outcomes, including timely completion, high quality thesis, good publication rates, independent researcher competency, and researchers ready for employment who successfully find employment within a reasonable time after completion.

Figure 10.4 shows level 4 split into four quartiles. Along the horizontal axis we have time to realization of the impact and on the vertical axis we have complexity. Complexity refers to the number of potential influencing factors on an impact, reflecting our Figure 10.1 example. In Figure 10.4 are a number of potential impacts of researcher development activity (for example, one of the earliest activities of the IEG was to 'brainstorm' what stakeholders felt were the potential impacts of researcher development. [See 2008 document for the original list and 2012 document for a cross correlation against real impacts realized]).

There will be 'target' impacts at the outset of designing and implementing a training and development intervention, but the complex context of the doctorate makes it difficult to prove causality between generic support and impact. Using this construction helps emphasize the issues and illustrate complexity to stakeholders and perhaps encourages realism in the practitioner and stakeholder. In terms of an impact methodology we now have a logic diagram to think about and a realistic foundation that takes the complex environment into consideration.

Assessment is more feasible when evaluation is embedded into any activity from the outset as part of a logical design of an activity to address an identified issue. It is harder to show effectiveness when assessment is an afterthought. It remains the case that a thorough evaluation is time expensive. For example, we need to improve time to submission of PhD thesis. Therefore we consider all the contributory factors to completing a PhD in good time, change the current environment to include a new generic support activity which we feel will logically lead to improvement, collect information through data collection, evaluation surveys, focus groups etc. along our logic diagram leading to a judgement as to whether any improvement in time to submission has actually been due to our implementation of our new activities.

Two further points on evaluation. Following a 'cohort' through an activity in longitudinal study, i.e. gaining a baseline assessment of where people are before an activity, responses during an activity and tracking after an activity helps support any claim of attribution. Secondly, challenges to evaluate what are quite nebulous terms such as the 'employability' of an individual need to be broken down in to

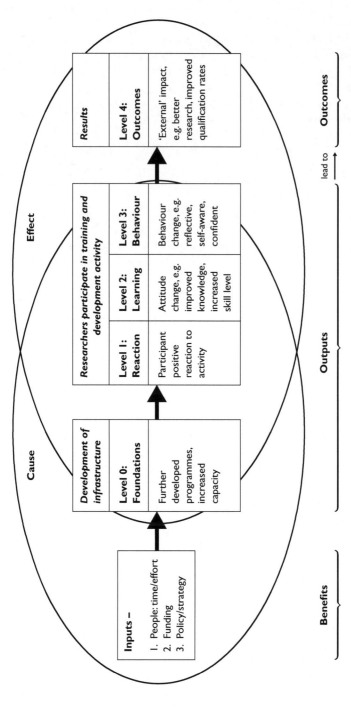

Figure 10.3 A schematic representation of a logic diagram for realization of impact from an increased investment in training and development activity

This example relates to the UK investment in training and development for postgraduate researchers and early career research staff following the UK Government Roberts' report (2002). (Source: Bromley, Metcalfe and Park [2008: 6], adapted from Kirkpatrick and Kirkpatrick [2006], reflecting critiques such as Kearns and Miller [1997]).

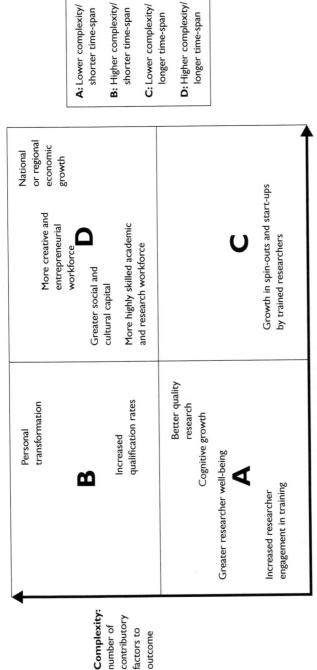

Figure 10.4 Level 4 of the impact framework expressed as four quartiles

component parts. What do we or a particular stakeholder mean by 'employability'? Is it that everybody gets a job after their PhD? Or that everybody gets the job they want after their PhD? Or perhaps it is that a programme of skills development provides wide ranging opportunities for researchers to develop skills that will aid them in finding employment in a broad range of sectors?

By way of summary a list of key methodological points emerged from the UK experience:

1 **Know** the aim of any activity at the outset, i.e. what is the identified need that led to the activity taking place? What impact is the activity designed to have?
2 **Know how the activity contributes to meeting the needs of different stakeholders**, i.e. the needs of researchers, practitioners, the institution, the funders of the activity, etc.
3 **Build in evaluation from the start.** Work through the logical thought process before designing any researcher training and development activity, such that evaluation is built in from the start and a logic diagram is constructed.
4 **Do a baseline assessment**, preferably at multiple impact levels, so you know where you are starting from before you implement the training and development activity to provide a means of comparison by which impact can be measured.
5 **Respect the issue of attribution.** Although direct causality is unlikely to be ultimately proven, consider what evidence can be collected to draw conclusions 'beyond reasonable doubt.'
6 **Don't make a judgement based upon only one source of evidence.** Acknowledge the potential for metrics to mislead when quoted as standalone figures. Collate both quantitative and qualitative information. Reinforce quantitative data with a narrative about the methodology that generated the data and supporting evidence of a qualitative nature.
7 **Appreciate the subjective nature of participants' views.** Always have additional supporting evidence when drawing conclusions from participants' views.
8 **Don't ignore the unexpected.** Design and evaluate activity based upon the aims of the activity, but do not ignore unintended outcomes that become apparent during an evaluation. They may be valuable and help focus future or new activity.

(Bromley and Metcalfe 2012)

It can be helpful to express some of the above in a report assessing and evaluating generic doctoral support. Tools, such as the 'evaluation map' shown in Figure 10.5, also support the application of the methodology and aim to ensure key points are covered in the design of an impact evaluation strategy.

	Evaluation map – the Concordat to Support the Career Development of Researchers						
	Issue	Drivers for change		Key stakeholders	Input(s)	Key implementation steps	Expected outcomes
		Carrots Why is change needed? Increased attractiveness and sustainability of careers, improved research impact	**Sticks** What happens if I/we don't change? Loss of attractiveness and sustainability of researcher careers in the UK				
Implementation Plan	**The need to:** 1. Increase the attractiveness and sustainability of research careers in the UK 2. Improve the quantity, quality and impact of research for the benefit of UK society and the economy	Increased attractiveness and sustainability of careers, improved research impact	Loss of attractiveness and sustainability of researcher careers in the UK	Research staff Principal investigators/supervisors Research funders UK Government Institutions Non-HE employers	Concordat signed by key stakeholders Establish baseline	Launch event June 2008 Concordat Strategy Group set up Implementation Coordinator recruited Vitae lead for implementation	1. Increased attractiveness and sustainability of research careers in the UK 2. Improvements to the quantity, quality and impact of research for the benefit of UK society and the economy
Logic Diagram	Logic steps to achieve outcomes	**Foundation 0:** Stakeholders will be aware of the Concordat	**Reaction 1:** Stakeholders' reactions to the Concordat (e.g. positive/negative views)	**Learning 2:** Stakeholders consider implications and plan change	**Behaviour 3:** Stakeholders implement change		**Outcomes 4:** There will be: 1. Increased attractiveness and sustainability of research careers in the UK 2. Improvement to the quantity, quality and impact of research for the benefit of UK society and the economy
Evaluation	Evaluation questions/Logic Step	**Foundation 0:** Is each stakeholder group aware of the Concordat?	**Reaction 1:** What are the reactions of each stakeholder group to the Concordat?	**Learning 2:** Have stakeholders developed any plans for change?	**Behaviour 3:** Have stakeholders implemented any plans for change?		**Outcomes 4:** Are there any indicators that a research career is more attractive? Are there any indicators that a research career is more sustainable? Has the quality, quantity & impact of research improved?
	Evidence	0	1	2	3	4	
	Potential sources of evidence (✓) to answer evaluation questions/key stakeholders at each level	CROS*/researchers	✓	✓	✓	✓	
		PIRLS*/principal investigators	✓	✓	✓	✓	
		HR Excellence*/institutions	✓	✓ (Action plans)	✓ (Monitoring report)	✓	
		Other, etc.	✓			✓	

NB: ▓ Shaded areas should link together in terms of content. Text in **bold** is common to any evaluation map. (Sources: *CROS: *Careers in Research Online Survey* [Vitae 2013a]; *PIRLS: *Principal Investigators and Research Leaders Survey* [Vitae 2013d]; *HR Excellence* [Vitae 2013b]).

Figure 10.5 An example evaluation map

So far we have covered how the impact framework can work as a guide to a methodology for evaluating impact, for example, for a training and development practitioner evaluating a particular workshop. Harking back to the common concerns raised earlier in this chapter we now need to look at how the impact framework also operated as a national translational and collatory framework. This is actually straightforward. The impact framework has a series of identifiable steps along a logical learning progression to impact. This means that regardless of how a practitioner actually evaluated their practice we need merely ask for any evidence of learning or behaviour change or a level 4 impact. Having the impact framework at the national level allowed practitioners to put forward any evidence they had from their work for each of the respective levels. This provided a common 'language' for the sector, a means to collate impact evidence from many different sources and provide a summarized view to national stakeholders such as the UK Research Councils in particularly through the 2010 IEG report (Bromley 2010).

Summary: answers to questions?

We return to the common concerns sighted at the beginning:

- *How can you prove a training and development activity led to any specific impact, particularly where an impact might be realized a significant time after any training and development intervention?*

The impact framework supports the design and implementation of a logical evaluation study based upon established methodological principles. The issues to be addressed are established at the outset, key influences understood, a baseline assessment carried out, quantitative and qualitative data collected against a logical framework, a cohort followed and individual findings collated and reinforced by a national collation of impact information. It must be firmly stated that ultimately this will not provide 'proof'; however, it will present a comprehensive package of information from which a judgement can be made about impact.

- *How can you assign attribution of an impact to a training and development intervention?*

The points raised in the discussion around 'proof' also hold here. However, key aspects are understanding the baseline environment such that the impact of changes to the environment can be contextualized, and understanding the potential influences of impact, those multiple outputs of completion times, publication, employability etc., from the outset. Also, following a cohort through a process (or in other words a longitudinal study) with specific detailed case studies will support any argument of attribution. Longitudinal studies are time costly, but it may be possible to obtain ethics approval and achieve publication as an additional benefit from the time spent.

- *What about metrics?*

Metrics are not an issue if they are always published with the narrative of how information was collected to produce the figures and also if they are published alongside qualitative information. Without the narrative and the qualitative information then any judgement on metrics alone is a judgement made on only part information. If improved attendances or evaluations are adequate for the stakeholders to whom you report, then this is the easiest data to produce. Nonetheless, as a teacher you should be aware that these are not gathering evidence of impact.

- *How can an evaluation methodology make practical sense in terms of useful implementation for a wide range of stakeholders?*

Hopefully the UK experience described above shows how an impact framework can work for varying levels of scale from an individual practitioner to that of a national government. Finally, the UK has made progress in measuring the impact of researcher training and development in recent years, but there is still much to do and realistically and inevitably it is still early days in understanding the impact of researcher development, particularly on some of those long term level 4 impact 'goals.' Time will tell!

Tony Bromley

The key suggestions from the UK entail systematic progression and gathering of data within a framework that is carefully thought through from the outset. The UK experience has established that it is unrealistic to seek rigorous quantitative evidence of the strength of generic doctoral pedagogy: too many factors impact upon the doctoral experience. Instead, one can gather attendance figures, student evaluations, unsolicited feedback, and signs of improvement in completion rates, output, employment success, and triangulate this evidence to show good practice beyond reasonable doubt.

Individual learning advisors teaching in programmes where the framework was not so deliberately constructed from inception also need to show the value of their work, either for funding purposes or to justify their place alongside the formal supervisory relationship. So Susan Carter and Deborah Laurs add another approach, a set of criteria immediately useful for individual ground level assessment, as another possible benchmarking tool for evaluative purposes.

Descriptors for generic doctoral support

In the interest of demonstrating a model of good pedagogy for generic support, we sought practitioners' views on what constitutes good practice. Contributors to this book and other professionals in the field – in generic settings in Australia, New

Zealand, the UK, the USA and Israel – came up with their descriptors. Garnered from individuals who did not consult with each other, these responses were treated as textual data and thematically categorized, with broadly seven criteria coming through as important. One contributor noted that generic pedagogy is about '*much more* than transferable skills;' the following list teases out the characteristics of good pedagogy, showing how generic support complements supervision, meets the responsibilities set up by universities advertising generic graduate attributes, and enables the creation of a healthy research community (Golde *et al.* 2006).

Practitioner criteria

Each of the following seven criteria was mentioned frequently; together, they convey a clear sense of how to demonstrate good practice and also what form sound pedagogy might take in the context of generic support. They speak back to the book's combined discussions. Each point is itemized, with comments from the data in quotation marks, before being presented altogether in a simple list below.

Merits positive student evaluation

Doctoral students are critical thinkers: their feedback can be trusted. It's important, then, that students 'feel generic support is worth the time' and say they 'find it relevant;' that they report 'feeling empowered and excited,' and that attendance numbers show their approval when they 'return for more.' It is good practice to evaluate regularly for both formative and summative purposes. Unsolicited student emails confirming value also signal beyond reasonable doubt that generic sessions are worthwhile.

Exemplifies strong teaching practice

Teaching should be strong, reflective, and careful. Classes should be 'interactive,' with discussion that 'engage[s] students with their research.' They must 'provide safe scaffolding' for the wide variety of students who attend, being aware of the multiple disciplinary and cultural differences, and wide range of methodologies, including 'non-Western frameworks.' They must thus be 'relevant to all students (e.g. not just those in Social Science).' Perhaps generic expertise is most evident when workshops are 'practical and useful;' 'provide tools;' and 'use good examples and models.' Indeed, because doctoral students are also fledgling academics, we suggest it is also good practice to overtly discuss pedagogy, describing the reasons for teaching decisions and inviting feedback, adding cognitive insight from a pan-university perspective.

Uses its clear overview of doctorate

Good generic support takes advantage of its own broader perspective. It 'gives larger context' and a 'conceptual framework.' By exploiting its discipline-crossing experience, it 'caters for multiple paradigms,' and ensures that 'collaboration across disciplines shows students their own disciplines more clearly.' In considering graduate attributes, generic support 'shows context for skills' and 'shows contingency of academic work.' Focusing on the apparatus of the doctorate means generic sessions are the places where attributes such as the ability to contextualize, work flexibly and interdisciplinarily if necessary, are likely to be established. (Making use of the exact language of the graduate attributes is a good strategy for reporting.) The generic focus is more likely to achieve this work than discipline-specific workshops; the purposes of the departmental and generic are different and complementary. This book has argued that the overview perspective is what distinguishes our area of expertise. Demonstrating this fact helps communicate our contribution to the institution.

Has benefit for the students' future

Responses from elsewhere endorsed the UK focus on future employability. Tertiary institutions have a responsibility to prepare their graduates well for whatever future lies ahead. This recognition comes through in many of the contributions to this book. It is crucial that generic support 'teaches transferable skills,' 'provides professional development,' 'opens multiple career possibility,' and 'helps students to realize their fullest potential.' In doing this, we contribute to the futures of individual students and their societies.

Provides community of practice collegiality

Literature shows that senses of isolation and alienation often underpin doctoral attrition (Ali and Kohun 2007). High non-completion rates signal 'wastage' for individuals, institutions and society. Generic support can go some way to remedying this when it 'validates student experience,' 'shares insider information,' 'shares experience,' and 'supports students for their relationships with supervisors and other academics.' If it makes the whole experience smoother and more pleasurable for doctoral students, word of mouth is recognized as the best advertising an institution can have. If it prevents more doctoral students from dropping out, government funding for successful completions recoups the university salaries of those who provide generic support. So the pastoral side of generic doctoral support has benefits financially as well as in terms of fulfilling responsibilities of care.

Aids students' identity transformation

We have noted throughout this book that progression through the doctoral degree causes a transformation of identity from student to novice independent researcher, and that this transformation, as literature confirms (Kamler and Thompson 2007), is sometimes troublesome. Arguably, transformation is interwoven with deep level learning (Marton and Säljö 1976) and threshold crossing (Kiley and Wisker 2009; Wisker and Robinson 2009). In this regard, generic doctoral support can 'help students to find their sense of self,' 'to become reflexive,' and 'to develop critical abilities.' Because it operates from an overview perspective, generic support has the potential to be 'mind expanding' and 'stretch students.' Cognizant of the degree's generic requirements, and the multiple successful theses that fulfil them, it 'develops the abilities to synthesize, argue, write, and manage time.' It can also safely 'encourage innovation' for those who wish to step outside the conventional. Away from the potential dependencies and tensions of the supervisory relationship, generic advice 'raises what Swales terms "rhetorical consciousness"' and 'teaches students to think for themselves.'

Fosters academic citizenship

Academic citizenship entails commitment to the service work that enables the university to run efficiently and ethically. It also entails fulfilling the university's responsibility to society. Because generic doctoral support 'develops understanding' and 'respect' through some of the criteria above (in particular, items 3–6) and because its pedagogy, in working across campus with such a variety of students, 'is inclusive,' it 'guards against threats to freedom of thought and develops students to take action as social watchdogs.' Although more true of some disciplines and students than others, this is a crucial dimension of universities' function, especially in the presence of potentially destabilizing financial and ecological tensions. For some of us, this holistic nature of generic work is amongst its most significant contributions.

We conclude this chapter by itemizing the criteria for strong generic support as a measuring tool for assessment. The list distils the contents and contribution of this book.

Assessment benchmarks:

1 Merits positive student evaluation.
2 Exemplifies strong teaching practice.
3 Uses its clear overview of doctorate.
4 Has benefit for the students' future.
5 Provides community of practice collegiality.
6 Aids students' identity transformation.
7 Fosters academic citizenship.

An anchor-stone holding our work firm, this list of our good-practice criteria closes the chapter.

Conclusion

This book has mapped out the possibilities and limitations of generic doctoral support in its borderlands between disciplines. The contact zone space where disciplinary cultures encounter each other is a dynamic one (Carter 2011c). It allows both what is distinctive to each and what is shared to become more evident – insight crucially relevant to doctoral students. Clarity with the generic conceptual framework enables them to contextualize their own research, developing understanding of their particular disciplinary epistemology, and to fulfil generic requirements. Generic support goes some way towards implementing institutional rhetoric about equity and graduate attributes. Yet, the contact zone is a risky place, requiring considerable cross-cultural savvy and some degree of luck and stamina in the face of restructuring likelihoods.

The contributions to this book are by no means exhaustive; nonetheless, they provide a composite picture of work across the interdisciplinary borderlands of the doctorate. Generic doctoral support, we argue, works alongside supervision at a similarly high level. We have shown how support from a 'genre of the thesis' perspective can alleviate supervisory responsibilities for students striving to produce good academic research writing. For example, generic support caters for the specific doctoral experience of part-time students; indigenous such as Māori in New Zealand; women; and those for whom English is not a first language. When specific equity groups are identified, their generic support sustains graduates who will be leaders in their own communities, contributing to a more equitable society. Generic support operates holistically to steer institutions towards their stated research goals. We show here that it contributes significantly more beyond the task of boosting institutional 'output.'

Generic doctoral collegiality activates a vibrant pan-university community of practice to support students psychologically and academically throughout the lengthy project. By considering institutional requirements and best strategies for future employment, it establishes understanding of academic citizenship. It improves many students' experiences, including for those who undergo discomfort or frustration as their identity is challenged and reconstructed over the duration of the research project. Improved experience in turn contributes to the reputation of the institution: potential future students pay attention to word-of-mouth recommendations based on actual experience. Viewed in this way, generic doctoral support is fiscally accountable: preventing attrition, fostering timely completion rates and enhancing the increase of research. At the same time, pan-disciplinary perspective allows rich research on the doctorate: many generic advisors contribute to research as well as drawing upon it.

We have noted too, however, that limitations and restrictions are tightening with the economic situation. Generic doctoral support often occupies a vulnerable position in institutions. The academic learning centres delivering this support are routinely restructured by senior administrators who want to make their mark. Sound pedagogy does not inform all changes. Tony Bromley (2013: 177) states boldly:

> it is better to invest effort in looking at why managers are negative towards training and development rather than introduce a new intervention...[which] may not have much chance of working until managerial culture changes regardless of any well thought out logic for intervention.

One theme of this book is the relentless reconfiguration of generic doctoral support, and the difficulty of accounting for ourselves because our contribution, although significant, is hard to quantify. With this in mind, we have also made suggestions as to how generic support might be assessed and evaluated. The book also serves as a reminder that, at the time when generic doctoral support was set up, funded and developed, it was often because institutions recognized persuasive fiscal motivations alongside ethical ones: Brailsford (2011), for example, surfaces the term 'wastage' from one university's senate's minutes from the late 1970s and early 1980s to describe high attrition. Generic support secures against such 'wastage' of institutional energy and of research endeavour. We suggest that it is economic good sense to make use of generic support for work relating to the genre of the doctorate, relieving supervisors of some of the burden at the same time as building on other generic advisors' academic expertise.

The borderlands that generic support occupies, like all such spaces, hold their own internal tensions. Generic support must ensure buy-in from academic staff across campus, often delicately negotiating the relationship between student and supervisor. Considerable professional integrity is required. We rely on supervisor trust and recognition, which we usually have, but not always. Additionally, our work must balance the comfortable homeliness of good pastoral care with the cutting rigour of strong innovative academic guidance.

Generic advisors should aim to provide practical support without seeming to use simple recipes for success that ignore the complexity of the work. We ought not to dumb down material in order to make things seem doable, nor crank up pedantry to parade our own erudition. The difficulties that students experience need to be acknowledged; our teaching aims to get students through those dark valleys of death to the doctorate. Ideally, generic support should be deep level, rigorous and research-informed and -informing. This book bespeaks the usefulness of research into the provision of generic support, arguing that it is an area of higher education's scholarship of teaching and learning and should be accepted as occupying a promising niche within education discourse.

To serve well, generic advisors will apply their expertise to particular contexts. Sometimes those who work generically tailor what they teach within broad discipline areas. Quite often, however, centrally-situated teachers involved in embedded workshops will make use of their overview understanding of the process and meta-cognitive dimensions of thesis writing – supported by discipline-specific examples. When they do this, they are not so much truly embedded within a discipline as incorporating their generic expertise into what could be seen as interdisciplinary teaching. It is certainly not our intention to suggest that generic work across campus is preferable to embedded work. Students often find meta-cognitive points more accessible when they are linked to their own immediate area of practice. One purpose of the book has been to delineate what is best supported generically as distinct from what belongs within disciplines.

For sometimes there are good reasons for not limiting doctoral support to what is embedded within disciplines. Many research challenges span across several disciplines: doctoral students strong in one aspect of their study can find themselves using unfamiliar methods. Students who lack motivation or have specific needs relating to age, gender or culture usually find it helpful to come together with others in the same position and address their doctoral challenges collectively.

The overview perspective is helpful, and supervisors don't always have it. Those who do, like deans of graduate studies, tend to be in highly demanding positions and lack the time to teach students in depth. We acknowledge the crucial significance of supervisors and supervision, with its associated pedagogy, but recommend this important work is properly triangulated with generic support to enable students to appreciate the meta-framework of research more clearly. We have found that discipline-specific epistemologies, ontologies and axiologies often become more patently obvious when inviting students to talk about what disciplinary variations imply and signal.

We have tried to capture some of the creative, diligent, careful work being done in this relatively new teaching environment. In part, this represents an attempt to delineate our area of expertise, showing how generic advisors differ from supervisors, and from those working tightly within disciplines. By doing so, we hope that we can show more clearly what it is that we contribute to the research projects we affect. There is more to be said about its pedagogy.

References

Acker, S. and Armenti, C. (2004) 'Sleepless in academia', *Gender and Education* 16(1): 3–24.
Ahmed, S. (2006) *Queer Phenomenology: Orientations, Objects, Others*, Durham, NC: Duke University Press.
Aitchison, C. (2009) 'Writing groups for doctoral education', *Studies in Higher Education* 34(8): 905–916.
—(2010) 'Learning together to publish: writing group pedagogies for doctoral publishing', in C. Aitchison, B. Kamler and A. Lee (eds) *Publishing Pedagogies for the Doctorate and Beyond*, London: Routledge, 83–100.
Aitchison, C. and Lee, A. (2006) 'Research writing: problems and pedagogies', *Teaching in Higher Education* 11(3): 265–278.
—(2010) 'Writing in, writing out: doctoral writing as peer work', in P. Thomson and M. Walker (eds) *Doctoral Student's Companion: Getting to Grips with Research in Education and the Social Sciences*, London: Routledge.
Aitchison, C., Catterall, J., Ross, P. and Burgin, S. (2012) '"Tough love and tears:" learning doctoral writing in the sciences', *Higher Education Research & Development* 3(4): 435–447. Online: http://dx.doi.org/10.1080/07294360.2011.559195 (accessed 10 May 2013).
Aitchison, C., Kamler, B. and Lee, A. (eds) (2010) *Publishing Pedagogies for the Doctorate and Beyond*, London and New York: Routledge.
Alexander, K. (2005) 'Liminal identities and institutional positioning: on becoming a "writing lady" in the academy', *Inkshed* 22(3): 5–16.
Ali, A. and Kohun, F. (2007) 'Dealing with social isolation to minimize doctoral attrition: a four stage framework', *International Journal of Doctoral Studies* 2: 33–49.
Arnold, J., Cohen, L. and Harpley, R. (2011) *Straight Talking: the Role of Non-Specialist Advice and Networking in Career Conversations for Researchers*, Cambridge: Careers Research and Advisory Centre (CRAC) Ltd. Online: http://www.vitae.ac.uk/CMS/files/upload/Vitae_Straight-talking_March_2012.pdf (accessed 13 May 2013).
Arthur, M.B., Claman, P.H. and DeFillippi, R.J. (1995) 'Intelligent enterprise, intelligent careers', *Academy of Management Executive* 9: 7–22.
Asmar, C., Mercier, O. and Page, S. (2009) '"You do it from your core": priorities, perceptions and practices of research among Indigenous academics in Australian and New Zealand universities', in A. Brew and L. Lucas (eds) *Academic Research and Researchers*, Maidenhead: Open University Press and McGraw Hill, 146–160.
Aspland, T. (1999) '"You learn round and I learn square": Mei's Story', in Y. Ryan and O. Zuber-Skerritt (eds) *Supervising Postgraduates from Non-English Speaking*

Backgrounds, Buckingham: Society for Research into Higher Education and Open University Press, 25–30.

Austin, A.E. (2002) 'Creating a bridge to the future: preparing new faculty to face changing expectations in a shifting context', *The Review of Higher Education* 26(2): 119–144.

Ball, C., Metcalfe, J., Pearce, E. and Shinton, S. (2004) *What Do PhDs Do?* Cambridge: UK GRAD. Online: http://www.vitae.ac.uk/CMS/files/1.UKGRAD-WDPD-full-report-Sep-2004.pdf (accessed 13 May 2013).

Bargar, R.R. and Duncan, J.K. (1982) 'Cultivating creative endeavour in doctoral research', *Journal of Higher Education* 53(1): 1–31.

Barnacle, R. and Dall'Alba, G. (2013) 'Beyond skills: embodying writerly practices through the doctorate', *Studies in Higher Education*. Online: http://dx.doi.org/10.1080/03075079.2013.777405 (accessed 7 April 2013).

Barnacle, R. and Usher, R. (2003) 'Assessing the quality of research training: the case of part-time candidates in full-time professional work', *Higher Education Research and Development* 22: 345–358.

Barnett, R. and Hallam, S. (1999) 'Teaching for supercomplexity: a pedagogy for higher education', in P. Mortimore (ed.) *Understanding Pedagogy and its Impact on Learning*, London: Paul Chapman, 137–154.

Barrie, S.C. (2004) 'A research-based approach to generic graduate attributes policy', *Higher Education Research and Development* 23(3): 261–275.

—(2006) 'Understanding what we mean by the generic attributes of graduates', *Higher Education*, 51: 215–241.

—(2007) 'A conceptual framework for the teaching and learning of graduate attributes', *Studies in Higher Education* 32(4): 439–458.

Barrie, S.C., Jain, P. and Carew, A. (2003) 'Generic graduate attributes: a research based framework for a shared vision', *Journal of Staff and Educational Development International* 7 (3): 191–199.

Barthel, A. (2007) 'John Grierson keynote: how do we communicate', paper presented at 8th Biennial Academic Language and Learning Conference, Melbourne, November.

Baruch, Y. and Hall, D. (2004) 'The academic career: a model for future careers in other sectors?', *Journal of Vocational Behavior* 64: 241–262.

Bash, L. (2009) 'Engaging with cross-cultural communication barriers in globalized higher education: the case of research-degree students', *Intercultural Education* 20(5): 475–483.

Bay of Plenty Polytechnic (2010) *Annual Report 2009*, Tauranga: Bay of Plenty Polytechnic.

Belcher, D. and Braine, G. (eds) (1995) *Academic Writing in a Second Language: Essays on Research and Pedagogy*, Norwood: Ablex.

Belcher, W.L. (2009) *Writing your Journal Article in 12 Weeks: A Guide to Academic Publishing Success*, Thousand Oaks: Sage Publications.

Bell, N. (2010) *Graduate Enrolment and Degrees: 1999 to 2009*. Washington, DC: Council of Graduate Schools.

Bentley, P.J. (2006) *The PhD Application Handbook*. Maidenhead: Open University Press.

Bhabha, H. (2004) *The Location of Culture. New Edition*, London and New York: Routledge.

Bieber, J. and Worley, L. (2006) 'Conceptualizing the academic life: graduate students' perspectives', *Journal of Higher Education* 77(6): 1009–1035.

Biggs, J. (1996) 'Western misperceptions of the Confucian-heritage learning culture', in D.A. Watkins (ed.) *The Chinese Learner: Cultural, Psychological and Contextual Influences*, Hong Kong: Comparative Education Research Centre, 169–206.

—(2003) *Teaching for Quality Learning at University*, 2nd edn, Buckingham: Open University Press/Society for Research into Higher Education.

Bologna Process Stock-Taking (2007) Online: http://www.ond.vlaanderen.be/hogeronderwijs/bologna/documents/WGR2007/Stocktaking_report2007.pdf (accessed 23 May 2013).

Borthwick, J. and Wissler, R. (2003) *Postgraduate Research Students and Generic Capabilities: Online Directions*, Canberra: Department of Education, Science and Training Research Evaluation Programme.

Boud, D. and Lee, A. (2005) 'Peer learning as pedagogic discourse for research education', *Studies in Higher Education* 30(5): 501–516.

—(eds) (2009) *Changing Practices of Doctoral Education*, London: Routledge.

Brailsford, I. (2011) '"The ha'porth of tar to save the ship": student counselling and vulnerable university students, 1965–80', *History of Education* 40(3): 357–370.

Brailsford, I. and Carter, S. (2010) 'Core and/or periphery: where's the heat coming from in graduate support?', *SEDA Educational Developments* 11(1): 23–26.

Brailsford, I., Carter, S. and Kelly, F. (2010) 'Evaluating a doctoral skills programme', in L. Stefani (ed.) *Evaluating the Effectiveness of Academic Development Practice*, New York: Routledge, 109–116.

Braine, G. (2002) 'Academic literacy and the nonnative speaker graduate student', *Journal of English for Academic Purposes* 1(1): 59–68.

Brause, R.S. (2000) *Writing your Doctoral Dissertation: Invisible Rules for Success*, London and New York: Palmer Press.

Brems, C., Baldwin, M.R., Davis, L. and Namyniuk, L. (1994) 'The imposter syndrome as related to teaching evaluations and advising relationships of university faculty members', *The Journal of Higher Education* 65(2): 183–193.

Bridgstock, R. (2009) 'The graduate attributes we've overlooked: enhancing graduate employability through career management skills', *Higher Education Research & Development* 28(1): 31–44.

Bromley, T. (2009) 'Evaluating training and development programmes for postgraduate and newer Researchers', in M. Gough (ed.) *Issues in Postgraduate Education: Management, Teaching and Supervision*, Society for Research into Higher Education series. Online: http://www.srhe.ac.uk/publications/guides_on_postgraduate_issues.asp (accessed 14 May 2013).

—(2010) 'The impact of researcher training and development: two years on', in J. Metcalfe (ed.) *Impact and Evaluation Group*. Online: http://www.vitae.ac.uk/CMS/files/upload/IEG_Development%20Report2010_soft%20copy.pdf and http://www.vitae.ac.uk/CMS/files/upload/Appendix%20final%20v2%20_3%20Sept%20logo.pdf (accessed 16 September 2012).

—(2013) 'Evaluating the impact of innovations in doctoral education in the UK', in M. Kompf and P.M. Denicolo (eds) *Critical Issues in Higher Education*. Rotterdam: Sense Publishers, 175–190.

Bromley, T. and Metcalfe, J. (2012) *The Impact Framework 2012: Revisiting the Rugby Team Impact Framework: Careers Research Advisory Centre (CRAC)*. Online: http://www.vitae.ac.uk/CMS/files/upload/IEG_Report_2012.pdf (accessed 16 September 2012).

Bromley, T., Metcalfe, J. and Park, C. (2008) *The Rugby Team Impact Framework: September 2008*. Online: http://www.vitae.ac.uk/CMS/files/1.Rugby%20Impact%20Framework_33.pdf (accessed 11 December 2013).

Brown, L. and Watson, P. (2010) 'Understanding the experience of female doctoral students', *Journal of Further and Higher Education* 34(3): 385–404.
Bruce, C. and Stoodley, I. (2009) 'A pedagogical framework for the technology disciplines. Paper 3, ALTC Fellowship 2008', *QUT*. Online: http://eprints.qut.edu.au/28536/ (accessed 11 December 2013).
Butler, J. (1990) *Gender Trouble: Feminism and the Subversion of Identity*, New York: Routledge.
—(1997) *Excitable Speech: A Politics of the Performative*, New York: Routledge.
—(1999) *Gender Trouble: Feminism and the Subversion of Identity*, New York: Routledge.
—(2004) 'Changing the subject', in S. Salih and J. Butler (eds) *The Judith Butler Reader*, Malden: Blackwell, 238–252.
Buxton, J., Carter, S. and Sturm, S. (2012) *Punc Rocks: Foundation Stones for Precise Punctuation*, Auckland: Pearson Education New Zealand.
Cadman, K. (1997) 'Thesis-writing for international students: a question of identity?', *English for Specific Purposes* 16(1): 3–14.
—(2000) '"Voices in the Air": evaluations of the learning experiences of international postgraduates and their supervisors', *Teaching in Higher Education* 5(4): 475–491.
Cameron, J. (1992) *The Artist's Way: a Spiritual Path to Higher Creativity*, London: Pan Books.
Cantwell, B. (2011) 'Academic in-sourcing: international postdoctoral employment and new modes of academic production', *Journal of Higher Education Policy and Management*, 33(2): 101–114.
Cantwell, R.D. and Scevak, J.J. (eds) (2010) *An Academic Life: a Handbook for New Academics*, Camberwell: ACER.
Carter, S. (2009a) 'Old lamps for new: mnemonic techniques and the thesis structure', *Arts and Humanities in Higher Education* 8(1): 56–68.
—(2009b) 'Volunteer support of English as an additional language (EAL) doctoral students', *International Journal of Doctoral Studies* 4: 13–25.
—(2010) 'Firming foundations for doctorate education in a shifting global environment: generic doctoral support', in V. van der Ham, L. Sevillano and L. George (eds) *Shifting Sands, Firm Foundations: Proceedings of the 2009 Annual International Conference of the Association of Tertiary Learning Advisors of Aotearoa/New Zealand (ATLAANZ)*, Auckland: ATLAANZ, 158–169.
—(2011a) 'Doctorate as genre: supporting thesis writing across campus', *Higher Education Research Development* 30(6): 725–736.
—(2011b) 'English as an additional language (EAL) viva voce: the EAL doctoral oral examination experience', *Assessment and Evaluation of Higher Education* 37(3): 273–284.
—(2011c) 'Interdisciplinary thesis practicalities: how to negotiate the borderlands', in J. Batchelor and L. Roche (eds) *Student Retention and Success: Sharing and Evaluating Best Practice: Proceedings of the 2009 Annual International Conference of the Association of Tertiary Learning Advisors of Aotearoa/New Zealand (ATLAANZ)*, Christchurch: ATLAANZ, 1–10.
—(2011d) 'Original knowledge, gender and the word's mythology: voicing the doctorate', *Arts and Humanities in Higher Education* 11(4): 406–417.
—(2011e) 'How to examine a thesis', *MAI Review* 4: 1–3.
Carter, S. and Blumenstein, M. (2011) 'Thesis structure: student experience and attempts towards solution', *Higher Education Research Development* 34: 95–107.

Carter, S., Blumenstein, M. and Cook, C.M. (2013) 'Different for women? The challenges of doctoral study', *Teaching in Higher Education* 18(4): 339–351.

Carter, S., Datt, A. and Donald, C. (2012) 'The pedagogy and practice of e-learning: looking backward to redirect the flow', in M. Protheroe (ed.) *Negotiating the River: He Waka Eke Noa, Proceedings of the 2011 Annual International Conference of the Association of Tertiary Learning Advisors of Aotearoa/New Zealand (ATLAANZ)*. Petone: ATLAANZ, 21–36.

Carter, S., Fazey, J., Geraldo, J.L.G. and Trevitt, C. (2010) 'The doctorate of the Bologna Process third cycle: mapping the dimensions and impact of the European Higher Education Area', *Journal of Research in International Education* 9(3): 245–258.

Carter, S., Kelly, F. and Brailsford, I. (2012) *Structuring your Research Thesis*, Houndsmills: Palgrave Macmillan.

Carter, S., Sturm, S. and Geraldo, J.L.G. (2012) 'Situating e-learning: accelerated precepts from the past', paper presented at the European Conference for Educational Research, Cadiz.

Casanave, C.P. and Hubbard, P. (1992) 'The writing assignments and writing problems of doctoral students: faculty perceptions, pedagogical issues, and needed research', *English for Specific Purposes* 11(1): 33–49.

Catterall, J. (2003) 'The language and academic skills advisor in the teaching partnership: what should be our role', in K. Deller-Evans and P. Zeegers (eds), *In the Future[...] Refereed Proceedings of the 2003 Biennial Language and Academic Skills in Higher Education Conference*, Adelaide: Student Learning Centre, Flinders University, 37–42.

Chanock, K. (2002) 'From mystery to mastery', in N. Trivett (ed.) *Changing Identities: Proceedings of the 2001 Australian Language and Academic Skills Conference University of Wollongong*, Wollongong, NSW: University of Wollongong.

—(2007) 'What academic language and learning advisers bring to the scholarship of teaching and learning: problems and possibilities for dialogue within the disciplines', *Higher Education Research and Development* 26(3): 269–280.

Cherry, N.L. (2005) 'Preparing for practice in the age of complexity', *Higher Education Research and Development* 24(4): 310–320.

Clanchy, J. and Ballard, B. John (1995) 'Generic skills in the context of higher education', *Higher Education Research & Development* 14(2): 155–166.

Clark, I.L. (2007) *Writing the Successful Thesis or Dissertation: Entering the Conversation*, Upper Saddle River: Prentice Hall.

Clerehan, R. (2007) '"Language staff lose academic ranking": what's new managerialism got to do with it?', *Journal of Academic Language and Learning* 1(1): A68–77.

Clughen, L. and Hardy, C. (2012) *Writing in the Disciplines: Building Supportive Cultures for Student Writing in UK Higher Education*, Bingley: Emerald.

Coffield, F., Moseley, D., Hall, E. and Ecclestone, K. (2004) *Should We Be Using Learning Styles? What Research Has To Say To Practice*, London: Learning and Skills Research Centre.

Cohler, B. and Hammack, P. (2007) 'The psychological world of the gay teenager: social change, narrative, and "normality"', *Journal of Youth and Adolescence* 36: 47–59.

Commons, K. and Gao, X. (2011) 'Excel on campus: a programme designed to increase international students' participation in learning', in *Design For Student Success: The 14th Pacific Rim FYHE Conference Proceedings, Perth, 28 June–1 July 2011*. Online: http://www.fyhe.com.au/past_papers/papers11/FYHE-2011/content/pdf/7B.pdf (accessed 10 September 2012).

Concordat to Support the Career Development of Researchers (2008) *An Agreement between the Funders and Employers of Researchers in the UK*. Online: http://www.vitae.ac.uk/CMS/files/upload/Vitae-Concordat-2011.pdf (accessed 24 September 2012).

Conrad, L. (2006a) 'Countering isolation—joining the research community', in C. Denholm and T. Evans (eds) *Doctorates Downunder: Keys to Successful Doctoral Study*, Camberwell: ACER Press, 34–40.

—(2006b) 'Developing the intellectual and emotional climate for candidates,' in C. Denholm and T. Evans (eds) *Supervising Doctorates Downunder: Keys to Effective Supervision in Australia and New Zealand*, Camberwell, VIC: ACER Press.

Conrad, L. and Phillips, E.M. (1995) 'From isolation to collaboration: a positive change for postgraduate women?', *Higher Education* 30: 313–322.

Conversation (2013) *New Research Network Aims to Boost Indigenous PhD Completion Rates*. Online: http://www.go8.edu.au/__documents/go8-policy-analysis/2013/the-changing-phd_final.pdf (accessed 5 September 2013).

Cook, A. and Leckey, J. (1999) 'Do expectations meet reality? A survey of changes in first year student opinion', *Journal of Further and Higher Education* 23: 157–171.

Cotterall, S. (2011) 'Doctoral pedagogy: what do international PhD students in Australia think about it?', *Pertanika Journal of Social Sciences and Humanities* 19(2): 521–534.

Cottrell, S. (2005) *Critical Thinking Skills: Developing Effective Analysis and Argument*, Houndsmills: Palgrave Macmillan.

Cram, F. (2001) 'Rangahau Māori: tona tika, tona pono', in M. Tolich (ed.) *Research Ethics in Aotearoa*, Auckland: Longman, 35–42.

Craswell, G. (2007) 'Deconstructing the skills training debate in doctoral education', *Higher Education Research and Development* 26(4): 377–391.

Craswell, G. and Bartlett, A. (2001) *Changing Identities: LAS advisers*. Online: http://learning.uow.edu.au/LAS2001/selected/craswell.pdf (accessed 20 August 2009).

Cryer, P. (2005) *The Research Student's Guide to Success*, 2nd edn, Buckingham: OUP.

Cumming, J. and Kiley, M. (2010) *Research Graduate Skills Project: Canberra Australian Learning and Teaching Council and The Australian National University*. Online: http://www.gradskills.anu.edu.au/sites/default/files/Part%201_adjusted.pdf (accessed 24 September 2012).

Daishonin, N. (1999) *The Writings of Nichiren Daishonin*, Tokyo: Soka Gakkai.

Dancik, B.P. (1991) 'The importance of peer review', *Serials Librarian* 19(3/4): 91–94.

Datt, D. and Carter, S. (2011) 'Engaging students online: "E ako"', *MAI Review* 3.

Debowski, S. (2012) *The New Academic: A Strategic Handbook*, Maidenhead and New York: Open University Press.

Deem, R. and Brehony, K.J. (2000) 'Doctoral students' access to research cultures – are some more equal than others?', *Studies in Higher Education* 25(2): 149–165.

Deloria, V. (1998) 'Intellectual self-determination and sovereignty: Looking at the windmills in our minds', *Wicazo Sa Review* 13(1): 25–31.

Denholm, C. (2006) 'Some personal obstacles to completion', in C. Denholm and T. Evans (eds) *Doctorates Downunder: Keys to Successful Doctoral Study*, Camberwell: ACER, 122–129.

Denholm, C. and Evans, T. (2006) *Doctorates Downunder: Keys to Successful Doctoral Study*, Camberwell: ACER.

Denicolo, P., Fuller, M. and Berry, D. (2010) *A Review of Graduate Schools in the UK*, Lichfield: UK Council for Graduate Education.

Denicolo, P. and Park, C. (2013) 'Doctorateness – an elusive concept', in M. Kompf and P. Denicolo (eds) *Critical Issues in Higher Education*, Rotterdam: Sense Publishers, 191–197.

Devenish, R., Dyer, S., Jefferson, T., Lord, L., van Leeuwen, S. and Fazakerley, V. (2009) 'Peer to peer support: the disappearing work in the doctoral student experience', *Higher Education Research and Development* 28(1): 59–70.

Devos, Anita (2008) 'When enterprise and equity meet: the rise of mentoring for women in Australian universities', *Discourse: Studies in the Cultural Politics of Education* 29(2): 195–205.

Durie, M. (2009) 'Towards social cohesion: the indigenisation of higher education in New Zealand', paper presented at Vice-Chancellors' Forum (VCF 2009): How Far are Universities Changing and Shaping our World. Kuala Lumpur, Malaysia, 15–19 June.

Edwards, A. (2010) *Becoming an Expert Practitioner: the Relational Turn in Expertise*, Dordecht: Springer.

—(2012) 'Expertise in the children's workforce: knowledge and motivation in engagement with children', in M. Hedegaard, A. Edwards and M. Fleer (eds) *Motives, Emotions and Values in the Development of Children and Young People*, Cambridge: Cambridge University Press, 173–190.

Elbow, P. and Sorcinelli, M.D. (2006) 'The faculty writing place: a room of our own', *Change* 38(6): 17–22.

Eley, A. and Murray, R. (2009) *How to be an Effective Supervisor*, Maidenhead: Open University Press.

Eliot, T.S. (1974) *Collected poems 1906–1962*, 2nd edn, London: Faber and Faber.

European Knowledge Society (2005) 'Salzburg Principles', *Bologna Seminar: Doctoral Programmes for the European Knowledge Society*. Online: http://www.eua.be/eua/jsp/en/upload/Salzburg_Report_final.1129817011146.pdf (accessed 24 September 2012).

Evans, C., Cools, E. and Charlesworth, Z.M. (2010) 'Learning in higher education – how cognitive and learning styles matter', *Teaching in Higher Education* 15(4): 467–478.

Evans, T.D. (2002) 'Part-time research students: are they producing knowledge where it counts?', *Higher Education and Research and Development* 21(2): 155–165.

—(2006) 'Part-time candidature—balancing candidature, work and personal life', in C. Denholm and T.D. Evans (eds) *Doctorates Downunder: Keys to Successful Doctoral Study in Australia and New Zealand*, Camberwell: ACER Press, 137–144.

Evans, T.D. and Pearson, M. (1999) 'Off-campus doctoral research and study in Australia: emerging issues and practices', in A. Holbrook and S. Johnston (eds) *Supervision of Postgraduate Research in Education (Review of Australian Research in Education 5)*, Melbourne: AARE, 185–205.

Evans, T.D., Evans, B. and Marsh, H. (2008) 'Australia', in M. Nerad and M. Heggelund (eds) *Toward a Global PhD: Forces and Forms in Doctoral Education Worldwide*, Seattle: CIRGE/University of Washington Press, 171–203.

Fegan, S. (2006) 'International students' expectations of speaking English in Australia', in J.A. Van Rij-Heyligers (ed.) *Intercultural Communications across University Settings: Myths and Realities*, Auckland: Communication Skills in University Education, 13–29.

Finke, L.A. (1992) *Feminist Theory: Women's Writing*, Ithaca and London: Cornell UP.

Flavell, J.H. (1979) Metacognition and cognitive monitoring: a new area of cognitive-developmental inquiry, *American Psychologist* 34(10): 906–911.

Flew, A. (1954) 'The justification of punishment', *Philosophy* 29: 291–307.

Flower, L. (1981) *Problem-Solving Strategies for Writing*, New York: Harcourt Brace and Jovanovich.

Forgasz, H.J. and Leder, G.C. (2006) 'Academic life: monitoring work patterns and daily activities', *Australian Educational Researcher* 33(1): 1–22.

Fotovatian, S. (2013) 'Three constructs of institutional identity amongst international students in Australia', *Teaching in Higher Education* 17(5): 577–588.

Fraser, C. and Ayo, L. (2010) 'The role of inter-faculty relationships in special project collaborations: a distinctly New Zealand experience', in M. Davies, M. Devlin and M. Tight (eds) *Interdisciplinary Higher Education: Principles and Practicalities*. Melbourne: Emerald, 255–267.

Freidson, E. (1994) *Professionalism Reborn: Theory, Prophecy and Policy*, Cambridge: Polity Press in association with Blackwell Publishers.

Galligan, L., Cretchley, P., George, L., McDonald, K., McDonald, J. and Rankin, J. (2003) 'Evolution and emerging trends of university writing groups', *Queensland Journal of Educational Research* 19(1): 28–41.

Gardner, S.K. and Gopaul, B. (2012) 'The part-time doctoral student experience', *International Journal of Doctoral Studies* 7: 63–78.

Gee, J.P. (2000–2001) 'Identity as an analytic lens for research in education', *Review of Research in Education* 25: 99–125.

—(2003) *What Video Games Have to Teach us about Learning and Literacy*, New York: Palgrave Macmillan.

Geraldo, J.L.G., Trevitt, C. and Carter, S. (2011) 'Realising the pedagogical potential of the Bologna Process third cycle', *Journal of Technology and Science Education* 1(2): 16–24.

Gilbert, R., Balatti, J., Turner, P. and Whitehouse, H. (2004) 'The generic skills debate in research higher degrees', *Higher Education Research and Development* 23(3): 275–288.

Glatthorn, A.A. (1998) *Writing the Winning Dissertation: A Step-by-Step Guide*, Thousand Oaks: Corwin.

Golde, C., Jones, L., Bueschel, A.C. and Walker, G. (2006) 'The challenges of doctoral program assessment: lessons from the Carnegie initiative on the doctorate', in P.L. Maki and N.A. Borkowski (eds) *The Assessment of Doctoral Education: Emerging Criteria and New Models for Improving Outcomes*, Sterling: Stylus, 53–82.

Goode, J. (2007) 'Empowering or disempowering the international Ph.D. student? Constructions of the dependent and independent learner', *British Journal of Sociology of Education* 28: 589.

Grant, B. (2003) 'Mapping the pleasures and risks of supervision', *Discourse: Studies in the Cultural Politics of Education* 24(2): 173–188.

—(2004) 'Masters and slaves: the twisted dialogues of supervision', in M. Kiley and G. Mullins (eds) *Quality in Postgraduate Research: Re-Imagining Research Education, Proceedings of the 2004 Conference*, Adelaide: Advisory Centre for University Education, University of Adelaide.

—(2005) 'Fighting for space in supervision: fantasies, fairytales, fictions and fallacies', *International Journal of Qualitative Studies in Education* 18(3): 337–354.

—(2006) 'Writing in the company of other women: Exceeding the boundaries', *Studies in Higher Education* 31(4), 483–495.

—(2008) *Academic Writing Retreats: A Facilitator's Guide*, Milperra NSW: HERDSA.

Grant, B. and Knowles, S. (2000) 'Flights of imagination: academic women be(com)ing writers', *International Journal for Academic Development* 5(1): 6–19.

Green, B. (2005) 'Unfinished business: subjectivity and supervision', *Higher Education Research and Development* 24(2): 151–163.

Green, P.J. and Bowden, J.A. (2010) 'Research training: supervising and managing research students', in R.D. Cantwell and J.J. Scevak (eds) *An Academic Life: A Handbook for New Academics*, Camberwell: ACER.

Grosz, E. (2005) 'Bergson, Deleuze and becoming', *Parallax* 11(2): 4–13.

Group of Eight (2013) 'The changing PhD: discussion Paper.' Online: http://www.go8.edu.au/__documents/go8-policy-analysis/2013/the-changing-phd_final.pdf (accessed 5 September 2013).

Grover, V. (2007) 'Successfully navigating the stages of doctoral study', *International Journal of Doctoral Studies* 2: 9–21.

Guerin, C. and Picard, M. (2012) 'Try it on: voice, concordancing and text-matching in doctoral writing', *International Journal of Educational Integrity* 8(2): 34–45.

Guerin, C., Xafis, V., Doda, D.V., Gillam, M., Larg, A., Luckner, H., Jahan, N., Widayati, A. and Xu, C. (2012) 'Diversity in collaborative research communities: a multicultural, multidisciplinary thesis writing group in Public Health', *Studies in Continuing Education* 35(1): 65–81.

Haas, S. (2012) 'Using story cards to facilitate reflective thought and dialogue about science writing', in L. Clughen and C. Hardy (eds) *Writing in the Disciplines: Building Supportive Cultures for Student Writing in UK Higher Education*, Bingley: Emerald, 143–168.

Halliday, M.A.K. (1994) *An Introduction to Functional Grammar*, 2nd edn, London: Edward Arnold.

Hammack, P., Thompson, E. and Pilecki, A. (2009) 'Configurations of identity among sexual minority youth: context, desire, and narrative', *Journal of Youth and Adolescence* 38: 867–883.

Hardy, C. and Clughen, L. (2012) 'Writing at university: student and staff expectations', in L. Clughen and C. Hardy (eds) *Writing in the Disciplines: Building Supportive Cultures for Student Writing in UK Higher Education*, Bingley: Emerald, 25–54.

Haynes, K., Metcalfe, J. and Videler, T. (2009) *What Do Researchers Do?*, Cambridge: Careers Research and Advisory Centre (CRAC) Ltd. Online: http://www.vitae.ac.uk/CMS/files/upload/Vitae-WDRD-by-subject-Jun-09.pdf (accessed 14 May 2013).

Henning, K., Ey, S. and Shaw, D. (1998) 'Perfectionism, the imposter phenomenon and psychological adjustment in medical, dental, nursing and pharmacy students', *Medical Education* 32(5): 456–464.

HERO Annual Report (1993) Auckland, New Zealand: University of Auckland.

Higher Education Academy (2012) *Student Experience Surveys*. Online: http://www.heacademy.ac.uk/student-experience-surveys (accessed 10 September 2012).

Hill, G. (2011) 'The (Research) Supervisor's Friend'. Online: http://supervisorsfriend.wordpress.com/ (accessed 17 December 2013).

Hinchcliffe, R., Bromley, T. and Hutchinson, S. (2007) *Skills Training in Research Degree Programmes: Politics and Practice*, Maidenhead: Open University Press.

Hodge, A. (ed) (2010) *Review of Progress in Implementing the Recommendations of Sir Gareth Roberts regarding Employability and Career Development of PhD Students and Research Staff*, Research Councils UK. Online: http://www.rcuk.ac.uk/documents/researchcareers/IndependentReviewHodge.pdf (accessed 11 December 2013).

Holland, D. and Eisenhart, M. (1990) *Educated in Romance: Women, Achievement, and College Culture*, Chicago: University of Chicago Press.

Holland, D., Lachicotte, W., Skinner, D. and Cain, C. (1998) *Identity and Agency in Cultural Worlds*, Cambridge, MA: Harvard University Press.

Holmes, J. and Riddiford, N. (2010) 'Professional and personal identity at work: achieving a synthesis through intercultural workplace talk', *Journal of Intercultural Communication* 22.

Holmes, L. (2013) 'Competing perspectives on graduate employability: possession, position or process?', *Studies in Higher Education* 38(4): 538–554.

Holton, E.F. (1996) 'The flawed four-level evaluation model', *Human Resource Development Quarterly* 7(1): 5–21.

Honey, P. and Mumford, A. (1986) *The Manual of Learning Styles*, London: Peter Honey.

Hood, S. (2008) 'Summary writing in academic contexts: implicating meaning in processes of change', *Linguistics and Education* 9(4): 351–365.

Hooks, B. (1994) *Teaching to Transgress: Education as the Practice of Freedom*, New York: Routledge.

Hooley, T., Kulej, M., Edwards, C. and Mahoney, K. (2009) *Understanding the Part-time Researcher Experience*, Cambridge: Vitae, CRAC. Online: http://www.vitae.ac.uk/CMS/files/upload/Part-time%20researcher%20experience.pdf (accessed 10 September 2012).

Hopwood, N. (2010a) 'Doctoral experience and learning from a sociocultural perspective', *Studies in Higher Education* 35(7): 829–843.

—(2010b) 'Doctoral students as journal editors: non-formal learning through academic work', *Higher Education Research and Development* 29(3): 310–331.

Hopwood N. and Paulson, J. (2012) 'Bodies in narratives of doctoral students' learning and experience', *Studies in Higher Education* 37(6): 667–681.

Howard, R. (1995) 'Plagiarisms, authorship and the academic death penalty', *College English* 57(7): 788–806.

Howie, P. and Bagnall, R. (2012) 'A critique of the deep and surface approaches to learning model', *Teaching in Higher Education* 17: 1–12.

Hutchings, C. (2006) 'Reaching students: lessons from a writing centre', *Higher Education Research and Development* 25(3): 247–261.

Hyland, K. (1999) 'Academic attribution: citation and the construction of disciplinary knowledge', *Applied Linguistics* 20(3): 341–367.

James, B. (2011) 'Silences, voices, negotiations: becoming a postgraduate research writer', Unpublished PhD thesis. University of Wollongong.

—(2013) 'Researching student *becoming* in higher education', *Higher Education Research Development* 32(1): 109–121.

Jamieson, R. (2007) *North Atlantic Drift*, Edinburgh: Luath Press.

Jarvac-Martek, M., Chen, S. and McAlphine, L. (2011) 'Tracking the doctoral student experience over time: cultivating agency in diverse space', in L. McAlpine and C. Amundsen (eds) *Doctoral Education: Research Based Strategies for Doctoral Students, Supervisors and Administrators*, New York: Springer, 17–36.

Johnston, S. (1997) 'Examining the examiners: an analysis of examiners' reports on doctoral theses', *Studies in Higher Education* 22(3): 333–347.

Jonas-Dwyer, D. and Pospisil, R. (2004) *The Millennial Effect: Implications for Academic Development*, Online: http://citeseerx.ist.psu.edu/viewdoc/download?doi=10.1.1.216.2538&rep=rep1&type=pdf (accessed 11 December 2013).

Jones, Alison (2012) 'Dangerous liaisons: Pākehā kaupapa Māori, and educational research', *New Zealand Journal of Educational Studies* 47(2): 100–112.

Jones, Anna (2009) 'Redisciplining generic attributes: the disciplinary context in focus', *Studies in Higher Education* 34(1): 85–100.
Kahaney, P. and Liu, J. (2004) *Contested Terrain: Diversity, Writing and Knowledge*, 4th edn, Michigan: University of Michigan Press.
Kamler, B. and Thomson, P. (2006) *Helping Doctoral Students Write: Pedagogies for Supervision*, New York: Routledge.
—(2007) 'Rethinking doctoral writing as text work and identity work', in B. Somekh and T.A. Schwandt (eds) *Knowledge Production: Research Work in Interesting Times*, London: Routledge, 166–179.
—(2008) 'The failure of dissertation advice books: toward alternative pedagogies for doctoral writing', *Education Researcher* 37(8): 507–514.
Kaplan, R.B. (1966) 'Cultural thought patterns in inter-cultural education', *Language Learning* 16(1–2): 1–20.
Kaplan, R.S. and Norton, D.P. (1992) 'The balanced scorecard: measures that drive performance', *Harvard Business Review* 70(1): 71–79.
—(1996) 'Using the balanced scorecard as a strategic management system', *Harvard Business Review* 74(1): 1–13.
Kearns, H. (2006) *The PhD Experience: What They Didn't Tell You at Induction*, Adelaide: Thinkwell.
—(2010) *The Crap Writing Tool*. Online: http://ithinkwell.com.au/resources/back_crap_writing.pdf (accessed 13 November 2012).
Kearns, H., Gardiner, M. and Marshall, K. (2008) 'Innovation in PhD completion: the hardy shall succeed (and be happy!)', *Higher Education Research Development* 27(1): 77–89.
Kearns, P. (2005) *Training Evaluation and ROI: How to Develop Value-Based Training*, London: Chartered Institute of Personnel and Development.
Kemp, D.A. (1999) *Knowledge and Innovation: a Policy Statement on Research and Research Training*, Canberra: AGPS.
Kiley, M. and Wisker, G. (2009) 'Threshold concepts in research education and evidence of threshold crossing', *Higher Education Research and Development* 28(4): 431–441.
King, J.E. and Cooley, E.L. (1995) 'Achievement orientation and the imposter phenomenon among college students', *Contemporary Educational Psychology* 20(3): 304–312.
Kirkpatrick, D.L. and Kirkpatrick, J.D. (2006) *Evaluating Training Programmes*, San Francisco: Berrett-Koehler Publishers Inc.
Knight, N. (1999) 'Responsibilities and limits in the supervision of NESB research students in the social sciences and humanities', in Y. Ryan and O. Zuber-Skerritt (eds) *Supervising Postgraduates from Non-English Speaking Backgrounds*, Buckingham: Society for Research into Higher Education and the Open University Press, 93–100.
Knowles, S.S. and Grant, B.M. (forthcoming) 'Walking the labyrinth: the holding embrace of academic writing retreats', in C. Aitchison and C. Guerin (eds) *Writing Groups for Doctoral Education and Beyond: Theory and Practice*, London: Routledge.
Kolb, D. (1984) *Experiential Learning: Experience as the Source of Learning and Development*, Englewood Cliffs: Prentice Hall.
Kreber, C. (2013) 'Empowering the scholarship of teaching: an Arendtian and critical perspective', *Studies in Higher Education* 38(6): 857–869.
Kress, G. (2004) *Before Writing: Rethinking the Paths to Literacy*, London: Routledge.
Krone, M. (2006) 'Managing the relationship with your supervisor(s)', in C. Denholm and T. Evans (eds) *Doctorates Downunder: Keys to Successful Doctoral Study*, Camberwell: ACER Press, 23–32.

Lam, A. (2007) 'Knowledge networks and careers: academic scientists in industry-university links', *Journal of Management Studies* 44(6): 993–1016.

Laurs, D.E. (2010) 'Collaborating with postgraduate supervisors', in V. van der Ham, L. Sevillano and L. George (eds) *Shifting Sands, Firm Foundations: Proceedings of the 2009 Annual International Conference of the Association of Tertiary Learning Advisors of Aotearoa/New Zealand (ATLAANZ)*, Auckland: Massey University, 18–30.

Lave, J. and Wenger, E. (1991) *Situated Learning: Legitimate Peripheral Participation*, Cambridge: Cambridge University Press.

Lea, M. and Street, B. (1998) 'Student writing in higher education: an academic literacies approach', *Studies in Higher Education* 23(3): 157–172.

Lee, A. (2012) *Successful Research Supervision*, London and New York: Routledge.

Lee, A. and Boud, D. (2009a) 'Introduction', in D. Boud and A. Lee (eds), *Changing Practices of Doctoral Education*, Oxon: Routledge, 1–9.

—(2009b) 'Framing doctoral education as practice', in D. Boud and A. Lee (eds) *Changing Practices of Doctoral Education*, Oxon: Routledge, 10–27.

Lee, A. and Danby, S. (eds) (2012) *Reshaping Doctoral Education: International Approaches and Pedagogies*, London: Routledge.

Leonard, D. (2001) *A Woman's Guide to Doctoral Studies*, Buckingham: Open University Press.

Lewis, C.T. (1995) *Elementary Latin Dictionary*, Oxford: Oxford University Press.

Loads, D. (2007) 'Effective learning advisers' perceptions of their role in supporting lifelong learning', *Teaching in Higher Education* 12(2): 235–245.

Lovitts, B.E. (2001) *Leaving the Ivory Tower*, Landham: Rowman and Littlefield.

—(2007) *Making the Implicit Explicit: Creating Performance Expectations for the Dissertation*, Sterling: Stylus.

Lundsteen, N. (2011) 'Learning between university and the world of work', unpublished PhD dissertation, University of Oxford. Online: http://www.bodleian.ox.ac.uk/ora/oxford_etheses (accessed 14 May 2013).

MAI Review (2012) Online: http://www.journal.mai.ac.nz/ (accessed 2 October 2013).

Mak, A.S., Westwood, M.J., Barker, M. and Ishiyama, F.I. (1998) 'Developing sociocultural competencies for success among international students: the EXCELL programme', *Journal of International Education* 9: 33–38.

Manathunga, C. (2005) 'Early warning signs in postgraduate research education: a different approach to ensuring timely completions', *Teaching in Higher Education* 10(2): 219–233.

—(2007a) 'Intercultural postgraduate supervision: ethnographic journeys of identity and power', in D. Palfreyman and D. McBride (eds) *Learning and Teaching across Cultures in Higher Education*, New York: Palgrave Macmillan, 367–376.

—(2007b) '"Unhomely" academic developer identities: more postcolonial explorations', *International Journal for Academic Development* 12(1): 25–34.

—(2011) 'Moments of transculturation and assimilation: post-colonial explorations of supervision and culture', *Innovations in Education and Teaching International* 48(4): 367–376.

Manathunga, C., Lant, P. and Mellick, G. (2006) 'Imagining an interdisciplinary doctoral pedagogy', *Teaching in Higher Education* 11(3): 365–379.

Marine, S. (2011) 'Stonewall's legacy: bisexual, gay, lesbian, and transgender students in higher education', *ASHE Higher Education Report* 37(4). San Francisco: Jossey-Bass.

Marton, F. and Säljö, R. (1976) 'On qualitative differences in learning: 1: outcome and process', *British Journal of Educational Psychology* 46: 4–11.

Mastekaasa, A. (2005) 'Gender differences in educational attainment: the case of doctoral degrees in Norway', *British Journal of Sociology of Education* 26(3): 375–394.

Matheos, K., Daniel, B.K. and McCalla, G.I. (2005) 'Dimensions for blended learning technology: learners' perspectives', *Journal of Learning Design* 1(1): 56–76. Online: https://www.jld.edu.au/article/view/9 (accessed 11 December 2013).

Maxwell, T.W. and Smyth, R. (2010) 'Research supervision: the research management matrix', *Higher Education* 59(4): 407–422.

McAlpine, L. and Amundsen, C. (2007a) 'Identity and agency: pleasures and collegiality among the challenges of the doctoral journey', *Studies in Continuing Education* 31(2): 109–125.

—(2007b) 'Academic communities and developing identity: the doctoral student journey', in P.B. Richards (ed.) *Global Issues in Higher Education*, New York: Nova Science Publishers, 53–83.

—(eds) (2011) *Doctoral Education: Research-Based Strategies for Doctoral Students, Supervisors and Administrators*, Dordrecht: Springer.

McAlpine, L. and Norton, J. (2006) 'Reframing our approach to doctoral programs: an integrative framework for action and research', *Higher Education Research and Development* 25(1): 3–17.

McAlpine, L. and Turner, G. (2011) 'Imagined and emerging career patterns: perceptions of doctoral students and research staff', *Journal of Further and Higher Education* 36(4): 535–548.

McAlpine, L., Jazvac-Martek, M. and Hopwood, N. (2009) 'Doctoral student experience in education: activities and difficulties influencing identity development', *International Journal for Researcher Development* 1(1): 97–109.

McArthur, T. (1998) 'GENERIC' *Concise Oxford Companion to the English Language*. Online: http://www.encyclopedia.com/doc/1O29-GENERIC.html (accessed 16 October 2012).

McCaffery, A. (2012) 'American Indian students: an exploration of their experience in doctoral programs', unpublished PhD dissertation. Seattle: University of Washington.

McGrail, M.R., Rickard, C.M. and Jones, R. (2006) 'Publish or perish: a systematic review of interventions to increase academic publication rates', *Higher Education Research and Development* 25(1): 19–35.

McWhinnie, S. (2010) *Stakeholders' Views of the Impact of Vitae and its Activities*, Cambridge: Careers Research and Advisory Centre (CRAC) Limited.

Melles, G. (2001) 'LAS centre identities and practices within higher education: fragments for negotiation', in B. James, A. Percy, J. Skillen and N. Trivett (eds) *Changing Identities: Proceedings from the National Language and Academic Skills Conference*, Wollongong: University of Wollongong. Online: http://learning.uow.edu.au/LAS2001/unrefereed/melles.pdf (accessed 5 February 2013).

Meloy, J.M. (2002) *Writing the Qualitative Dissertation: Understanding by Doing*, 2nd edn, Mahwah: Lawrence Erlbaum Assocs.

Melville Jones, H. (1996) 'Teaching critical thinking in a faculty of education', *ERA-AARE Joint Conference*. Online: http://www.aare.edu.au/abs96.htm (accessed 24 August 2012).

Mercer, C., Andersen, P., Booth, W., Hocquard, T., Kelly, M., Williams, M. and Wood, P. (2006) 'Making time to write', *New Zealand Nursing Review* 9(1): 14.

Metcalfe, J., Thomson, Q. and Green, H. (2002) *Improving Standards in Postgraduate Research Degree Programmes*, Bristol: Higher Education Funding Councils for England, Scotland and Wales.

Mewburn, I. (2010) *The Thesis Whisperer*. Online: http://thesiswhisperer.com/ (accessed 11 December 2013).

Meyer, J.H.F. and Boulton-Lewis, G. (1997) 'Variation in students' conceptions of learning: an exploration of cultural and discipline effects', *Higher Education Research and Development* 18: 289–302.

Milne, A.A. (1961) *The House at Pooh Corner,* London: Methuen and Co.

Moore, S. (2003) 'Writers' retreats for academics: exploring and increasing the motivation to write', *Journal of Further and Higher Education* 27(3): 333–342.

Morita, N. (2000) 'Discourse socialization through oral classroom activities in a TESL program', *TESOL Quarterly* 32(2): 279–310.

—(2009) 'Language, culture, gender, and academic socialisation', *Language and Education* 23(5): 443–460.

Morley, L., Leonard, D. and David, M. (2002) 'Variations in vivas: quality and equality in British PhD assessments', *Studies in Higher Education* 27: 263–273.

Morris, S. (2011) 'Doctoral students' experience of supervisory bullying', *Pertanika Journal of Social Sciences and Humanities* 19(2): 547–555.

Mullen, C.A., Fish, V.L. and Hutinger, J.L. (2010) 'Mentoring doctoral students through scholastic engagement: adult learning principles in action', *Journal of Further and Higher Education* 34(2): 179–197.

Murray, R. (2011) *How to Write a Thesis*, 3rd edn, Maidenhead: Open University Press.

—(2012) 'Social writing', in L. Clughen and C. Hardy (eds) *Writing in the Disciplines: Building Supportive Cultures for Student Writing in UK Higher Education*, Bingley: Emerald, 30–45.

Myburgh, C.P.H., Niehaus, L. and Poggenpoel, M. (2002) 'International learners' experiences and coping mechanisms within a culturally diverse context', *Education* 123(1): 107–130.

Nagata, Y. (1999) '"Once I couldn't even spell 'PhD student', but now I are one!" Personal experiences of an NESB student', in Y. Ryan and O. Zuber-Skerritt (eds) *Supervising Postgraduates from Non-English Speaking backgrounds*, Buckingham: Society for Research into Higher Education and Open University Press, 15–24.

National Archives: HM Treasury (2002) *SET for Success: Final Report of Sir Gareth Roberts' Review*. Online: http://webarchive.nationalarchives.gov.uk/+/http://www.hm-treasury.gov.uk/ent_res_roberts.htm (accessed 10 September 2012).

Nerad, M. (2010) 'Globalisation and the internationalisation of graduate education: a macro and micro view', *Canadian Journal of Higher Education* 40(1): 1–12.

Nesbit, P. (2004) 'The motivational journey', in S. Burton and P. Steane (eds) *Surviving Your Thesis*, London and New York: Routledge, 97–109.

Neumann, R. (2007) 'Policy and practice in doctoral education', *Studies in Higher Education* 32: 459.

Neumann, R. and Tan, K.K. (2011) 'From PhD to initial employment: the doctorate in a knowledge economy', *Studies in Higher Education* 36(5): 601–614.

O'Connor, P. and Petch, M. (2012) 'The embodied writer: Merleau-Ponty, writing groups and the possibility of space', in L. Clughen and C. Hardy (eds) *Writing in the Disciplines: Building Supportive Cultures for Student Writing in UK Higher Education*, Bingley: Emerald, 75–98.

References

Paltridge, B. and Harbon, L. (2006) 'Intercultural competencies and the international experience', in J.A. Van Rij-Heyligers (ed.) *Intercultural Communications across University Settings: Myths and Realities*, Auckland: Communication Skills in University Education, 55–66.

Paltridge, B. and Starfield, S. (2007) *Thesis and Dissertation Writing in a Second Language: a Handbook for Supervisors*, London and New York: Routledge.

Paré, A. (2011) 'Speaking of writing: supervisory feedback and the dissertation', in L. McAlpine and C. Amundsen (eds) *Doctoral Education: Research-Based Strategies for Doctoral Students, Supervisors and Administrators*, Dordrecht: Springer, 59–74.

Park, C. (2007) *Redefining the Doctorate: A Discussion Paper*, York: Higher Education Academy.

Parry, S. (2007) *Disciplines and Doctorates*, Dordrecht: Springer.

Pawson, R. and Tilley, N. (1997) *Realistic Evaluation*, Thousand Oaks: SAGE Publications.

Pearce, L. (2005) *How to Examine a Thesis*, Maidenhead: Open University Press.

Pearson, M., Evans, T. and Macauley, P. (2004) 'The working life of doctoral students: challenges for research education and training', *Studies in Continuing Education* 26(3): 347–353.

Percy, A. (2011) 'Making sense of learning advising: an historical ontology', unpublished PhD dissertation. University of Wollongong. Online: http://ro.uow.edu.au/cgi/viewcontent.cgi?article=4363&context=theses (accessed 11 December 2013).

Phillips, E.M. and Pugh, D.S. (1994) *How to get a PhD: A Handbook for Students and their Supervisors*, 2nd edn, Buckingham: Open University Press.

Phipps, A. (2003) 'Languages, identities, agencies: intercultural lessons from Harry Potter', *Language and Intercultural Communication* 3(1): 6–19.

Pilbeam, C., Lloyd-Jones, G. and Denyer, D. (2012) 'Leveraging value in doctoral student networks through social capital', *Studies in Higher Education*, DOI:10.1080/03075079.2011.636800.

Pratt, M.L. (1992) *Imperial Eyes: Travel Writing and Transculturation*, London: Routledge.

Prensky, M. (2001) 'Digital natives, digital immigrants part 1', *On the Horizon* 9(5): 1–6.

Prior, P. (2001) 'Voices in text, mind, society: sociohistoric accounts of discourse acquisition and use', *Journal of Second Language Writing* 10(1): 55–81.

QAA (The Quality Assurance Agency for Higher Education) (2004) *Code of Practice for the Assurance of Academic Quality and Standards in Higher Education: Section 1: Postgraduate Research Programmes*. Online: http://www.qaa.ac.uk/Publications/InformationAndGuidance/Pages/Code-of-practice-section-1.aspx (accessed 28 March 2013).

—(2011) *Doctoral Degree Characteristics*, Gloucester: The Quality Assurance Agency for Higher Education.

—(2012) *UK Quality Code for Higher Education Part B: Assuring and Enhancing Academic Quality: Chapter B11: Research Degrees*, Gloucester: The Quality Assurance Agency for Higher Education. Online: http://www.qaa.ac.uk/Publications/InformationAndGuidance/Documents/Quality-Code-Chapter-B11.pdf (accessed 24 September 2012).

Ramsden, P. (1979) 'Student learning and perceptions of the academic environment', *Higher Education* 8(4): 411–427.

—(2003) *Learning to Teach in Higher Education*, 2nd edn, London: Routledge Falmer.

Reeploeg, S. (2010) 'Intercultural opportunities and regional identity: Nordic voices in Scottish literature', *eSharp: Uniting Nations: Risks and Opportunities* 15: 112–132.

References

Reeves, J. (2007) 'Getting beyond supervision', in R. Hinchcliffe, T. Bromley and S. Hutchinson (eds) *Skills Training in Research Degree Programmes: Politics and Practice*, Berkshire: Open University Press, 151–162.

Reeves, J., Denicolo, P., Metcalf, J. and Roberts, J. (2012) *The Vitae Researcher Development Framework and Researcher Development Statement: Methodology and Validation Report*, Cambridge: Careers Research and Advisory Centre (CRAC) Ltd.

Ring, P.S. and Rands, G.P. (1989) 'Sensemaking, understanding and committing: emergent interpersonal transaction processes in the evolution of 3M's microgravity research program', in A.H. Van de Van, H.L. Angle and M.S. Poole (eds) *Research on the Management of Innovation: the Minnesota Studies*, New York: Ballinger, 337–366.

Roberts, G. (2002) *SET for Success: the Supply of People with Science, Engineering and Technology Skills*, London: UK Government Department of Trade and Industry and Department of Education and Skills. Online: http://www.vitae.ac.uk/policy-practice/1685/Roberts-recommendations.html (accessed 24 September 2012).

Rosen, M. and Oxenbury, H. (1989) *We're Going on a Bear Hunt*, London: Walker.

Rountree, K. and Laing, T. (1996) *Writing by Degrees: a Practical Guide to Writing Dissertations and Research Papers*, Auckland: Longman.

Rowarth, J. and Green, P. (2006) 'Sustaining inspiration and motivation', in C. Denholm and T. Evans (eds) *Doctorates Downunder: Keys to Successful Doctoral Study*, Camberwell: ACER Press, 112–119.

Rowland, S. (2006) *The Enquiring University: Compliance and Contestation in Higher Education*, Maidenhead: Open University Press.

Royal Society (2010) *The Scientific Century: Securing our Future Prosperity*, London: The Royal Society Science Policy Centre. Online: http://royalsociety.org/uploadedFiles/Royal_Society_Content/policy/publications/2010/4294970126.pdf (accessed 14 May 2013).

Rudestam, K.E. and Newton, R.R. (2001) *Surviving your Dissertation: A Comprehensive Guide to Content and Process*, 2nd edn, Thousand Oaks: Sage Publications.

Ryan, J. and Viete, R. (2009) 'Respectful interactions: learning with international students in the English-speaking academy', *Teaching in Higher Education* 14(3): 303–314.

Ryan, Y. and Zuber-Skerritt, O. (1999) 'Supervising non-English speaking background students in the globalized university', in Y. Ryan and O. Zuber-Skerritt (eds) *Supervising Postgraduates from Non-English Speaking Backgrounds*, Buckingham: Society for Research into Higher Education and the Open University Press, 3–11.

Salmon, P. (1992) *Achieving a PhD: Ten Students' Experience*, London: Trentham Books.

Samuelowicz, K. (1990) 'Profession, emerging profession or... a bag of tricks? Learning skills counsellors in Australian tertiary education institutions', in M. Kratzing (ed.) *Proceedings of Eighth Australasian Language and Learning Conference*, Brisbane: QUT Counselling Services, 99–118.

Samuels, L. (2002) 'Relinquish intellectual property', *New Literary History* 33(2): 357–374.

Savin-Williams, R. (1998) *'And Then I Became Gay': Young Men's Stories*, New York: Routledge.

Scarry, E. (2001) *On Beauty and Being Just*, London: Duckworth.

SET for Success: Final report of Sir Gareth Roberts' review [2002], 'Section 4: postgraduate education'.

Siepmann, D. (2006) 'Academic writing and culture: an overview of differences between English, French and German', *Meta: Journal des Traducteurs/Meta: Translators' Journal* 51(1): 131–150.

Simon, R. (1995) 'Face to face with alterity: postmodern Jewish identity and the eros of pedagogy', in J. Gallop (ed.) *Pedagogy: The Question of Impersonation*, Bloomington and Indianapolis: Indiana University Press, 90–105.

Sinclair, A. (2000) 'Women within diversity: risks and possibilities', *Women in Management Review* 15(5/6): 237–245.

Sinclair, M. (2004) 'The pedagogy of "good" PhD supervision: a national cross-disciplinary investigation of PhD supervision', *DEST*. Online: http://www.tempus.ge/files/PhD/phd_supervision.pdf (accessed 1 December 2013).

Singh, M. (2009) 'Using Chinese knowledge in internationalising research education: Jacques Ranière, an ignorant supervisor and doctoral candidates from China', *Globalisation, Societies and Education* 7(2): 185–201.

Singh, M. and Chen, X. (2012) 'Generative ignorance, non-Western knowledge and the reshaping of doctoral education: arguing over internationalising Western-centred programs and pedagogies', in A. Lee and S. Danby (eds) *Reshaping Doctoral Education: Changing Programs and Pedagogies*, London and New York: Routledge, 187–203.

Skillen, J. (2006) 'Teaching academic writing from the "centre" in Australian universities', in L. Ganobcsik-Williams (ed.) *Teaching Academic Writing in UK Higher Education: Theories, Practices and Models*, Basingstoke: Palgrave Macmillan, 140–153.

Smith, L. (1999) *Decolonizing Methodologies: Research and Indigenous Peoples*, London: Zed Books.

Spillett, M.A. and Moisiewicz, K.A. (2004) 'Cheerleader, coach, counsellor, critic: Support and challenge roles of the dissertation advisor', *College Student Journal* 38(2): 246–256.

Stacy, H. (1999) 'The law, policies and ethics: supervising postgraduate NESB students in an era of internationalisation', in Y. Ryan and O. Zuber-Skeritt (eds) *Supervising Postgraduates from Non-English Speaking Backgrounds*, Buckingham: Society for Research into Higher Education; Open University Press, 75–90.

Stanford University Division of Literatures, Cultures and Languages (2012) *The Future of the Humanities PhD at Stanford*. Online: https://www.stanford.edu/dept/DLCL/cgi-bin/web/events/humanities-education-focal-group-discussion-future-humanities-phd-stanford (accessed 14 May 2013).

Starfield, S. (2010) 'Fortunate travellers: learning from the multiliterate lives of doctoral students', in P. Thomson and M. Walker (eds) *The Routledge Doctoral Supervisor's Companion*, London: Routledge, 138–146.

Statistics New Zealand (2006) *2006 Census Data*. Online: http://www.stats.govt.nz/Census/2006CensusHomePage.aspx (accessed 30 November 2013).

Stefani, L. (2013) 'Performance measurement for academic development: risk or opportunity?', *International Journal of Academic Development* 18(3): 294–296.

Stokes, E. (1985) *Maori Research and Development: A Discussion Paper*, Wellington: National Research Advisory Council.

Strauss, P. (2012) ' "The English is not the same": challenges in thesis writing for second language speakers of English', *Teaching in Higher Education* 17(3): 283–293.

Strauss, P., Sachfleben, A. and Turner, E. (2006) 'Talkback: empowering EAL thesis writers', in J.A. Van Rij-Heyligers (ed.) *Intercultural Communications across University Settings: Myths and Realities*, Auckland: Communication Skills in University Education, 174–188.

Subcommittee, CQA (2008) *European Higher Education Area: the Bologna Process*, Toronto: Council of Ministers of Education, Canada.

Surgeons' Hall (2012) *Surgeons' Hall: a Unique Edinburgh Venue*. Online: http://www.surgeonshall.com/ (accessed 10 September 2012).

Swain, E. (2007) 'Constructing an effective "voice" in academic discussion writing: an appraisal theory perspective', in A. McCabe, M. O'Donell and R. Whittaker (eds) *Advances in Language and Education*, New York: Continuum, 166–184.

Swales, J. (1996) 'Occluded genres in the academy: the case of the submission letter', in E. Ventola and A. Mauranen (eds) *Academic Writing: Intercultural and Textual Issues*, Amsterdam: John Benjamins, 45–58.

Swetnam, D. (2003) *Writing Your Dissertation*, 3rd edn, Oxford: How to Books Ltd.

Symons, M. (2001) 'Learning assistance: enhancing the PhD experience', in A.B. Mercer (ed.) *Postgraduate Research Supervision: Transforming (R)elations*, New York: Peter Lang, 101–112.

Thaman, K.H. (2008) 'Nurturing relationships and honouring responsibilities: a Pacific perspective', *International Review of Education* 54: 459–473.

Tinkler, P. and Jackson, C. (2000) 'Examining the doctorate: institutional policy and the PhD examination process in Britain', *Studies in Higher Education* 25(2): 167–180.

—(2004) *The Doctoral Examination Process: a Handbook for Students, Examiners and Supervisors*, Maidenhead: Open University Press.

Tonso, K. (2006) 'Student engineers and engineer identity: campus engineer identities as figured world', *Cultural Studies of Science Education* 1: 272–307.

Trafford, V.N. and Leshem, S. (2002) 'Starting at the end to undertake doctoral research: predictable questions as stepping stones', *Higher Education Review* 34(4): 31–49.

—(2008) *Stepping Stones to Achieving your Doctorate*, Maidenhead: Open University Press.

—(2009) *Stepping Stones to Achieving your Doctorate*, 2nd edn, New York: McGraw Hill.

Trivett, N., Skillen, J. and James, B. (2001) 'New partnerships in supporting postgraduate research', in *Proceedings of 24th International HERDSA Conference*. Newcastle, NSW (8–11 July).

Trumble, W.R., Stevenson, A., Bailey, C. and Siefring, J. (2002) *Shorter Oxford English Dictionary: on Historical Principles*, 5th edn, Oxford: Oxford University Press.

UK GRAD Programme (2001) *Joint Statement of the UK Research Councils' Training Requirements for Research Students*. Online: http://www.vitae.ac.uk/cms/files/RCUK-Joint-Skills-Statement-2001.pdf (accessed 17 October 2012).

—(2002) *Profiting from Postgraduate Talent: Report of a Conference held on 11 June 2002*, Cambridge: Careers Research and Advisory Centre (CRAC) Limited.

Universities Australia (2010) *Universities Australia Strategy for Women: 2011–2014*, Online: http://www.universitiesaustralia.edu.au/women (accessed 18 April 2012).

University of Worcester (2011) *Facts and Figures*. Online: http://www.worcester.ac.uk/discover/facts-and-figures.html (accessed 17 October 2012).

Ur, P. (2003) 'Shattering the myths', *ETAI Forum* 14(2): 62.

Vitae (2004) *'What Do PhD's Do?': 2004 Analysis of First Destinations of PhD Graduates*. Online: http://www.vitae.ac.uk/CMS/files/1.UKGRAD-WDPD-full-report-Sep-2004.pdf (accessed 10 May 2013).

—(2008) *Rugby Team Impact Framework*. Online: http://www.vitae.ac.uk/CMS/files/1.Rugby%20Impact%20Framework_33.pdf (accessed 24 September 2012).

—(2009) *What Do Researchers Do? First Destinations of Doctoral Graduates by Subject*. Online: http://www.vitae.ac.uk/CMS/files/upload/Vitae-WDRD-by-subject-Jun-09.pdf (accessed 16 April 2013).

—(2010) *Researcher Development Framework*. Online: http://www.vitae.ac.uk/researchers/428241/Researcher-Development-Framework.html (accessed 12 December 2013).
—(2011) *Annual Report Cambridge*, Cambridge: Careers Research and Advisory Centre (CRAC) Limited.
—(2013a) *CROS: Careers in Research Online Survey*. Online: http://www.vitae.ac.uk/policy-practice/143071/Careers-in-Research-Online-Survey-CROS.html (accessed 25 May 2013).
—(2013b) *European Commission 'HR Excellence in Research' Badge*. Online: http:vitae.ac.uk/policy-practice/303561/European-Commision-HR-excellence-in-research-badging.html (accessed 25 May 2013).
—(2013c) *KE Scotland 2012 Conference: Booking Form*. Online: http://www.vitae.ac.uk/policy-practice/73511/Part-Time-Researcher-Conference-registration-of-interest.html (accessed 25 May 2013).
—(2013d) *PIRLS: Principal Investigators and Research Leaders Survey*. Online: http://vitae.ac.uk/policy-practice/448681/Principal-Investigators-and-Research-Leaders-Survey-PIRLS.html (accessed 25 May 2013).
Vygotsky, L.S. (1978) *Mind in Society*, Cambridge, MA: Harvard University Press.
—(1986) *Thought and Language*, Cambridge, MA: MIT Press.
Walker, M. (2006) *Higher Education Pedagogies: A Capabilities Approach*, Maidenhead: Open University Press.
Walker, M. and Thomson, P. (2010) *The Routledge Doctoral Supervisor's Companion: Supporting Effective Research in Education and the Social Sciences*. Oxon: Routledge.
Webber, M. (2009) 'The multiple selves and realities of a Māori researcher', *MAI Review* 1.
—(2012) 'Edge-walking: The multiple selves and realities of a Maori researcher', Keynote address at the Academic Identities Conference, Auckland.
Weber, L.E. and Duderstadt, J.J. (2006) *Universities and Business: Partnering for the Knowledge Society*, London: Economica.
Weick, K. (1995) *Sensemaking in Organizations*, London: Sage.
Wenger, E. (1998) *Communities of Practice*, Cambridge: Cambridge University Press.
Wertsch, J. (1991) *Voices of the Mind*, Cambridge, MA: Harvard University Press.
West, R. (1998) 'Review of higher education financing and policy (West Committee)', *Learning for Life: Final Report*, Canberra: AGPS.
Wheeler, S. (2012) Thinking in networks. Online: http://steve-wheeler.blogspot.co.nz/2012/08/thinking-in-networks.html#!/2012/08/thinking-in-networks.html (accessed 14 August 2013).
White, B. (2011) *Mapping your Thesis: The Comprehensive Manual of Theory and Techniques for Masters and Doctoral Research*, Camberwell: ACER.
Williams, J.B. and Jacobs, J. (2004) 'Exploring the use of blogs as learning spaces in the higher education sector', *Australasian Journal of Educational Technology* 20(2): 232–247.
Williams, L.R.T. (2007) 'A transformative model and programme for indigenous advancement through higher education, research and capability building', *International Journal of Diversity in Organizations, Communities and Nations* 6(6): 17–22.
Willison, J. and O'Regan, K. (2008) *The Researcher Skill Development Framework*. Online: http://www.adelaide.edu.au/rsd/framework/ (accessed 12 December 2013).
Wilson, K., Li, L.Y. and Collins, G. (2011) 'Co-constructing academic literacy: examining teacher-student discourse in a one-to-one consultation', *Journal of Academic Language & Learning* 5(10): A139–A153.

Wingate, U. (2006) 'Doing away with "study skills"', *Teaching in Higher Education* 11(4): 457–469.

Wisker, G. (2001) *The Postgraduate Research Handbook: Succeed with your MA, MPhil, EdD and PhD*, Hampshire and New York: Palgrave Macmillan.

—(2005) *The Good Supervisor*, Basingstoke: Palgrave Macmillan.

—(2008) *The Postgraduate Research Handbook*, 2nd edn, Hampshire and New York: Palgrave Macmillan.

—(2012) *The Good Supervisor*, 2nd edn, Basingstoke: Palgrave Macmillan.

Wisker, G. and Robinson, G. (2009) 'Encouraging postgraduate students of literature and art to cross conceptual thresholds', *Innovations in Education and Teaching International* 46(3): 317–330.

Wisker, G., Robinson, G., Trafford, V., Warnes, M. and Creighton, E. (2003) 'From supervisory dialogues to successful PhDs: strategies supporting and enabling the learning conversations of staff and students at postgraduate level', *Teaching in Higher Education* 8(3): 383–397.

Woodward, D., Denicolo, P., Hayward, S. and Long, E. (2004) *A Review of Graduate Schools in the UK*, Lichfield: UK Council for Graduate Education.

Woolf, V. (1947) *Mrs Dalloway*, London: Hogarth.

Wu, S. (2013) 'Filling the pot or lighting the fire: cultural variations in conceptions of pedagogy', *Teaching in Higher Education* 7(4): 387–395.

Yeh, C.C. (2010) 'New graduate students' perspectives on research writing in English: a case study in Taiwan', *Journal of Academic Language and Learning* 4(1): A1–A12. Online: http://journal.aall.org.au/index.php/jall/article/view/115 (accessed 1 May 2013).

Zamel, V. (1995) 'Strangers in academia: the experiences of faculty and ESL students across the curriculum', *College Composition and Communication* 46(4): 506–521.

Zerubavel, E. (1995) 'The rigid, the fuzzy, and the flexible: notes on the mental sculpting of academic identity', *Social Research* 62(4): 1093–1106.

Index

Academic career preparation *see* Careers
Academic culture *see* Culture
Academic identity formation 2–3, 11, 30, 36–37, 51–67, 69, 76–80, 85, 87, 103–106, 112, 115–118, 135, 137–140, 163–165; in writing 87, 103, 112, 115, 118
Accountability 58, 63, 66, 83, 128, 134, 147, 166
Arts *see* Humanities
Assessment of generic support 70, 88–90, 134, 147–164
Australia (context for generic support) 59, 74, 75ff, 125, 128

Belongingness *see* Homeliness/unhomeliness
Benchmarking 25, 77, 161–164 *see also* Assessment
Blogs 122, 128–131
Bologna process 8–9, 14

Careers 3, 13–17, 24, 26, 133–146, 159
Critical thinking skills 9, 31, 44–50, 53–56, 70, 73, 108, 110–111, 143–145, 164 *see also* Graduate attributes
Collaboration 15–16, 20, 23, 25, 31, 36, 38, 39, 63, 74, 75, 90, 109, 123–124, 127, 128, 130, 137, 154–155
Community/ies of practice 39, 53, 75, 90, 97, 121, 128, 163, 164
Completion of doctorate 2–3, 10, 13, 17, 19–20, 25, 26, 37, 39, 40, 43, 52, 58, 71, 78, 80, 83, 106–107, 113, 118, 147, 153, 155, 160, 163, 166
Critical theory/analysis *see* Critical thinking skills, Theory

Culture 2–3, 30, 32, 45–46, 52, 54, 57–84, 162, 166; academic culture (including discipline, research, policy, institutional) 7, 16, 20, 36, 43, 105, 128, 138–145, 151, 165
Curriculum 13, 19, 86, 134, 140

Descriptors/criteria for generic support 10, 12, 147, 161–164
Definition of generic 9–12
Digital media 118, 121–131
Doctoral stages *see* Completion of doctorate, First year, Mid-stage, Final stage

English as an additional language (EAL) 67, 69–83, 111
e-learning *see* Digital media
Effectiveness 11, 15, 26, 38, 42, 69, 73, 79, 83, 105, 108, 109, 125, 136, 142, 150, 155
Employability 10, 13, 16, 65, 151, 155, 158, 160, 163
Equity 25, 29, 51–67, 70, 122, 153, 165
Evaluation *see* Assessment
Excellence in Cultural Experiential Learning and Leadership (ExcelL) 79
Exclusion 27, 52, 75 *see also* Isolation, Homeliness/unhomeliness

Feedback 21–22, 30, 35–36, 58, 65, 73, 79, 104–106, 107–109, 115, 121, 145, 150, 162 *see also* Student feedback (on generic support)
Final stage of doctorate 42, 92–96, 110, 127, 153
First year of doctorate 22, 24, 90, 113

Index

Gay *see* Gender
Gender 2–3, 14, 37, 51, 53–59, 167
Generic definition *see* Definition of generic
Genre 2, 9–12, 30, 58, 70, 101, 103–105, 112–113, 118, 165–166
Global(ization) 8, 61, 67, 82–83, 134
Graduate attributes 9, 14, 44, 56, 127, 162–163, 165 *see also* Transferable skills

Heteronormativity 54 *see also* Equity
Homeliness/unhomeliness 52, 72–74, 112, 166 *see also* Exclusion, Isolation
Humanities (discipline) 11, 24, 28, 64–66, 73, 87, 112, 140
Hubs (Vitae, UK) 15, 123–124

Identity *see* Academic identity formation
Impact of doctoral support 15–17, 74, 86, 135, 147, 147–161 *see also* Assessment
Imposter syndrome 57, 85, 106
Indigenous 3, 59–63, 165
Individual support *see* One-to-one support
Induction to the doctorate 8, 12, 26, 88, 126, 136
Insider/outsider 7, 52, 54–55, 67, 70, 112, 160 *see also* Homeliness, Isolation, Exclusion
Instability of generic situation in institution 13, 147, 166
Intercultural skills 79–80
Interdependency 51, 58–59
Interdisciplinarity 28, 65, 77, 82, 97, 107, 109, 112, 163, 165, 167
International doctoral students 2, 3, 14, 17, 29, 31, 38–41, 45–46, 69–83
Internationalization 70, 75, 77–78, 134
Intrapreneurship 16, 142
Isolation 11, 19, 22, 56–58, 118, 163 *see also* Belongingness, Exclusion, Insider/outsider

Kaupapa Māori 63–64
Kemp Higher Education initiatives 128
Key performance indicators 65, 149
Knowledge (functioning/declarative) 135

LBGT (lesbian, bi-sexual, gay, transgender) *see* Gender
Learning advisors 1, 7, 9, 10, 12, 19–20, 29–32, 51–52, 71, 73, 83, 87, 103–106, 110–111, 115, 122, 128, 135, 145, 147–155
Loneliness *see* Isolation

Māori *see* Indigenous and Kaupapa Māori
Massification of education 56, 134
Measurement *see* Assessment
Mid-stage of doctorate 94
Multidisciplinarity 82

Neoliberalism in academia 64
NESB students *see* English as an Additional Language (EAL)
New Zealand (context for generic support) 3, 13, 22, 59–63, 67, 70, 74, 77, 85, 125–126
Ngā Pae o te Māramatanga 60–61 *see also* Māori and Indigenous

One-to-one support 20, 24, 29–31, 35–36, 61–62, 73, 82, 96, 103, 110
Online *see* Digital media
Oral examination of doctorate 12, 39, 42–43, 70, 87–91
Overseas doctoral students *see* International

Part-time doctoral students 28, 118, 119–128, 165
Pedagogy 1–3, 7–8, 12, 16, 19, 53, 72–73, 82, 98, 104, 109, 122, 128–131, 148, 161–167
Professional doctorates 14
Publication (developing skills in) 3, 11; thesis by publication 22, 28, 65, 89, 97–110, 139, 151, 155, 160

QAA / QAAQC (Quality Assurance Agency / QAA Quality Code) 13–17, 27, 150
Queerness *see* Gender

RCUK (Research Council UK) 17, 150, 152
Reading skills 31, 71–74, 80–82
Research skills 2, 8, 10, 14, 20, 26–27, 31
Researcher identity *see* Academic identity formation
Restructuring (of generic doctoral support) 23, 96, 145, 147, 165–166
Retreats *see* Writing retreats
Roberts' report 7–8, 13–14, 17, 27–28, 38, 123, 147–148, 151–152
Rugby: Rugby Group 15; Rugby Policy Forum 149–150; Rugby Team Impact Framework 147

Index

Salzburg principles 14–15
Sciences *see* STEM skills
Senior management 13, 52, 147
STEM skills (science, technology, engineering and mathematics) 11, 13, 17, 27, 28, 142
Social sciences 24, 28, 65–66, 73, 87
Student feedback (on generic support) 11, 22, 45, 56, 108, 161–162
Summer school 41, 126–27
Supercomplexity 7
Supervision: generic support for managing supervision 21, 23–25, 29, 38–39, 40–43, 70, 110, 128; interface and complement between generic and supervisory advice 1–3, 8–9, 10–13, 15–16, 19, 29–32, 46, 53, 57, 61–62, 75–76, 78–79, 83, 97, 99–101, 103–106, 113, 127–129, 135–137, 141, 154–155, 161–167

Theory 2, 7, 28, 43–50, 52, 53–56, 72, 74, 111–112, 117–118, 152
Thesis-writing 2, 11, 20, 22, 29–30, 39, 71, 83, 85–118, 165
Tino rangatiratanga 60 *see also* Māori and Indigenous
Transculturation 71–73
Transferable skills 2, 7, 10–11, 13, 27, 133, 136, 141–142, 145, 162–163

UK (United Kingdom context for generic support) 7–8, 10–17, 26–29, 38, 40–43, 65, 121–124, 133, 136, 141–144, 147–161
UK Grad Programme 13–14
UKCGE (UK Council for Graduate Education) 16
Under-represented groups *see* Equity
Unhomeliness *see* Homeliness
University (as context for generic doctoral support) 7, 9–12, 14–17, 20–21, 23, 25–27, 38, 51–52, 60–61, 66, 71, 77, 79, 83, 91, 104, 128–131, 134, 136, 138, 140, 162–167

Vitae / Vitae Research Development Programme 14–17, 123–124, 133, 136, 141–144, 147, 149–159
Viva voce *see* Oral examination
Voice (doctoral) 21–22, 30, 37, 53, 58, 67, 81, 86–87, 97, 111
Vulnerability of generic situation *see* Instability of generic situation in institution

Women *see* Gender
Workshops (specific generic) 8, 11–12, 19, 20–22, 26, 28, 36–50, 71–80, 96–98, 109–112, 124
Writing retreats 56–59, 61–62, 97, 106–109

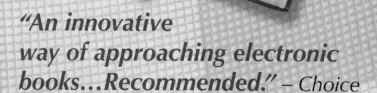